A HARPERS & QUEEN PUBLICATION

THE OFFICIAL
F·O·O·D·I·E
H·A·N·D·B·O·O·K

ANN BARR & PAUL LEVY

Be Modern-Worship Food

EBURY PRESS
LONDON

Published by Ebury Press
National Magazine House
72 Broadwick Street
London W1V 2BP

First impression 1984

ISBN 0 85223 343 4 (paper)
ISBN 0 85223 348 5 (hardback)

Artist Diana Gold
Picture researcher Anne-Marie Ehrlich
Jacket photograph by Jhon Kevern
Editor Anna Selby
with design help from Ted Kinsey

Computerset in Great Britain by
MFK Typesetting Ltd., Saffron Walden, Essex
Printed in Great Britain at the
University Press, Cambridge

Thanks

Many people provided ingredients for this book. We wish to thank particularly Foodies and Foodie-watchers Alexandra Artley, Fiona Bailey, Frances Bissell, Catherine Bond, Charles Bricker, Susan Campbell, Martin Cropper, Anthony Gardner, Sheila Hale, Philip and Mary Hyman, Jocelyn McCurdy, Penelope Marcus, Jonathan Meades, Patrick O'Connor, Michael Pye, Alistair Scott, Stephanie Turner and Julia Watson. And like Foodies everywhere, we owe a debt to those distinguished people listed in the Foodie Who's Who.

We are grateful to David Dimbleby for coining the word Grapie, and to many people who gave us unwitting help by writing scholarly books, in particular Quentin Crewe, for *Great Chefs of France*, and Christopher Driver, for *The British at Table 1940–1980*. Andrew Barr supplied the very old jokes.

It would still have been a stodgy mixture without the design of HARRY GREEN.

The authors would like to state that the information contained in this book was checked as rigorously as possible before going to press. Neither the authors nor the publishers can take responsibility for any changes which may have occurred since, nor for any other variance of fact from that recorded here in good faith. The authors were unable to obtain all the information they wanted, especially for the Foodie Who's Who. They would be very grateful for any further details or corrections from readers, so as to improve future editions.

CONTENTS

CONTENTS

PART TWO
THE FOODIE EATS OUT

PART THREE
THE GLOBAL FOODIE

CONTENTS

PART FOUR
A FOODIE WHO'S WHO
(and an index, too)

COOK BOOK

You are, probably. A Foodie is a person who is very very very interested in food. Foodies are the ones talking about food in any gathering – salivating over restaurants, recipes, radicchio. They don't think they are being trivial – Foodies consider food to be an art, on a level with painting or drama. It's actually your *favourite* art form.

What does a Foodie look like? Like anyone else. Burns on the back of the wrists, perhaps – from getting pots out of the oven. Fatness – no. Foodies are from the ambitious classes, who know about exercise and bran. Characteristic clothing – no. Foodies can be anything from lawyers or musicians to farmers (strangely, the ones who do best in cookery competitions are doctors).

Don't Foodies smell of garlic? Yes, and of coriander and cumin too, probably. But so do many Europeans, Indians and Chinese who have No Palate. Foodies are *all* palate, with a vestigial person attached.

The way you tell a Foodie is by listening. The mouth will declare its passion. To hear a Foodie talk to another Foodie is like overhearing lovers. Lots of little hums, lip-smacking – mmmm puh puh puh puh. Cries of 'Yes! Yes!' All that is happening is that they agree on Harrods' cheese department.

You feel no need to conceal your – excitement (it used to be called greed). The sinners today are those who buy their cheese in plastic-wrapped portions and rely on the label to know whether it's Gouda or Gorgonzola. Nowadays you are ashamed *not* to have a huge, rapacious, experienced, palpitating palate. A Foodie even exaggerates his enthusiasm in conversation to warm up the bond with the Foodie he is talking to. Food talk is the *staple* diet of social intercourse now. Foodism crosses all boundaries and is understood in all languages. Food is the frontier to be on.

You are the New Man – and the New

Young American Foodies discover What Really Matters at La Varenne School of Cookery in Paris

Foodie clichés

I read cookery books like novels.
This is *delicious* beside the Mediterranean/ Aegean/Caspian/Yangtze, but it doesn't travel.
The longer the name the better the wine.
People who are good cooks are good at love.
I've had a wild goose (or something) in the freezer for two years. I must get round to making a cassoulet (or something).
He or she (fellow Foodie) knows *nothing* about food.

Woman. You believe you are impervious to fads, a setter not a follower of trends. You are not a fanatical jogger, squash addict or tennis bum. You know what exercise is *for* – to give you an appetite.

You are the New Traveller. You have no interest in unclimbed Everests, unexplored continents, unknown jungles, uncharted seas or unjust deserts. You

know why man travels – to get to lunch. Or dinner. You have no need of atlases when you voyage, for you mostly voyage through France. Your Gault-Millau restaurant guide is the only text you require – sic itur ad astra: the only stars worth scaling are those in Michelin.

So, proud possessor of a Gault-Millau, user of Michelin, are you a Foodie?

Is the grass green? Is the Pope Catholic?

'Breakfast, dinner, lunch and tea are all the human frame requires,' Hilaire Belloc wrote. Just so. You know a great secret. The Purpose of Life is Eating Well.

But pigs can eat well. The Foodie *thinks* about eating. The Foodie *talks* about eating. The *unexamined meal* is not worth eating.

What is new about an interest in food? Everyone knows some older person who was called a 'gourmet' before the term 'Foodie' arrived (Foodies and Foodism were christened by *Harpers & Queen* in August 1982). But Foodies *are* new, children of the consumer boom. The gourmet was typically a rich male amateur to whom food was a passion. Foodies are typically an aspiring professional couple to whom food is a fashion. *A* fashion? *The* fashion. Couture has ceded the centre ground to food.

Foodism being fashion, you don't live with the same menu for years – you discover, embrace, explore minutely, get bored, and move on tomorrow to fresh meals and pastas new.

Foodies are pleased with the state of their art. It has made them into an elite, an international elite with branches in every country. Foodism is a good ism – it is helpful to planet earth rather than doing any harm; Foodism is glamorous; Foodism is fun. 'I am a Foodie' is as proud a boast as the old Roman citizen's 'Civis Romanus sum'. 'I am a Roman citizen', 'I am a Foodie': what they both mean is 'I am a winner'. Eating is a vocation worth devoting your life to. 'Yes! Yes!' Mmmm mmmm puh puh puh puh.

F·O·O·D·I·E·B·O·R·E·S

THE COFFEE BORE

The coffee bore prefers the berries of the coffee tree of the Coffea arabica species. He dislikes rubbishy robusta (which you can spot by its smaller beans), but often has to settle for it. It is *very* difficult to buy 100 per cent arabica coffee, though it is indigenous to Ethiopia and still grows wild there. The third species, C. liberica, is chiefly of interest to Liberians, and there are relatively few Foodies in Liberia.

Robusta *is* more robust than arabica – it is less disease-prone, hardier, higher yielding and grows at lower altitudes – and is thus perfect for making non-Foodie instant coffee. Arabica is softer, less harsh in flavour and more aromatic. The ideal Foodie coffee is high-roast all-arabica. It is not just expensive, it is rare. One British supermarket now sells a 75/25 arabica/robusta blend, but only medium-roast. The real bore wants the slightly bitter, burnt caramel flavour of high-roast beans.

Coffee gives a bonus to bores: it has regional differences. This means that the bore can dismiss a brew with a knowing 'Ugh! Rioy,' signifying coffee from Rio, the least desirable of Brazil's crop. Or sigh, 'Mmmm. Santos,' when he wants to let his audience know he knows they are drinking Brazil's best.

The coffee bore mugs up these facts, and many more, from Claudia Roden's *Coffee, the* book on the bore's table of the same name.

Bores brew espresso only – ie, each cup is made on purpose, expressly, and not left around to stew. Percolators are *out* (they *boil* the coffee), and vacuum (drip) methods are not much favoured (they take too long, and sometimes the coffee is cold before it's ready to serve). Melitta filters and cafetières with metal mesh filters are approved – so long as they're kept scrupulously clean.

But the best methods are Italian, and make coffee by forcing steam under pressure through very finely ground coffee. It is best when just made; but some bores make twelve cups in the Moka Express and store it in a vacuum flask.

Bores drink coffee black, without sugar. Except for breakfast, when they take milk; for preference, puffed up with steam as capuccino (this is a current Foodie fad). They do not despise Turkish coffee – when drunk in Turkey or Greece. And they *do* drink décaf as well as vraicaf, but only if it has been properly brewed, from decaffeinated arabica beans. (Robusta is too robust for the caffeine-sensitive: the less good the bean, the more the caffeine.)

WARNING ABOUT BORES IN GENERAL

This animal cannot be confined in one area for long. He or she is always on the way from one territory to another. When the bore has exhausted a subject (and you), he or she will be off to devastate another area of food. Your only chance is to DESTROY HIM NOW.

ARE YOU A FOODIE?

Eleven tests of taste

1 What do you feel at the thought of missing a meal?
A Relieved   **B** Hungry   **C** Incredulous

2 Do you taste your companion's food when dining out?
A Never   **B** If you live with him or her
C Always

3 Who is the British Royal Foodie?
A The Prince of Wales   **B** The Princess of Wales
C The Queen Mother

4 Who would you rather dine with?

Guess who's coming to dinner? President Jelly Bean and Prime Minister Chicken Véronique

A President Reagan   **B** Mrs Thatcher
C President Mitterrand

5 What are these symbols?

A Cheese soufflés   **B** Trees   **C** The highest awards for cooking given by the Gault-Millau restaurant guide

6 What is the correct wine to drink with Chinese food?
A None   **B** House white   **C** Chablis or old claret – but not with the sweet and sour

7 What is the most important invention since the wheel?
A Atomic power   **B** The microchip   **C** The food processor

8 What do you think of tomato ketchup?
A Nice   **B** Nasty   **C** What is tomato ketchup?

9 What is a mango?
A A device for ironing sheets   **B** A tropical fruit
C A garnish for a plate with thin slices of rare breast of duck

10 What really matters?
A Wealth   **B** Health   **C** That the fish is not overcooked

11 What is this?

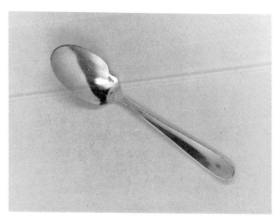

A A bonsai-gardening tool   **B** A surgical instrument   **C** A sauce spoon

Test your Foodietude on p 144

PART ONE
THE FOODIE AT HOME

WOULD YOU HAVE BEEN A FOODIE?

Dates that changed the Foodie world

30,000 BC Homo sapiens appears

8,000 BC First agricultural settlements. Chasseur does not at first realise what has happened

5,000 BC First loaf to leave a trace (Bulgaria)

AD 135 Dispersion of Jews from the Holy Land sends a nation of future Foodies out into the world

13th C Hangzhou goes food-mad: the first Foodie city

1256–1323 Marco Polo publishes an account of his travels to China, India and other eastern countries which alerts the West to different ways of eating

Das ist der edel Ritter · Marcho polo von

14th C Japan becomes vegetarian. Raw fish given a 200-year sabbatical

1453 Constantinople taken by Turks, to the constanternation of traders (Venetians, Genoans, etc) who had shipped eastern spices from there, the end of the overland spice route, to sell in Europe

1488 Bartholomew Diaz rounds Cape of Good Hope. Spices can come by sea

1492 Christopher Columbus discovers the West Indies. A new land for food to come from

1499 Amerigo Vespucci charts the South American coast. Ditto

1519 Magellan begins first round the world voyage, linking the food sources

1570 First printed picture of a place setting with fork: in *Cuoco Secreto di Papa Pio Quinto* by Bartolomeo Scappi

1584 Sir Walter Raleigh begins colonising Virginia and brings potatoes to Britain (and tobacco – but who cares about that?)

1600 English East India Co founded, start of the British love affair with curry and kedgeree

1620 Pilgrim Fathers settled in New England, with their English recipe books

1641 Japan excludes all foreigners in order to refine cuisine

1765 The first 'restaurant' in Paris opened by Boulanger the soupseller. The traiteurs sued in 1765 to stop him selling his dish of sheep's feet in white sauce; he won. His soups were called 'restaurants' because restorative and after the lawsuit the name moved to the shop

1770 Captain Cook lands in Australia, linking the other continents with the New Zealand kiwi fruit that was to put the novelty into nouvelle cuisine

1782 The first real restaurant, La Grande Taverne de Londres, opened in Paris by Beauvilliers with a choice of dishes served at individual tables

1789 Marie Antoinette says 'Let them eat brioches'

1789 The French Revolution puts the aristocrats' cooks on the market. There are already about 100 restaurants in Paris

1800 The stove is invented by Benjamin Thompson, Count Rumford: American born, lived in Britain. He also invented a keep-hot coffee pot

1803 First restaurant guide: the *Almanach des Gourmands* in Paris

1804 There are 500–600 restaurants in Paris: a 500 per cent growth in five years

1845 Eliza Acton's *Modern Cookery* published

1850s Service à la Francaise (all food on the table at once) gives way to service à la Russe (courses)

1861 Mrs Beeton's *Household Management* published

1864 Phylloxera starts its 30-year creep through French vineyards from the Gard in the south

1869 H. J. Heinz start canning in Pittsburgh. First British factory 1925. The slogan '57 varieties' underestimates the number. Foodies shudder

1874 The Wine Society founded in Britain

1900 Michelin run a motorist's guide to French restaurants

1903 Escoffier's *Guide Culinaire* published

1905 Emigration of Russian and Polish Jews to US and Britain. Lower East Side and Whitechapel burst with borscht and bagels

1906 Vitamins discovered by F. G. Hopkins

1906 Kellogg's start making cornflakes in Michigan. First British factory in 1938

1917 Bolshevik Revolution: the end of cooking in Russia. 'Let them eat koulibiac'

1917 Prohibition in USA, until 1933

1919 Break-up of the Austro-Hungarian Empire: beginning of the end of a great cooking style. Goodbye gulyás. Sacher Torte stays

1923 Clarence Birdseye starts frozen food in US

1926 Michelin starts merit star system

1928 'Ali-Bab' publishes *Gastronomie Pratique*

1930s	German Jews moving to Britain and US. The spread of strudel
1939	Second World War robs Europeans of cuisine and, often, adequate food
1940	Food rationing starts in Britain
1941	*Gourmet* magazine founded in America
1946	First shipment of bananas for six years arrives in Britain – the ship that launched a thousand bananas flambées
1950	The Good Food Club launched in Britain
1950	Elizabeth David's *A Book of Mediterranean Food* published
1951	First *Good Food Guide* published, editor Raymond Postgate
1950s	Frozen food taking over from tins
1955	Fernand Point, of La Pyramide, Vienne, father of nouvelle cuisine, dies
1954	Commercial television in USA. Television Act in Britain. Food advertising on the box. Food rationing ends in Britain
1955	McDonald's hamburgers begin McDonaldisation of the world. They reach Britain in 1974

1956	America's first Kentucky Fried Chicken appears. Colonel Sanders sells his chicken for a 'royalty' of 1 cent per piece. Originally, he'd had a store that had closed down – this was the beginning of the KFC empire. In 1984, it is selling

	16–20 million meals a week in 50 different countries
late 1950s	Marks & Spencer diversify into food
1959	Mario and Franco's Trattoria Terrazza opens in London, launching the tiled-floor, red-chaired, deafening-din Italian restaurants
1961	Craig Claiborne publishes the *New York Times Cook Book*
1962	Henri Gault and Christian Millau publish the *Guide Juillard* to Paris, which becomes the *Gault-Millau* (1969)
1962	*Sunday Times* starts colour magazine, bringing Foodism to the massed middle classes of Britain
1960s	The whole-food movement gives Foodies something to half-like – 'the speckled beige band'
1960s	A barbecue in every garden. And Tandoor ovens come to western restaurants
1963	Mr Kuo, chef of the Chinese Embassy in London, defects and starts first non-Cantonese restaurant in Britain, at Willesden. This short step is like the Long March to Foodies
1968	Claudia Roden's *A Book of Middle Eastern Food* published. A new planet swims into Foodies' ken
1971	*Campaign for Real Ale* (CAMRA) founded in Britain. Fs don't say I Am a CAMRA, but the Cs are on the right track
1972	Richard Mabey's *Food For Free* published in Britain
1973	'Nouvelle cuisine' christened by Gault and Millau in an article in the *Gault-Millau* magazine October issue
1973	Sainsbury, British Foodie grocers since 1869, go public
1974	Heinz take salt out of their baby foods

1974	Piers Paul Read publishes *Alive*, an account of cannibalism in the Andes
1975	Commercial television starts in France
1976	First book by a nouvelle cuisine chef – if only Michel Guérard had called it that instead of *Cuisine Minceur*
1977	Monosodium glutamate scare. Chinese Restaurant Syndrome was the herpes of the Seventies
1977	John and Karen Hess's *The Taste of America* grills American food critics and the food business for their disservices to food
1979	Alan Davidson publishes the first number of *Petits Propos Culinaires*
1979	Alan Davidson and Theodore Zeldin hold first International Food Symposium at St Antony's College, Oxford
1980s	New York goes food-mad. Paris goes food-mad
1982	Wine boxes arrive, but not for Foodies
1982	Madhur Jaffrey's book and BBC television programme *Indian Cookery*: another new planet swims into Foodies' ken
1982	'Foodies' described and christened in *Harpers & Queen* August issue
1984	The *Harpers & Queen Official Foodie Handbook* by Ann Barr and Paul Levy published in Britain

Whole-Foodier than thou

Laura and Richard Whole-Foodie have a *totally* organic marriage. Even their wedding cake was like a brown iced stone. During their early Friends of the Earth period, she started keeping bees in their dusty London garden while he encouraged the clover. Later they hived off to the country (a rambling Old Rectory in Wiltshire) where Laura keeps millions of bees, grows a field of sunflowers and Richard drones on about wild food for free.

Laura's sunflowers are grown by the most primitive organic methods and she has them refined into oil at home by an assistant. Her four naturally-childbirthed children (Richard helped deliver them at home by candlelight and Mozart) *loathe* the sight of wholemeal bread. Down in the village shop where the real country people buy ready-made cakes and frozen peas, the young Whole-Foodies long for soft, sliced white and real (bought) sausages.

Most of the Rectory garden is never mowed. It is grazed instead by a flock of Jacob sheep who turn it every year into a sea of muddy tussocks. The Whole-Foodies are not vegetarian. Every spring, Laura chases luckless lambs round the garden, trying to shoo them into the back of a shooting break. Baa-ing behind the dog guard, they are driven through fresh, bendy lanes to the slaughter. The next day, the evil deed done, Laura is begging borrowed space in half the freezers in Wiltshire. She tells her tearful children self-sufficiency requires sacrifices. ('Yes, of the weakest,' sobs her eldest.)

Richard Whole-Foodie loves to forage. He says the fields and the sea-shore are Nature's larder. When it comes to mussels, however, the sea-shore is more like Nature's Fortnum & Mason. The Wild Foodie sum works out like this:
2½ hour drive to the beaches of Dorset + chocolate bars to bribe children to gather buckets of mussels + au pair's overtime + new wellies for four = 25p per mussel.

The ordinary Foodie sum works out like this:
go to good fishmonger + go home = 20p per pound.

But Richard is as stubborn as a moule.

Every October the children are roped in again: this time as mushroom-gatherers. Richard is Fungus the Foodie-Man and he has every fungus book there is. Even the two-volume Romagnesi. For the Wild Foodie autumn is a season of mists and mellow fruitfulness, close bosom friend of the vomiting son. Laura will never forget how she stopped the children making an omelette with an Amanita phalloides.

As a cook, Laura is insipid. She thinks of herself as a Foodie but urban Foodies see the fallacy in her belief that anything you grow yourself must be good. All her food looks khaki and tastes of mushy beans.

Laura has never mastered a simple vinaigrette dressing. She uses funny health food-shop oils instead of olive oil. Even her lambs die in vain. Their meat is always cooked until grey, pitted with too much rosemary and garlic and served with the usual mush. The dogs get given a lot of it but they hate the rosemary and garlic (grr-rr-oan).

The Whole-Foodies' salads should be absolutely delicious – they grow rocket, land cress, radicchio, mâche, four or five kinds of lettuce, chervil and chives, escarole, romaine, sorrel, ornamental cabbages, nasturtiums and dandelions, which Laura carefully blanches. The salad looks rainbow not khaki but the taste is shrouded in her pervasive dressing, malt-vinegared and safflowered to death.

Boiled eggs are her best thing, from free-range hens which eventually go the way of the lambs.

All meals are eaten on an 18-foot pine refectory table that Foodies dread. Not only have they the food to face, but backache from sitting for two hours on long benches, with the wriggling, wrangling children.

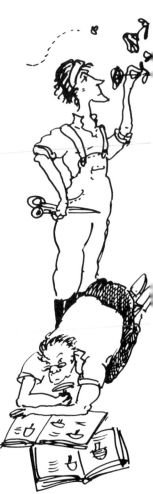

The squalor scholar cook

Barbara Bookish is deeply admired by the other scholar cooks. Her contributions to Alan Davidson's and Theodore Zeldin's Oxford Symposium on Food are eagerly awaited every summer, as she always has something original to say. Her paper on yeast doughs under Louis XIV enthralled the conference.

Dr Bookish lives in a dark house in North Oxford. It used to be *Doctors* Bookish, but her husband moved to Berkeley with a student. He left Dr Bookish their valuable collection of pre-Columbian cooking pots.

Every post brings enquiries about 'foodways'. Is it true that the first recorded reference to Black Forest cake is 1934? What is the origin of the poubelle de table? What does she think of the Portuguese navigator's report that he was given maize in West Africa two years before Columbus sailed to the New World? She knows these letters keep her in touch, but they do interrupt her work-in-progress, on the history and use of the gas oven.

When Lord Forte endowed a chair of Gastronomic Studies at Oxford, Dr Bookish was the obvious choice.

Professor Bookish never ceases the mental fight. She thrives on the vigour and excess of her collection of mediaeval texts. 'Take spynaches,' her favourite receipt begins, 'Parboyle hem in seething water. Take hem up and hewe hem in two. Fry hem in oile clene.'

She likes to say she cooks in exactly the same way. She is rather proud she can never remember how many minutes to the pound a sirloin of beef needs, and instead of consulting Mrs Beeton or Prue Leith, she turns to Wyken de Worde's *Book of Kerving*, with its recipes that begin 'Breke that deer', 'spoyle that hen', 'splat that pyke' or 'dismembre that heron'. Her rare guests are delighted as she quotes these colourful phrases while struggling with the door of her ancient oven. But when the roast is finally brought out, they see that it is undercooked, overcooked or burnt. In deference to the scholar cooks' interest in fish, she has tried serving this, but an American professor who dined with her says he saw her filleting a plaice with nail scissors.

She literally has no time for food. Her cheerful cleaner Mrs Sloppet buys it – dyed kippers, biscuits, tea and fruit yoghurt. Professor Bookish wishes she could be bothered to get a new kitchen knife – the tip of it broke while she was levering off the chutney lid last winter.

At night she lies in bed ticking off items in booksellers' catalogues ('Anon. My Lady's Closet of Receipts Open'd. 1690. 96 pp. Some foxing. Lacks boards. £180'). Around her stand stacks of faded volumes, all with paper slips marking passages of importance. In the morning she will answer that West African maize query. Now, she sleeps off the effects of a fat text gobbled at a sitting, content in the knowledge that the proper study of mankind is food.

Made in Paris

Frank George has been called 'Gorgeous George' by his friends ever since High School in his home town of Lawrence, Kansas. One of the middle-aged mid-western ladies whom Frank 'walks' every Saturday night to Paris restaurants says his com-plexion reminds her of oyster mushrooms.

He gained his first gastronomic experience in the restaurants of Chicago and at the famous Le Français at Wheeling, Illinois, where he went as often as he could persuade boyfriends to take him when he was at the University of Illinois.

Though his most ardent admirers were professors, they could do Frank few favours when he graduated. Economic hard times meant that the obvious doors open to a talented black American – law, dentistry, business school – were shut.

Still, a rich theologian from the University of Chicago offered to sponsor Gorgeous George in Paris for a year, and he managed to find a place on a basic catering course. The next year he apprenticed himself to a minor chef, for almost no money. But he had succeeded in getting into the system – and in learning to speak French.

Always versatile, Frank was taken up by the French woman owner of a not very prominent cookery school outside Paris, and proved useful in swelling the number of American ladies taking the course. He comes back to the city at weekends, to his tiny flat from which you can see the Beaubourg.

Frank is assiduous in keeping up his Paris contacts. He still knows every maître d'hôtel and sous chef in the city – intimately. Consequently he is an authority on the politics of the kitchen, and therefore an invaluable source of information for American journalists.

Frank is aware that he is only one of an entire squad of American Foodies making their living in France. He is slightly envious of Robert Noah, who had the good idea of a three-star restaurant table-booking service for Americans. But there is a lot of camaraderie amongst the Foodie Americans in Paris, who see themselves as the successors to Gertrude Stein, Scott Fitzgerald and Ernest Hemingway. As a generation, though, the Foodies are very far from lost.

Paris c'est un dump

François Fourchette is an administrator working for the Monoprix chain, for whom he manages six shops in the middle of France. He lives in the gastronomic desert of Clermont-Ferrand, and thanks God that Roanne and the Troisgros are less than a 100-kilometre drive away.

Jean-Pierre Billoux's station restaurant at Digoin is also just possible, and the flesh-pots of Lyon are accessible for a long weekend, but François ultimately depends on his local, La Poularde at Montrond-les-Bains. François is trend-conscious and fou about food, subscribes to the Gault-Millau magazine, and doesn't admit to *owning* a copy of Michelin. He wishes M Randoing, the ancient chef of La Poularde, was more experimental, but has noticed a huge improvement since the new man, Gilles Eteocle, joined the kitchen brigade. Still, La Poularde is *cheap*. It has a 130F menu, which is very important, as François takes the whole family there, including all three children and sometimes his wife's mother, for lunch every Sunday.

Saturdays, in the season, are given over to la chasse. The trouble is that, like the peasants, François and his bourgeois friends will shoot anything that moves, and the peasants have not left a lot. His wife hates cooking game, and despairs that her freezer is almost completely filled by the haunch of marcassin or sanglier that François seems to bag every year, as well as by any songbirds that have escaped the peasants' limed twigs.

François is a serious Foodie. Not only does he spend a fifth of his life in restaurants, he also belongs to the Club des Cent, and regards being a fin bec as nearly a full-time job. He is bringing up the eldest boy to be just like his papa: to wear English clothes and drink Scotch, to affect to loathe Paris and Parisians and to be fussy about food.

Poor Madame Fourchette longs for

Monoprix to transfer François to Paris, or at least to the suburbs of Paris, where she could get a job, live in a small flat instead of their large house, have a bonne, instead of doing all the housework herself, and buy the family's food from the traiteur – ready-made and ready to reheat.

The gorgeous East in me

Nyree Nymph O'Manioc, born in Townsville, Australia, formed an interest in Asian food when she escaped to Sydney and shared a rooming-house with a group of Asian students.

She could never decide what she liked best, her Korean lover's kim chee, her Vietnamese's spring rolls or her Indian's murgh vindaloo. But she copied down the recipes for each into her turmeric-stained cloth notebook.

After university, Nyree, like everybody of her generation, made a bee-line for London. She bypassed the Earl's Court ghetto, touched down in Mayfair and NW1 and became a travel courier, taking package tourists to her beloved East.

Nyree was an erratic tour leader. The young males of her flock tended to be very happy, but she sometimes mislaid a temple, and had instead to take the whole group to the local restaurant. Her vividness and knowledge always turned these diversions into much more valuable cultural experiences.

Nyree's second career is the reduced essence of her first. She gave the recipes from her cloth-bound notebooks to the Australian literary agent with whom she was currently eating and sleeping. He sold world rights to Hamlyn, and the rest is publishing history. Nyree's sunny Sydney kitchen is the workshop where she manufactures her annual cookery book. These become more accurate, precise and ethnic every year, yet sales figures are not improving. Could it be that the stilt-village recipes in her *Malaysian Kampong Cookery* are too specialised?

Now 40, she is torn between marrying the Foodie anthropologist at Sydney University who helped her with her last three books, or going off to Latin America. She tells herself there are several countries not yet on the culinary map, but which would be sure to deeply delight the First World. (Tomorrow to fresh blood, and pampas new.)

Foodies on ice

Vera and Ronny Similitude put the kitsch in kitchen. Just after the War, they fell in love between the gleaming aluminium vats in a British catering college and they have been happily sculpting food ever since.

Vera and Ronny never realised that food has a natural shape of its own. A carrot is a carrot is a carrot. They think of food as soft squashy stuff (that can be squeezed out of a forcing bag) or hard stuff (that can be carved into something *spectacular*).

Even at catering college one artist recognised another. By day Vera and Ronny were streets ahead of other students as they cleverly piped creamed potatoes into squiggles, rolled coloured marzipan into Christmas novelties, turned tomatoes into water-lilies, radishes into roses and sponge cakes into crinoline ladies. By night, Vera released her spun-sugar hair from its hygienic catering-college net and moulded it with a trace of rose-scented shellac from a squeezy bottle. Then she and Ronny went Old-Time dancing.

Beneath the glittering, faceted globe at the Birmingham Locarno (with her tulle frock nice and stiff) Vera thought how lucky she and Ronny were. Their life stretched ahead. At work and play they moved in a world of real artistic beauty.

Over the years, when it came to ice carving, Ronny became a virtuoso. Like Michelangelo who simply 'released the form imprisoned in the block', Ronny goes to a cold store, stares at a huge block of ice and sees a swan, a penguin with a cheeky face or a Dutch clog filled with tulips. For romantic private occasions he can do a very popular bluebird of happiness or cupid poised on a heart. Ronny and Vera can also turn lard, butter or sugar into incredible representations of town halls, parish churches and football stadiums. One triumph was a true to scale model in

best English butter of the Cheddar Gorge commissioned by the Milk Marketing Board for a promotional dairy party. Beautifully back-lit and with parsley for trees, it fairly took one's breath away.

Vera and Ronny regret they were born just too late for the golden age of the ocean liner, where they could have floated and sculpted, carved and spun. The great London hotels have come to realise that such naive artfulness destroys many customers' appetites. But Vera and Ronny are properly appreciated in the provinces.

For municipal banquets and receptions in the Midlands, they make rubbery little canapés, fill a large carved ice bucket with prawn cocktail, and cleverly fold crisply starched linen napkins into bishops' mitres or into water-lilies with a bread roll hidden inside. Whether fork luncheon or evening function, 'It were champion,' says Councillor Bunright.

Vera and Ronny Similitude are aware they could make a fortune on the country-club circuit in America but they would never dream of emigrating. They are artists and *patriots*. They aspire to join the self-selected, self-financing British 'Culinary Olympics' team, who go to Frankfurt every four years in a so-far vain search for medals. Vera and Ronny have a fantasy that in 1988 they will win for Britain – the Torvill and Dean of the food world.

The all-American Foodie

Ernest Sams (his friends, naturally, call him 'Uncle'), born in 1943, is a restaurateur in Minnesota. He is an American Foodie chauvinist. Sams says that his was the first restaurant in America to have native morels on the menu, that he introduced wild turkey and buffalo steaks, and that no one ever bothered to gather the local huckleberries until he made a pie of them.

Ernest claims to have persuaded the owners and chefs of East Coast restaurants such as the Quilted Giraffe, Hubert's, the Four Seasons and the River Café of the virtues of Bay scallops and fiddlehead greens, and to have preached the merits of Laurie Chenel's California chèvre to Michael's of Santa Monica.

In short, Sams takes the credit for inventing the American nouvelle cuisine that is now sweeping the country. Without him, he says modestly, the American sturgeon would have become extinct (no gold caviar!) and no one would bother to grow 'arugula' (which an earlier generation knew was a native plant and called by its correct name – rocket). Ernest spends much of his time talking to zoology and botany departments on the telephone.

He has become fat, bald and lumberjacketed in the quest for the Holy Quail. Yet he has still to find a native game bird cheap and good enough to put on his menu – someone should tell him that American pheasant would taste less like cardboard if it was hung for a week before being cooked. But he has made contact with the local blue-collar hunting fraternity, who have guaranteed him venison. The deer-hunters would be upset to learn of Ernest's annual 'fact-finding' trips to France, and to the west coast to rip off the new recipes at Chez Panisse – and of the much younger boyfriend he keeps in the apartment above the restaurant.

At present, Ernest's big headache isn't people or venison, but vegetables, which are coarse and, on the whole, too large to be good eating. He is negotiating with a farmer in California to grow a French variety of green bean, pencil-thin and tender. They will certainly be the world's most expensive green beans. In the meantime, the food at the Yankee Doodle Stewpot could be improved, if the chef-patron would spend more time stirring the casseroles and less time patting himself on the back in articles about the early days of the American Foodie Movement.

A second-generation Foodie is as rare as a white truffle

You are about to be born, to Foodie parents. You will be that rarity in the Foodie world, someone who was born not converted. There will be more of you in the future, but at present you are an infant pioneer – a person with roughly 70 years of service to food in front of you: 51,100 major meals. They will pass all too fast.

You have made arrangements to take your first in San Francisco rather than Los Angeles, New York rather than Boston, Chicago rather than St Louis, London rather than Manchester and Lyon rather than Paris; if you are in the eastern hemisphere you have chosen Hong Kong in preference to Manila and Tokyo to Sydney. Above all you have avoided eastern Europe.

You will spend the next four to six months at your mother's breast, laying down a sensible nutritional foundation, in preparation for the solid business of a lifetime. If you've been born in America, your parents will have no problem weaning you on to a Foodie diet; but if you've had the bad luck to be born somewhere where Beechnut Baby Foods (sugar-free, salt-free, additive-free) are not sold, your parents will make a thorough search of the shops of North London or around the rue de Rosier in Paris: Beechnut Foods are also kosher.

After teething comes the serious task of learning to eat properly. Your parents will be vigilant about your sugar and animal fat intake, because they know that, as an adult Foodie, you will be prone to overweight; they want to give you the best possible start in the lifetime's struggle.

Foodie parents will see that the infant Foodie gets most of his protein from innocuous sources such as chicken and fish. They are certain that the uncorrupted palate will always prefer chèvre to mousetrap and olives to sweets. However, rather than let Nanny or Granny put this to the test, your parents lug you with them as they make their annual pilgrimage to the three-star restaurants of France. Remember to be very quiet in your portable chair under the table, and your kind parents will slip you a corner of truffle. You may not be so lucky as the child whose first experience of dining-out was purée de pommes de terre prepared by Paul Bocuse himself at Collonges au Mont d'Or, but good parents will see to it that you taste your first truffle as soon as you can chew.

Your favourite sound will be the popping of corks. While your parents won't begrudge you the odd sip of Roederer Cristal 1976, it would be better not to get tipsy the first time, lest your parents succumb to the pressure of the puritanical and cut off the supply.

The next few years will present you with problems that are almost entirely negative: how to avoid school meals; how to say no gracefully when your peers want to spend their pocket money on Big Macs; how not to give offence to other children's mothers who offer jellies and sticky buns and British sausages at children's parties. You will acquire cunning and guile as you slip away to spend your pocket money on avocados, smoked salmon, fresh mangoes and hand-dipped chocolates. You will have no objection to sharing these – no Foodie is mean about food – but your allowance is not big enough for you to keep the table you are being brought up to maintain.

As a Foodie teenager, you begin to *know* you are different. Naturally, you worry about whether you will ever be like most people your own age; but as your real friends obviously share your tastes, it is not really difficult to come out of the larder and admit to yourself and others that your condition can only be shared with a small group of similarly obsessed adults. At least you are spared the problem of confessing to your parents – they know already.

A born Foodie

Your parents, though Foodies, may object to your training as a chef the minute you leave school, and insist on your going to university. In this case, you will probably provide yourself with some good books by Julia Child and Anton Mosimann, make sure that your digs have adequate kitchen facilities, and neglect your lectures for the next three or four years, while you teach yourself to cook. If you go to Oxford, Cambridge or Harvard, you will be able to find a group who share your priorities and you will spend your university career around the dinner table, not the seminar table. If you are not so lucky, you can probably do a course at a good provincial university in history of art or something that will fit you for your subsequent career. History of art will be a help in suggesting ways of decorating a plate.

There are more Foodies in medicine than any other job. Until 1984, there was never a year when one or even two of the finalists in the *Observer* Mouton Cadet competition, the toughest of the amateur cookery competitions, was not a doctor. Law is an obvious alternative (you become a barrister by eating your Dinners), or accountancy, but the quickest and easiest route to job satisfaction is food journalism. The trouble with that is it's pretty full up. And Foodie journalists don't retire, they die on the job like limpets.

Chef's whites wedding

When in search of a mate you make certain to concentrate on what really matters – eating out and shopping for food – and don't squander your money and time on visits to the theatre, concerts, the cinema or bed. Plays and concerts are a problem for Foodies – do you eat before or after? You always discuss it, decide neither would be fair to the food, and skip the performance.

A Foodie's wedding must be gastronomically memorable, and mass catering is the enemy of the good. Christenings present fewer problems – if you see that all the godparents are Foodies it will be possible for the champagne to be vintage and the caviar black.

A Foodie's marriage is a partnership in passion. It is far more important that the lamb isn't overcooked than that the other person caters to your sexual foibles. As they say in the north of England, anybody can fook, but not many people can cook.

A Foodie marriage is very often homosexual, but that doesn't matter amongst Foodies. Being Foodie is so much more important. Many, many Foodies spend their lives with the wrong sex. And if after thirty years of marriage or partnership you discover you are really gay, or heterosexual, you wouldn't dream of doing anything about it. Breaking up a home is one thing, breaking up a kitchen is quite another. You don't want to waste even a week looking for another partner who understands exactly how you like your magret de canard.

Foodie couples don't *share* the cooking

SEX on a PLATE

Oral sex is the Foodies' favourite kind – good practice. The average person starts being interested in food at 25. Most Foodies are first generation because 1) it is an upwardly mobile activity, 2) it is an activity of the 1980s. However, in the Sixties, there was a foretaste of Foodism among the flower children. Just to remind you – in case you are a twenty-five-year-old Foodie too young to remember – the flower children thought they had invented sex, peace 'n' love, because sex, peace 'n' love looked completely different seen through the diamond skies of drugs. The hippies did something they called 'plating', which they also thought they had invented (the Romans called it cunnilingus and fellatio and thought *they* had invented it). The hippies tried decorating the plates with cottage cheese, chocolate sauce, champagne and strawberry mousse. (When the straight world was shocked by Brando buttering buns in *Last Tango in Paris*, it hadn't been paying attention.) Then the head shops (head shops, 25-year-olds, sold the hippies their joss sticks, drugs, Tarot books and so on) came up with aids to plating – strawberry, mint and vanilla flavours in tubes. There were even *edible knickers*.

This just proves how tastes change. In the Foodie Era these disgusting artificial substances would be spat out by even the keenest lover, and he/she would immediately *leave* the person who had such a blot on his/her plate. In a British television programme in June 1984, a teenage boy said he smeared his girlfriend with baked beans and licked them off. But no Foodie had to hear this – no serious Foodie would watch a programme called *Sex Matters*.

Just before Lettice got married, one of her friends warned her: 'I hope you'll be able to stand Tom. He's obsessed by F!' 'That's a relief,' said Lettice. 'I was beginning to wonder.'

They were booked at a three-star French hotel for their honeymoon, and when they got to the bedroom, Tom said, 'I have been waiting so long for this. Up to now, I have only been able to taste half the pleasure of life. What I thought was, we could just be straightforward for four days, and after that we could experiment and try things on the side and make our own combinations.'

'That sounds fun,' said Lettice.

'I reckon we can do two serious sessions a day if we keep our strength up by walks and naps,' said Tom.

'How organised you are,' said Lettice.

'All we have to do now is get ready,' said Tom, going into the bathroom. Lettice pulled off her clothes and jumped into bed. Tom came out. 'Oh no, aren't you feeling well?' he said. 'I *was* looking forward to having somebody to eat with.'

– there would be murder. In 80 per cent of Foodie marriages, the man cooks; in the other 20, he shops. There is something of la vie bouleversée (upside-down cake) in all Foodie marriages. You can tell who dominates by who says 'What would you like me to order, darling?' in a restaurant.

The cook in the family gets home as early as possible and cooks for three hours. Foodies rarely have children or pets. They haven't the time or money to spare. Food takes it all. Food is their children. That

11	dimanche avril		S. Jules	12	lundi avril
S. Stanislas	recettes	dépenses		recettes	dépenses
Pravons in garlic			Toms birthday		
Salade niçoise			Foie gras, tarct (aux truffes)		
Roast duck			Haricots verts beurres		
Cheese			Le veau au citron, panné		
Marghautas			Les dattes fraiches		
1964 Ducru Beaucaillou			Sorbet au limon		
Mirabelle			1964 Ch. Margaux		
			1959 Ch. Ducru Beaucaillou		
			Tom says its the best birthday meal he's ever had in his life and worth waiting 38 years for!		
total			**total**		

Croque-monsieur (pour 4 personnes)

Coupez en triangle les tranches très fines de pain de mie. Beurrez légèrement. Mettez sur une tranche de pain une tranche de jambon de la même épaisseur, puis une tranche de gruyère très mince. Recouvrez avec une autre tranche de pain. Faites dorer rapidement au beurre.

Si vous voulez que vos croque-monsieur soient moins gras, beurrez les deux tranches de pain et passez-les au four très chaud.

Décoration

Pour décorer un gâteau d'anniversaire, découpez des lettres dans de l'angélique, de l'orange confite; ou bien tracez des lettres sur un papier blanc, découpez l'intérieur de ces lettres, appliquez légèrement le papier sur le gâteau, puis saupoudrez largement de sucre glacé ou de poudre de chocolat. Le plus délicat : retirer le papier !

Dear Diary ... from the diary of London Foodie Frances Bissell

---

Zoologists and anthropologists have described pair-bonding, the process by which animal and human couples become permanently paired – a gradual habitation, nothing instant like 'with this ring I thee wed'. Foodies are lucky in that their rituals of shopping, preparation, eating and loading the dishwasher are so repetitive and comforting that anyone married to or living with a Foodie soon feels completely trapped, like a patient in a hospital.

The organisation *never sleeps* (there is always something soaking or marinating or ripening or hanging or thawing). There are big cycles and little cycles, rituals for time of day and time of year. ('We always have wild goose at

The FOODIE of

whom Cod hath joined

Christmas. Annabel sends us a kilo of Belles de Soisson beans from France, 100 francs a kilo. We put them into soak on Christmas Eve, for cassoulet on Boxing Day.') Cooking keeps the Foodie family together – and non-Foodies inferior.

You are buoyed up by the expectation of more meals and by the soothing routines. (In a minute, nurse will be along with macaroons and Lapsang Souchong for your tea.)

Foodie quarrels are different too: hardly anyone says 'I can't stand another moment of her and her bloody lamb.' And you can't get divorced – who would get custody of the food processor?

Foodies don't want children is one reason for most Foodies having bangers-and-mash parents. They are *converts* – with all a convert's zeal. You can identify that rare specimen – a Foodie child – by its agility with chopsticks (the sign used to be whether it liked avocado pears). The other children in the kindergarten dislike Foodie children because they say 'My mummy doesn't let me eat chocolate. We have proper food.' The Foodie pet if it exists is a cat. Dogs interfere with the shopping and need walks. Fresh air adds something powerful to appetite that Foodies can't measure so resolve not to try again. The Foodie couple know the cat would like the chicken bones but you give them to the stock – you consider the stock's need is the greater.

Foodies don't have mid-life crises; they have diabetes and coronaries caused by overeating. The biggest problem in a Foodie's middle-age is making his visits to the fat farm frequent enough to avoid taking any more exercise than a trot to the shops. Divorce is seldom a problem with Foodies; after all, both partners have something in their lives to which they are mutually devoted, and to which they pay a great deal more attention than they do to each other. The Foodies' seven-year itch can easily be assuaged by the discovery of a new type of pasta; and any passion you conceive over 40 is likely to be for a new sauce.

In Foodie marriages, there are no such things as battered wives; rather there is a question of who gets the batterie de cuisine if you *were* to divorce – but usually this is too tricky to allow the marriage ever to dissolve.

If you've been a good and generous host, you can anticipate, after the last grande bouffe, that your surviving Foodie friends and relations will see that your funeral baked meats are up to your standards. It should not be beyond the imagination of a Foodie executor to invent an all-black menu.

More pages from Frances Bissell's food diary

MESSAGER

FÉVRIER

MESSAGER

gousses
cuill.
citron.
frire.

	RECETTES	DÉPENSES
gue		

JEUDI **10** MAI

STE SOLANGE   MESSAGER

PIZZA AU FROMAGE

SAMEDI **11** FÉVRIER

N.-D. LOURDES   MESSAGER

CRÊPES À L'ANANAS

Faites 2 crêpes par personne et tenez-les au chaud. Écrasez le
contenu d'une grosse boîte d'ananas en tranches brisées après
avoir enlevé le jus. Fourrez chaque crêpe avec cette purée. Rangez
les crêpes roulées dans un plat, saupoudrez de sucre et flambez
au rhum.

	RECETTES	DÉPENSES
Dinner for Myra		
salad of pleurottes + quails eggs		
ravioli with chicken, herbs + ricotta		
noisettes of venison, pear jelly, purée of celeriac green beans		
cheese		
pears in caramel		
Crémant de Bourgogne		
1982 Bourgogne Aligoté		
1977 Sassicaia		
1980 Ch. Guiteronde		AUX

2 poi...
une tranche de jambon...
omelette avec 6 œufs. Sur l'omelette...
tomate. Couvrez avec les tranches de jambon.

	RECETTES	DÉPENSES
		·
fresh spinach ravioli with walnut sauce		
samphire ~ melted butter		
fillets of turbot with champagne + coriander sauce, raddiccio beans.		
cherries, passion fruit sorbet		
Henriot Champagne.		
	TOTAUX	

VENDREDI **11** MAI

STE ESTELLE   MESSAGER

BOUCHÉES DE MOULES

Cuisez à feu vif 1 l 1/2 de moules avec 1 échalote et 1 verre de
vin blanc. Décortiquez les moules. Garnissez-en des croûtes à
bouchées réchauffées au four. Passez le jus de cuisson. Faites-le
réduire de moitié. Liez avec 1 petit pot de crème. Versez dans les
croûtes.

Champagne
Chablis 1er cru
1978
1975 Ch. Larose
1975 Ch. Trintaudon
1975 Ch. des Combes

	RECETTES	DÉPENSES
Graeme + Margaret for dinner		
salade de poissons crus à la nivèche		
agnolottis au ris et rognons de veau sauce morilles		
magrets de canard au gelée d'arêtes et de cassis, haricots verts, purée d'ail et de pommes de terre		
salade tiède de mâche et de radiccio aux lardons de canard		
soufflé au...		

DIMANCHE **8** JUILLET

ST THIBAUT   MESSAGER

TOURNEDOS AUX ABRICOTS

...sauter deux moitiés d'abricots par personne, salez, poivrez
...ernir les tournedos cuits à point. Ajoutez autour salade ou
...pois.

	RECETTES	DÉPENSES
samphire ~ melted butter		
ravioli with walnut sauce		
turbot salad with coriander mayonnaise ~ new potatoes		
feta cheese		
cherries		
1982 Chablis 1er Cru Montmain		
	TOTAUX	

HOW FODDER BECAME THE MOTHER OF INVENTION

The history of Foodism

The Foodie movement did not start with a sizzle in any one person's brain-pan. It did not start with a group of intellectuals drawing up a manifesto, like Surrealism – though the leaders are intellectuals, and most of them know each other by now. Mass Foodism surged up in the 1980s all over the developed world, with more than one rising agent. The political climate was moist enough, the economy warm enough. And there was room in the kitchen: the supermarket chains were selling all the ordinary food there were stomachs for; the food industry needed Foodies to create new tastes for others to follow.

The archetypal Foodie couple, kept close by their passion and proud the world doesn't share it, jabbing at each other's plates with greedy forks in a restaurant and murmuring Mmmm puh puh puh puh and PRONOUNCING JUDGEMENT, has suddenly become a million diners, a million brains all concentrated on the next meal and the last meal and the meaning of meals and not feeling at all guilty about it.

Forward from the back burner

Old-fashioned people brought up to despise the body cannot understand all this fuss about food. Even the early Foodies were astonished to discover that their passion has been elevated to an art, and a smart art – *required* for high status. But it was predictable. The Me Generation that Tom Wolfe christened in 1976 had run out of areas of self to wallow in. AIDS and herpes made sexual freedom dangerous; and one can only exercise so many hours a day. Drugs kill – after incapacitating. Dressing in the latest fashion had begun to seem old-fashioned. Travel – in search of *what?* As for the inner landscape of Me, what's in one's head soon palls if there isn't much in one's head.

The palate was the answer – a living sensitive thrilling new place to be Me. Food was ready to move forward from the back burner. Food was a craze whose time had come.

And it was swallowed whole by a *class* whose time had come – the *aspiring* class. Old-fashioned rich people are as useless to Foodism as it is to them. They can dine well at home. The *aspiring* class go to restaurants. They used to be called the middle class, but now, as the Eighties arrived, they were out to buy the whole chain of stores and reduce the upper class to a quaint specialist department patronised by a few discriminating aspirers. This new type had been making its tastes and values felt in the market-place for almost twenty years before it was identified. In Britain, the founding of the Social Democratic Party in 1981 was a response to the new ways of thinking. Raphael Samuel, a British academic, remarked in 1982 that 'sensual pleasures, so far from being outlawed, are the very field on which social claims are established and sexual identities confirmed. Food, in particular, a post-war bourgeois passion (an SDP admirer has called it "the opium of the centrist classes"), has emerged as a crucial marker of class.'

Too right, Raph. In 1983 in America, two different sets of writers defined the new people. Marissa Piesman and Marilee Hartley in *The YUPPIE Handbook* ('the state-of-the-art manual for Young Urban Professionals'), published in January 1984, used the term already current in New York. Cathy E. Crimmins in *The Official Young Aspiring Professional's Fast-Track Handbook* (October 1983) called them YAPs. In Britain in November 1983, *Harpers & Queen* christened the equivalent type the Noovos or Noovs, from nouveaux riches.

And, suddenly, the whole monstrous crowd of streak-haired arrivistes was seen to have been fertilising the soil for new restaurants of every kind. Because it is

KNOCK KNOCK.
Who's there?
SAM.
Sam who?
SAMPHIRE'S THE BURNING
TOPIC THIS YEAR.

Getting ready for the evening's onslaught: Boulestin, Covent Garden

erupted with a gush of comment on Foodies and Foodie things like butter spurting from a pierced chicken Kiev.

In December 1983, the feminist journalist Jill Tweedie of the *Guardian* came out *against* Foodism. She said she had been 'a Foodie' for 25 strenuous years ('I blame Elizabeth David, it was she who began it all') and was going to stop wasting time in the kitchen. But she is fighting against history. The trend is towards more various, subtler, more time-taking Foodism.

Hot-plates of the world

It takes several things to support a Foodie culture: high-class shops, fast transport bringing fresh produce from the land, enlightened well-paid eater-outers who will support the whole expensive edifice, lower-paid workers to make the food. Suddenly they are all present.

New York is the hot-plate of Foodism. As *The Times* (London) admitted in December 1983, New York is 'the eating capital of the world, a city devoted to its stomach'. Paris, with its high-speed trains setting out for Lyon's three-stars every hour, used to be the city most obsessed by food. As Emma Rothschild had put it in 1980, 'In Paris, high cuisine is for the first time a more or less genuine mass mania.' In an article in *The London Review of Books*, she compares Paris in the 1980s to another food-mad city, Hangzhou in the thirteenth century. She suggests that a pinch of politics is necessary to make a city food fou – political pride but also political insecurity, so the citizens become culinary chauvinists.

The great cities of the West *quiver* with culinary chauvinism – not only the native porky chauvinism of the citizens for the reputation of their city, but the fiery individual chauvinisms of the 200 or so other nationalities who will have set up restaurants there. The modern restaurant

YAPS, Yuppies and Noovs who pay the bill for the Food Movement. You could say that *all* YAPs, Yuppies and Noovs are Foodies. In fact, Marileee Hartley says she had planned to write a book about the eating habits of the breed, then expanded it to cover all YAPspects.

In the twenty years before, there had been plenty of signs that food was heating up – cookery book sales soaring, television programmers putting gimmicky television cooks into the schedule, travel agencies concocting gastronomic tours, new restaurant guides challenging fat Mich.

Foodism heats up

'Foodies' were formally christened by *Harpers & Queen* in an article called 'Cuisine Poseur' by three staff writers and several freelances in August 1982. (Paul Levy edited it anonymously, having signed an agreement not to sue for the libellous things written about him, the greedy 'King Foodie'.) At last the phenomenon had a name. Newspapers, magazines and books

world is the exact opposite of a melting pot. The deep and natural conceit of the French and the Chinese as being the *only* cuisine suffers the daily insult of sharing the same Manhattan street with the barbarians – and *each other*.

The cuisine of France was idolised by the rest of the world before the Second World War. Everyone knew of the great restaurants, the Foodie route to the south (pok pok pok pok past the poplars of the Route Nationale 7), the miraculous meals produced in ugly little villages where you happened to stop. But the war slammed the dining-room door. In Europe, it was not *fashionable* to be a Foodie (not possible, either). Spartan values reigned. As Jane Grigson says, 'Making a virtue of endurance, we added butter, cream, wine and olive oil to the list of deadly sins, or the unpardonable extravagances.' Expectations were put away. In *The British At Table* (1944) John Hampson was not sure they would ever be brought out again. 'Nothing will bring back the days of cheap proficient domestic labour. Shall we know again the days when wine and oil are plentiful, or have such glories gone, like the past, forever? Much can be said in favour of modern kitchens. Will they degenerate into mere cubby-holes in which to heat the dull contents of tins, jars and cardboard boxes?'

Too wrong, Sadsack. The fat future was about to reach you. The door to joy was opened again for the British by Elizabeth David, who had lived abroad but had not published anything except some articles in *Harper's Bazaar* before she brought out, with no fanfare, *A Book of Mediterranean Food* in 1950 and *French Country Cooking* in 1951. Their impact was extraordinary, even for a literary nation like the English, who learn everything through reading. They read Elizabeth David, tried it, and fell in love. Meat, sugar, butter and cream were still rationed and there was a £50 limit on foreign travel. But the British, and other northern Euro-

peans, and the Americans, took the road to southern Europe. The sun, the sun! The Mediterranean, thyme, wine, French food and heat dazzled and intoxicated people who had been starved of them for at least twelve years.

'Basil then was no more than the name of bachelor uncles, courgette was printed in italics as an alien word, and few of us knew how to eat spaghetti or pick a globe artichoke to pieces': Jane Grigson. A Forties Foodie will never forget the moment when you first found the succulent artichoke base under its coolie hat of spiky leaves.

Foodism fills out

As fast as the war had shrunk people's expectations, the years after the war expanded them. Like a speeded up Chaplin film, people devoured each new flavour madly before the next knocked it out of fashion, and the next and the next and the next. What memories (oh, Proust, oh Françoise's boeuf à la mode) will rise if in some Foodie fossil's house we taste again:

- a cup of (watery) hot chocolate
- a thin, gristly minute steak
- Cona coffee that has boiled
- coffee-bar cappuccino in a Pyrex cup
- green salad in a rancid wooden bowl
- bananas flambées
- tinned pineapple chunks in Grand Marnier.

They were the Foodie food of the time in Britain, no matter how revolting they seem now. In the blasé 1980s, Raphael Samuel did encounter past-shock. He was served a meal by a friend *just like the meals they had shared twenty years earlier*. Dr Samuel was astonished by his own disapproval. The friend had *not moved on*. Foodies consider it a moral duty to evolve. Food carries the obligations of fashion.

The post-war intelligentsia were the first generation to consider food impor-

Sorry Mr. Proust, the madeleines are off.....

tant. It may have been because the outer world seemed to be reducing their opportunities. Graduate wives were discovering that motherhood was no fun without help. The *Manchester Guardian* ran an article called 'Housebound' by Betty Jerman in 1960 that provoked a deep wail of response. The whole monstrous heap of pre-Habitat sofas was seen to have been fertilising the soil for dissatisfactions of every kind.

Only cooking came up to expectations. Frustrated housewives were slightly more fulfilled if they followed Elizabeth David.

In America, where Elizabeth David's books had been published in 1958, the young Sixties radicals were also keen on food. Staff members of the *New University Thought* magazine at the University of Chicago used to have feasts of teriyaki or moussaka in their office ('the NUT-house'). Members of SLATE (Student Liberals Against the Establishment? No one can remember) at Berkeley combined left-wing activity with boozy inactivity at Radical Picnics in the Napa Valley. The Berkeley Gourmet Marching and Chowder Society had a chapter in Cambridge, Massachusetts, for Harvard and MIT students – members drank burgundy (by some freak, it was cheaper than claret) and drove out to Medford on Sunday mornings for dim sum at Peking-on-the-Mystic. And some of the Sixties druggies even discovered food – via the recipe for hashish fudge in *The Alice B. Toklas Cookbook*.

Now that they are in their forties, the radical movement has gone off the boil for most, but they are Foodier by far. Foodism is a kind of radicalism, they tell themselves – going to the source, cleaning up the sauce. Alice Waters, who had been a student activist, opened the most famous Foodie restaurant of the West Coast, Chez Panisse, in Berkeley in 1971.

American Foodies weren't, like the British, all taught by one writer. They had several – Craig Claiborne, Samuel Chamberlain, Louis Diat, Irma Rombauer. But they turned to their stomachs after post-war experiences – European travel, the growth of consumerism, a change of attitude towards their immigrant populations. The immigrant recipes became something to be collected, not despised and exchanged for peanut-butter-and-jelly sandwiches. Germany was thumping out Volkswagens again. In the late Fifties,

TEN RECIPES THAT SHOOK THE WORLD

1

BRION GYSIN'S HASHISH FUDGE

FOODIES TAKE A TRIP

This recipe was responsible for many Sixties Druggies becoming Seventies Foodies. Orignially found in the pages of *The Alice B. Toklas Cook Book*, 1960, tattered Xeroxed copies of it circulated on half the campuses of America, and one or two even made their way to England. It is, of course, quite illegal to possess the cannabis sativa with which to make this recipe, but it's actually quite good even without its principal ingredient. Anyway, you can always pretend it's got hash in it, and wallow in a bit of culinary nostalgia. Incidentally, if you should break the law, do remember that the effects of the illegal substance tend to last until excreted. Verb sap.

Do not try to make this in a food processor – the texture will be nasty, and it'll take all day to clean the machine. In a mortar grind coarsely 1 tsp black peppercorns, a grated whole nutmeg, 1 tsp coriander seeds and 4 sticks of cinnamon. Then chop finely with a heavy knife 8–12 stoned fresh dates, the same of dried figs, plus 24 almonds and a dozen Brazil nuts. Pulverise as much hash as you like and mix it, plus the spices, fruit and nuts into 115 g (4 oz, ½ US cup) of unsalted best butter, kneaded with 225 g (8 oz, 1⅓ US cup) brown sugar. Roll into a cake or make into walnut-sized balls. 'Two pieces are quite sufficient,' warned Miss Toklas.

Americans who drank wine drove a Volkswagen. Radicalism + burgundy = VW.

Affluence plus consumerism was soon to equal a Cuisinart.

Cuisine-in-exile

America already had a Chinese restaurant in every small town (just as Britain had an Indian restaurant in every small town) – because Chinese labour had built the railways. And every American town has a greasy spoon run by a Greek. Both America and Britain had big Italian populations. But after the war, huge numbers of people left the poor countries, or were driven out, and went to the richer countries. America attracted Korean greengrocers and Japanese sushi chefs as well as Haitian taxi-drivers. Britain reaped new populations from the Commonwealth. Since the EEC was founded, Chinese restaurateurs have been colonising West Germany and Scandinavia.

A cuisine-in-exile used to take time to develop (Foodies have changed that). In the Fifties and Sixties, a foreign culture could not produce a great restaurant until there was a network in the new country to support it – a jumble of humble restaurants, importers and markets. Italian cuisine rose into sight at the Trattoria Terrazza in Soho in 1959. The white-tiled red-chaired Italian restaurant designed by Enzo Apicella for Mario and Franco was the smartest place to eat in London in the early Sixties, and it gave birth to many noisy bambini. All Foodies know the story of Mr Kuo, Pekinese chef at the Chinese embassy in London, who asked for political asylum in 1963 and started the first good non-Cantonese restaurant, in Willesden. Before then 'Chinese' restaurants in Britain and America did not serve the regional haute cuisine of Peking, Canton and Sichuan.

All British students had eaten 'Indian food' at Indian restaurants because it was cheap and culturally familiar since the nineteenth century. Then, suddenly, in the early Eighties, the whole monstrous heap of steaming curry was seen to have been fertilising the soil for new plants of every kind. There were smart South Indian vegetarian restaurants, Mogul restaurants, even the elegant Bombay Brasserie in Kensington.

In 1982, British cooks had been introduced to the subtleties of Indian cuisine by Madhur Jaffrey's television series and book, both called *Indian Cookery*. Since television, an entire new cuisine can become familiar to millions of people in a few months, by a series reinforced by a paperback. Or the revelation can come merely through a paperback. In the last

President Giscard d'Estaing waving his magic baguettes. When he went to Peking in 1980 he was almost knocked over by the waves of Peking cuisine coming the other way. But he pressed on with the determination of a starving man, because Paris has few real Chinese restaurants

★ ★ ★ ★ ★ ★ ★ ★ ★ ★

Old joke
'Waiter, waiter, there's a fly in my soup!'
'Keep your voice down, sir, or they'll all want one.'
Nouvelle joke
'Waiter, waiter, this isn't raspberry vinegar, it's plain vinegar.'
'Keep your voice down, sir. This is the last drop of plain vinegar in town.'

fourteen years, authentic versions of three major cuisines have become accessible to English-speaking cooks, each through a successful book: Indian, Middle Eastern (Claudia Roden's *A Book of Middle Eastern Food*) and Italian (Marcella Hazan's *Classic Italian Cookbook*).

America has had close links with Japan since the nineteenth century. Now, San Francisco, New York and Los Angeles offer as much variety in Japanese restaurants as Tokyo. Planes fly into London every day with Pacific fish for the sushi bars, and return to Tokyo via Paris with fresh foie gras and truffles.

Air freighting of food is so taken for granted that foreign restaurants – such as the three or four Korean restaurants in London – are starting up in cities where there is no base of native workers. They hope to survive by attracting businessmen and Foodies. They are competing with the other ethnic restaurants for 'customers from a common pool of floating eaters – a new phenomenon of the twentieth century', as Christopher Driver, former editor of the *Good Food Guide*, observes in his book *The British at Table 1940–1980*.

Being able to get fresh summer produce all year round does make life more difficult for the Foodie – 'the season' has been part of the aesthetics of cooking since early Chinese times. But Foodies keep the ingredient 'time of year' in their meals, no matter that it is artificial. The first new potatoes, the first grouse, the first broad beans and the last raspberries.

Society cooks

Before the Second World War, you had to cook badly if you cooked at all – to show you were used to employing a cook. After the war, the upper and middle classes took to cooking with zeal. It was like the old joke: 'Is this what the working class call ****ing? It's too good for them.' Before the war, talking about food was gross, swapping recipes unthinkable. By 1960, food chat and recipe-exchange were required of the society wife. (In the Eighties, middle-class husbands are more interested in recipe-swapping than in wife-swapping.)

The young ladies' cookery schools, such as Rosemary Hume's Cordon Bleu in London, which she reopened in 1945 with Constance Spry, taught mostly classic French methods, and Emma and Melissa sallied forth to get jobs cooking for boardrooms or ski chalets or Mediterranean villas or shooting lodges. By the 1970s and '80s, being able to cook was the favourite passport to travel and social life of upper-class European girls. Planes were flying out every day with debutante cooks for the holiday chalets.

The daughters of the former domestic servants preferred to work in factories or offices. They did not learn how to cook – they were too busy. The food manufacturers were delighted to help by selling them tins and packets. Frozen food, which arrived in the mid-1950s, was a great improvement and with its precise instructions put crisper vegetables on their plates than they had ever had before.

The spread of supermarkets and the start of food advertising on television took Foodism to the masses (commercial television began in 1954 in both Britain and America). Television channels had cookery programmes – Julia Child in America and Philip Harben on the BBC. After Philip Harben the BBC got stodgier and less Foodie with Fanny and Johnny Cradock and Delia Smith.

British newspapers launched colour supplements to catch the food, furniture and fashion advertisements. The *Sunday Times* launched its supplement in 1962, the *Daily Telegraph* and *Observer* in 1964 (the *News of the World*, *The Mail on Sunday* and *Sunday Express* each launched a supplement in 1983). In America, supplements ('the rotogravures') had been added to papers since before the war. The *New*

York Times Sunday Magazine has carried arch-Foodie Craig Claiborne's recipes since 1975, a formula now imitated by every American Sunday newspaper; and most dailies have food supplements during the week.

By 1970, all the colour-photograph articles and cookery books made the smart Foodies uneasy – they don't like seeing their subject dished up for the masses. Cuisine began to seem suburban. Every last bad cook was putting wine and mushrooms into the sauce. 'French cuisine', in the dark culinary hours before the dawn, was debased and was everywhere – in hotels, big restaurants, little restaurants and even in pubs.

Nouvelle machine

T hen, suddenly, in the early Seventies, the whole monstrous heap of meunière was seen to have been fertilising the soil for new plants of every kind. Nouvelle cuisine (p 62) was the most vigorous, springing up in France itself, sundering the old alliance of flour and butter, and the très riches sauces. Nouvelle cuisine requires a lot of old-fashioned puréeing, whisking and mincing and would not have got out of restaurants if the food processor had not arrived at the same time. Nouvelle cuisine and the machine formed a new alliance. The Robot Chef in France, the Cusinart in America and the Magimix in Britain allowed the ordinary Foodie to rape the carrots, julienne the légumes, grate the Parmesan, mince the fish and purée the spinach and pear along with his leaders Bocuse and Guérard.

At the same time, the general market in food and drink became as stiff as a properly made polenta and began to fragment at the edges and become more particular, more *Foodie*. All the fresh cream the ordinary cook could use was already being sold to her – she had to be turned into a

customer who would say 'Where is the crème fraîche please?' That is why supermarkets now stock croissants, fresh pastas, overpriced moules marinières already washed and sauced in plastic buckets. (One Foodie couple quarrelled as they finished trying these, and pelted each other with the shells. They made up on the happy calculation that the mark-up for unfortunates who can't make their own was either fourteen or fifteen times the price of the mussels and the bucket.) But the supermarkets hope their Foodie customers (class AB and C1 socio-economically) will buy mountains of moules and eventually set an example to all the Ds and Es lower down the scale. It's the Foodies' A-ness the marketing buggers want.

Foodies and the ad-man

T he big newspaper and magazine publishing groups realised in the Seventies that they too had to 'go up-market' to stop television putting them out of business by taking most of their advertising revenue. Television, they saw, could reach a much bigger audience with its appeals to 'Buy X's instant coffee'. But the advertisement cost £7,000 for 30 seconds. To the maker of real coffee, it was not worth paying that to reach 6½ million people, only 50,000 of whom had the developed taste to buy his coffee: and each of those would be shocked to see *my* coffee, which I considered the proof of a sophisticated palate, being vulgarised on commercial television. The newspapers and magazines were very glad that *they* still had the snob advertisements. And those with big circulations made their editorial policy snobbier rather than less snobby (going *down*-market is always the temptation in lean times – and for those in second place).

The placing of the vast sums of food and drink advertising still going into print was decided by a very simple calculation:

the advertising agency divided the circulation (and readership) of the publication by the cost of the ad. The paper with the biggest AB circulation for the smallest advertising rate got the business. (The Ds and Es were reached on television.)

This was much too coarse a sieve to use for the new finely fragmented food market. The big publications and the brand-leader foods were sitting on top of the mesh and growing, the smaller publications and rarer brands were pouring down the drain and going out of business in a steady stream –
when –
suddenly the whole monstrous heap of business lunches was seen to have been fertilising a dead idea.

In 1968, Tim Joyce at the British Market Research Bureau had invented a hair sieve. This was called the Target Group Index, the TGI. The TGI measures consumer preferences for brands of goods from shampoo to chocolate biscuits to cars by door-to-door interviews, and relates those to the viewing of television and reading of newspapers and magazines. The TGI is like a satellite.

Look down from the TGI and you can target your advertisement, exactly.

The new method was in use in America in 1968, but in Britain it took until 1972.

The TGI was a godsend to upmarket newspapers and magazines. It revealed, for example, that *more* men in total who read *Harpers & Queen* (circulation in 1972, 68,000, colour page advertisement, £540) were heavy wine and mineral-water users and expensive holiday-takers than men who read *Vogue, Punch, House & Garden* or the colour supplements – all of whom had higher circulations and higher advertising rates. Advertisements started to go into the appropriate shop-window rather than the largest shop-window, to the health of smaller publishers. By the second half of 1983, as the market fragmented yet more finely, the snobby glossy magazines were the only magazines in Britain which gained rather than lost readers (as well as making a fat profit) – elitism was growing, in reading as in shopping.

It was all part of the move up-market that people were making, as higher wages and shorter hours allowed those with jobs to experiment and enjoy themselves.

Advertisements financed the growth of Foodism

Foodies fight on

At the same time, fast-food shops sprang up to feed the new street-life – a leisurely river of floating eaters. The good-quality American hamburgers and real-cream ice-cream and Italian pizzas, slammed out in clean stylish surroundings, were wonderful for young people, although Foodies would never go into such a place. They hate what they call 'junk food', and some pretend never to have tasted Heinz tomato ketchup ('You mean that red stuff in the plastic tomatoes?').

They wage war against the fast-food chains. Foodies will fight for what they believe in. They are always attacking Pennsylvania Dept of Agriculture regulations – or EEC regulations, in the case of Britain. They get furious with the big farmers. They Save Old Seeds. Foodies' campaigns are all the more fun because the fight does not expose the fighter to risk. Foodies are revolutionaries who will never get hurt. Who does not believe in better, purer food?

Another contemporary campaign was the rescuing of regional cookery. All over the world, there was a rejection of the grand hotel tradition, as chef-patrons sprang up like wild mushrooms. At home there was a rediscovery of home cooking – what grandmother made. Countries fragmented into lots of little cuisines at the Foodies' touch. (Elizabeth David had seen France that way twenty years earlier.)

Jaw, jaw, jaw

It all made food talked about. The end of the first phase of Foodism came with a picnic, not *utterly* different from the Radical Picnic at Napa in 1960. This picnic was indoors, but there were some of the same Foodies, twenty years on, and much redirected idealism, and a lot of publishing gossip. Mmmm puh puh puh puh. It was the third Oxford international food symposium organised by ex-British-ambassador Alan Davidson and Oxford don Theodore Zeldin at St Antony's in September 1981 (it started in 1979 and was repeated, growing each time, in 1980, 1981, 1983, and 1984). There they all were, the Foodies of the world. They had come from Japan, Africa, America, New Zealand, Canada, and Europe, of course. Each British delegate brought a contribution to the buffet table for lunch – mango tart (Sonia Blech), pastries stuffed with aubergine (Claudia Roden), smoked scallops (Elizabeth Evans), coffee brewed in the scientific Foodie's own replica of Count Rumford's coffee pot (physics professor Nicholas Kurti).

The delegates were thrilled to see each other: 'I always go *straight to your shop* when I arrive in New York.' 'I'm such a fan.' 'Your book is my bible.' 'I do hope you won't mind, but can you sign it for me?' 'Your paper on fiddlehead ferns sounds fascinating.' 'Are you going to speak in English or French?' The greyness of the Oxford skies and the ugly, airport-like, Ladies' lavatory-inadequate building were forgotten as Foodies heard their heroes and heroines read papers on the first loaf (baked in Bulgaria 7,000 years ago) and Bogus Cuisines (Alan Davidson's obsession). The world's Foodies could not help greeting each other, even during the lectures, with little smiles and bows and whispers of recognition. 'Hel*lo*.' 'A*llo*.' '*Hi*.'

Foodism had arrived. It will not go away.

Where a Foodie meets a Wholefoodie coming through the rye

You are what you eat' is the Foodie's favourite metaphysical maxim. By it you mean 'The unexamined meal isn't worth eating'. Your store of memory and desire is almost entirely meals. Your second favourite maxim is 'It is impossible to have too much of a Good Thing', eg caviar (stiff with killer salt), clotted cream (solid cholesterol) or sirloin steak (layered cholesterol).

Foodies worry about their health, because they are modern people, but they would never let it get between them and food. They have borrowed a few ideas from that other post-war phenomenon, the Wholefoodies. They are also mad about vegetables, like the Wholefoodies' food-political ally, the vegetarians. But the three groups are marked by mutual disapproval.

The Speckled Band

Sub speciae aeternitatis – or even on a moment's reflection – it is obvious that Wholefoodies are in fact only Halffoodies. Wholefood freaks (and the shops that cater for them) care deeply about the quality of food – as raw ingredients. Their nuts, pulses and grains are the best, so is their flour and bread. Moreover they are not, like vegetarians, open to the charge of mere crankiness. They may be over the top about organic methods of farming, but everyone knows that the only edible chickens, at least in Britain, are free-range ones from wholefood shops.

The reason Wholefoodies are only Halffoodies is that they don't care what happens to the ingredients. An over-cooked free-range chicken is very nearly as bad as an over-cooked battery chicken (except that the battery bird tastes of fish).

Nouvelle version of an Old Joke

Three men went on a camping holiday. Tom the Foodie said only he was allowed to cook. While the others swam, boated, walked and sunbathed, Tom planned the night's menu and made expeditions to the village shop (a country Fauchon, naturally, for Tom chose the campsite) and read his cookery books and wrote his food notes and sent postcards to Foodies all over the world and cooked and arranged the food on plates in delicious mouthfuls like a picture and lectured on the subtle assemblage of tastes. All the other two wanted after their exercise was beans, bacon and beer. They asked if they could cook a meal. Tom said no, he had a delicate palate and had to do all the cooking.

This went on for another two days, until John had a bright idea. He told Tom that he had discovered a farmhouse which made a rare local cheese and he would see if he could get some. Tom frowned, but said all right. The night's menu, he announced, was lentil salad, lamb and aubergine stew, and chocolate mousse – but it was still worrying him.

John carried out his plan. He got a cow-pat from a field, wrapped it up, brought it back and gave it to Tom. Tom opened it, and his face fell. John felt ashamed. Tom said in a very reproachful voice: 'I am sorry you did this. I can see the week has been wasted. You haven't understood at all what I have been trying to do for you.' John felt a real heel, and said: 'It was only a joke. I realise I have been beastly. I just thought it smelt like those cheeses you like.' Tom said: 'The fact that this is a cow-pat is nothing. I could have cooked this cow-pat so that it was quite delicious. What makes me sad is that you hadn't noticed that tonight's menu already has too much brown in it.'

And Wholefoodies actually believe virtue has a colour – speckled beige – and a texture – moist and fibrous, like pig food. At many Wholefoodie meals, *everything* is beige to look at and drudgery to chew. Wholefoodies lack the *aesthetic attitude* to food that characterises the true Foodie.

Turd time lucky

Foodies start the day on bran, and then forget about their bowels. Foodies care about what they put into themselves, but there is a kind of health-food freak who cares desperately about what comes out. This subject is dreary, Foodies consider. As novelist and fart-food columnist of the

Guardian Colin Spencer said in *Good and Healthy*, 'The excreta of vegetarians is by far the healthiest: stools should be soft and fall lightly into a pyramid shape. Compact stools are not a sign of a healthy diet.' Foodies care about the saucepan, not the lavatory pan.

Vegetable, die

The main thing Foodies have against vegetarians is that Veggies are against fish, and also that 'they *cannot* cook vegetables.' Like Wholefoodies, they go for the speckled beige moist fibrous approach to vegetable-cooking. A vegetarian meal can literally make you vomit, if the beans or lentils are soaked too long and have started to ferment or germinate. Two hours is long enough soaking for young haricots. Twenty-four and you'll shortly be rushing to the lavatory. (Better to boil for ten minutes, and cool in fresh water, before starting the cooking proper.)

Foodies say vegetarians have *negative* criteria for food: no animal flesh and – for extremist 'Vegan' vegetarians – nothing of animal origin. Foodies have a *positive* criterion: it must be, if not The Best, at least Good.

Foodies think that many vegetarians allow their diet to be dictated by sentiment: 'I gave up eating meat the day I saw a calf on his way to market; his eyes met mine, and . . .' Foodies are only sentimental about quality. They are ruthless about the means to the end. Foie gras would be on the menu every week except for the cost. ('It's no longer done to nail the goose's feet to the floor of the barn; they're all *conditioned* nowadays – they *like* being force-fed.')

Foodies visiting southern China or Hong Kong seek out the experience of tasting dog or snake. ('Wokking the dog. Eating them is quite the best thing to do with them.')

A healthy attitude in a Foodie body

Foodies consider their own ways the best balanced and healthiest. None is so dim as to neglect the findings of science. Weight, naturally enough, is The Enemy. But Foodies, although always slimming, are never on a diet. Diet books are a million-dollar (and pound and franc and Deutschmark) industry, but if their writers had to sell their wares to Foodies they would starve. So far as Foodies are concerned, Tarnower, Pritikin, Atkins, Mayo and Eyton are, or ought to be, merely the names of famous murder victims. Most Foodies think the F-Plan Diet is something to do with sex. And, as they in any case live permanently on a high-fibre diet, they have no need of a book telling them to eat baked beans.

Foodies Know. They were the first to recognise the validity of Dr Denis Burkitt's findings, published in the 1970s, about the lack of roughage in the western diet. All-Bran and muesli are found in every Foodie's larder, and few Foodies haven't a sack of bran for adding to the

The Foodie cupboard is always bare, according to the Foodie: 'There is *nothing* in the house.' It is like the woman with £4,000's worth of clothes but nothing to wear. Foodies always have a hoard of food which cost them approximately £400 ($600, 4600 F, 1600 DM, 160,000 yen) – £200's worth in the store cupboard, £200's worth in the freezer; not to mention the £400 tied up in wine. But you think you have zilch. When, with a flourish, you produce the spinach soufflé with its anchovy sauce, you know you're a genius who's *done it again*, never mind who else takes miracles for granted.

NB If you are wondering about tomatoes, Foodies keep whole ones in the freezer for cooking.

. . . .

KNOCK KNOCK.
Qui est là?
RAVIOLI.
Did you tell the police or was it someone you know?

Foie gras makes decent people and vegetarians see red (those poor geese). But Foodies are ruthless about the means to the end (foie gras is their favourite shade of pink)

tuna fish in tin
anchovies
olives, walnut oil (huile de noix)
Soy - 2 kinds (dark and light)

cheap French eau de vie, last year's Christmas pud
FISH soup in tins (French!), 1 or 2 tins artichoke bottoms
1 huge and 1 very large tin escargots, jar pimentos
Amora Dijon mustard. girolles, tin pleurottes,
mushroom ketchup, tin choucroute garni,
& 3 foil packets of choucroute.

VINEGARS - homemade fruit vinegar (raspberry, blackcurrant)
redcurrant
Balsamic vinegar (aged strong Italian wine vinegar
champagne vinegar, homemade red and white
(made from the dregs of glasses
Alum for pickling. Meaux mustard (for cooking), capers,
mustards.

CHINESE preserved bean curd
chungking pickled turnip
tinned bamboo shoots
Hoisin sauce, Hunan dried soy bean
with chilli

5 spice mixture, preserved radish with chilli
chinese rice vinegar, sesame oil,
dried black mushrooms, pea starch noodles,
dried Mo-er mushrooms.

VIETNAMESE tunngot (pimento puree)
INDIAN 10 different pickles and chutneys
(homemade)
6 packets poppadums
MIDDLE EAST tahini (jar), orange flower
water, harissa (hot pepper sauce),
1 tin vine leaves.

tin rillettes d'oie, tin smoked oysters, 2 tins expensive sardines (connét.able), tuna in water,
tuna in peanut oil, (American) 2 jars maple syrup, 1 corn syrup, worcester sauce, tabasco sauce,
tin green peppercorns, apricot jam, jar horseradish, natural clams in broth (vongole- Italian jar)
polenta (cardboard tube), tin green olives, 2 tins rouille Marseillaise, tin confit de poule,
cornflower, bag of grits, selection of dried pasta, sachets Harvest Gold dried yeast, icing sugar,
caster sugar, preserving sugar (not enough to do anything with), 2 packets Rakusen's matzo meal,
cooking salt, 2 packets brown rice, pearl barley, dried flageolets, 2 kinds lentils (brown and orange)
cannellini (white haricot beans), sunflower seeds, dried currants,   trail mix (dried fruit etc)
fruit muesli, All-Bran bran, tin Dorset Knobs (rusks), sea salt,   ratafias, cayenne
amaretti de Saronno (with the papers), packet of jumbo oats,
bicarbonate of soda, crab boil (for boiling shellfish in), paprika
bag whole nutmegs, jar cloves,
packet Maurice Mességué's rosemary (from Fleurance)
saffron, pistachio nuts

pine nuts,   vanilla sugar
walnuts,   dried ceps
gumbo filé   poppy seeds
mace blades

lead beans for baking pastry blind,
All the standard spices in their original jars
jar bay leaves, big jar vinaigrette,
huile noisette (HAZELNUT),
4 kilo tin calamata, Greek-as-well- but cheap!
Litre of Lucca, corn oil (Waitrose)
MANY MANY tisanes and teas,
coffee black beans (deep freeze)

strings of garlic and pepper (French or
Hungarian)

Several kinds of chillis,

Honey (Provence etc.) Jams and Jellies:
redcurrant, blackcurrant, gooseberry,
sage and mint, American wild rice,
semoule for couscous

DAGO IN SEARCH OF GREENER
PASTAS: THE FOODIE STORE
CUPBOARD, ITALIAN DIVISION

Pasta is faster. With these ingredients, which no
self-respecting Foodie is ever without, like-minded
friends can be feasted – and non-Foodies overawed
– in minutes.

• Wedges of fresh parmesan and pecorino cheese,
mozzarella and ricotta, mascarpone
• pancetta, sliced
• jars of: crema di carciofi (artichoke paste) and
sun-dried tomatoes (the home-made pesto is in the
freezer)
• Balsamic vinegar
• Tuscan olive oil (the best is made by A. & M.
Zyw at Poggio Lamentano, Castagneto Carducci)
• a white truffle packed in tissue in a jar of rice (in
season) or a tube of white truffle paste
• garlic, basil (fresh or frozen in freezer trays),
tomatoes (fresh, tinned or frozen)
• anchovies in brine
• packets of Arborio rice, dried farfalle, stellini,
penne, rigatoni, trenette, vermicelli and ziti.
Tagliatelle in the freezer.

home-made bread. You know that bran prevents all ailments, from haemorrhoids to heart disease; that oat bran is even better for you (but harder to find) than wheat bran; that it is necessary to eat more complex carbohydrates and less protein, and that sugar is Out. You also know, but ignore the fact, that we all eat too much salt. A few years ago, Craig Claiborne, cookery editor of the *New York Times*, underwent a conversion, and tried to persuade his readers to leave the salt out of his recipes. Foodies all over America tried to eat – and cook – without salt for a year or so; but most gave it up as a very bad job, and are waiting for science to invent an adequate salt substitute. Foodies are not fanatics – except about food itself. The salt stays on the table, in its mill.

TEN RECIPES THAT SHOOK THE WORLD

THAT ONE'S NICE, THIS ONE'S GENUINE

LA (VRAIE) SALADE NIÇOISE

Jacques Médecin, the Reagan-loving, American-talking Mayor of Nice, who has quarrelled with novelist Graham Greene (whom he successfully sued for libel), is the leading Foodie of Provence. In his *Cuisine Niçoise* we learn that the Real Thing consists only of raw ingredients – except for hard-boiled eggs – that it may not, under any circumstances, include boiled potatoes or green beans, and is not dressed with vinaigrette, but the tomatoes are salted three times 'and moistened with olive oil'. He does allow either raw broad beans or thinly sliced raw artichokes, depending on the season, but not both. Apart from these, he also allows that the Niçois themselves nowadays break the rules by including *both* anchovies and tuna fish in the same salad. Médecin calls for a salad bowl rubbed with garlic, into which he puts 10 tomatoes, quartered and salted, 3 quartered hard-boiled eggs, 12 anchovy fillets or 300 g (12 oz) canned tuna, 1 peeled and sliced cucumber, 2 thinly sliced green peppers, 6 sliced spring onions, 200 g (½ lb) shredded small broad beans *or* 12 shredded tiny globe artichokes, 100 g (4 oz) black olives, 6 shredded basil leaves and 6 tbs of olive oil. Foodies forget about making SN with leftover boiled potatoes. You start from scratch now, for a taste of your own Médecin.

Greens in Judgement

Lettuce consider salad

Foodies spend their salad days avoiding the eating patterns of their native countries and aping those of others. British Foodies would have to be tortured before they gave their families the proverbial meat and two veg. American Foodies feel the same about serving the salad before the main course, as is done in every Howard Johnson's, every country club and every greasy spoon in the land.

The habit of salad first has an honourable ancestry. As usual, it is the British and French, who now eat their salad after the main course, who have changed their custom: the American pleb practice is the older. Salads were included in the gustus, the first course of Roman times, and according to C. Anne Wilson's *Food and Drink in Britain*, simple green salads remained a first-course dish in Tudor times. By Elizabeth I's reign, though, the salad was no longer simple. The French salade panachée and salade composée had caught on, adding vegetables, fruit and hard-boiled eggs to the basic leaves. These were for special guests and occasions, and could be a first course or the main meal. They were the predecessors of the seventeenth-century grand salads called salmagundi, ornate edifices based on cooked or cured meats and fish. Tomatoes have dominated cooking even more than the thing Foodies call 'the bully' – the onion. The tomato, from the New World, was used by the Spanish cooked and in salads in the sixteenth century, as Gerard notes in his *Herball*, 1597. In the eighteenth century they were called love apples in English, Italian and French because they were thought to be aphrodisiacs. Hannah Glasse has a recipe using them in *The Art of Cookery*, 1747. But it was not until the nineteenth century that they started to paint Britain and America red, pushing out of recipes the more subtle flavours of the onion family, particularly the shallot (a substitution deplored by Foodie historians John and Karen Hess). Recently, the tomato has got married to Basil.

The flowers of the nasturtium, brought back from Peru, were eaten in European salads in the seventeenth century – also its peppery buds and leaves.

In 1664, John Evelyn wrote a pamphlet describing how the gardener could produce salads in England all year round. In 1699, he gave a rule for salad in his *Acetaria*: 'every plant should come in to bear its part, without being over-powered...'

Laitue, Brute

Salads were dressed then, as now, with basic vinaigrette (French dressing). The sickly horrors of American Thousand Island, tomato-flavoured 'French', and blue cheese dressing were unknown even to the gross-feeding Romans. The British cousin of these horrors is salad cream (Heinz launched their salad cream on the British market in the late Twenties): the colour of

A Foodie-approved salad: surly red radicchio, burly mâche and curly endive

mayonnaise but of pouring consistency and sweetish. Foodies use real mayonnaise, though not on salads – with cold poached fish, for instance, or oeufs mayonnaise. They either make the mayonnaise themselves, drip-drip-dripping the olive oil in, or serve Hellmann's with apologies. A mayonnaise-based sauce is acceptable however with crudités, the raw vegetable first course that has inched across the Channel to Britain and then across the

Atlantic in the last ten years. Crudités have got ever more fantastical, like the feathered decorated hair-dos in the age of the pompadour. One of the restaurants on Tahiti Plage at St Tropez served amazing crudités at the end of the Seventies. The slab of cork supporting the raw vegetables needed two waiters to bring it to the table. It had, as well as the usual carrots, celery, fennel, cucumber, radishes and spring onions, groups of whole baby globe artichokes, thick asparagus spears, tiny courgettes, thick slices of celeriac and slender French beans.

The most complicated early dressing was probably like that devised in verse by the Reverend Sydney Smith, the English Foodie Divine who lived from 1771 to 1845. The third couplet is quoted by all Foodies; the final couplet is said to be taught by some to their children to say last thing, instead of 'Now I lay me down to sleep'.

To make this condiment your poet begs
The pounded yellow of two hard-boiled eggs;
Two boiled potatoes, passed through kitchen sieve,
Smoothness and softness to the salad give.
Let onion atoms lurk within the bowl,
And, half-suspected, animate the whole.
Of mordant mustard add a single spoon;
Distrust the condiment that bites so soon;
But deem it not, thou man of herbs, a fault
To add a double quantity of salt;
Four times the spoon with oil of Lucca crown,
And twice with vinegar procur'd from town;
And lastly o'er the flavour'd compound toss
A magic soupçon of anchovy sauce.
Oh, green and glorious! Oh, herbaceous treat!
'Twould tempt the dying anchorite to eat;
Back to the world he'd turn his fleeting soul,
And plunge his fingers in the salad bowl!
Serenely full, the epicure would say,
'Fate cannot harm me, I have dined today.'

Jane Grigson quotes this in her *Vegetable Book*, and specifies 125g (4oz) of potato, 1 tsp of mustard and anchovy sauce, 2 tsps of salt, 4 tbs of oil and 2 tbs of vinegar, served with watercress, cos lettuce (Romaine) or chicory (endive).

The grandest houses in Sydney Smith's time did not have courses, but service à la Française: everything was put on the table at once and left to get cold; diners would eat only what they could reach. In the 1850s this gave way to service à la Russe, which still prevails: food brought to the table course by course, and served hot to each diner. In the march of dishes, a simple green salad came after the main course, to help digestion. This is still the sequence with all the French, with American

Foodies, and with the British upper and middle classes – the only British who eat green salad. The other ranks continue to think salad means beetroot, usually soaked in malt vinegar, with a single lettuce leaf, a slice each of tomato and cucumber, and the dreaded salad cream.

Burning your salad bowl

Green salad was a password among the France-lovers among the British before and during the Second World War. In each class there were a tiny minority who embraced French culture – the films, the paintings, the food. This green salad party lived in a fantasy of Abroad, as Raphael Samuel remarked. He has unearthed a subsection who believed an *un*dressed salad was a cultural statement. Vinegar was said to destroy the vitamins, or thin the blood. Malt vinegar is still a stain on the character to all Foodies. After Elizabeth David's books, the green salad party became the majority. A wooden salad bowl was as essential to a proper wedding as new sheets. Until the 1970s the wedding present salad bowl took the spiritual place of the open fire or household gods. The wooden O continued to be sacred while its handmaidens, such as the garlic crushers, came and went. It was wiped not washed. No one liked to admit that every salad tasted of the ones that had gone before. The bowl had become impregnated and was rancid. Its wooden salad spoons and forks were also impregnated and rancid. Suddenly a Foodie announced that she always used a glass bowl. What a blinding thought! Foodies of the world united to throw out their wooden ones. One Foodie had a bonfire of all his Foodie friends' wedding present bowls.

Salad tasted like a different dish in a china or glass bowl. But those didn't last long. Nouvelle cuisine arrived to attack the principle of a communal salad from which you could fish the bits you wanted, and substituted tiny amounts of radicchio and rocket arranged beautifully on individual plates in the kitchen and set in front of you, as a first course.

The two NC salads that Foodies like are either warm sautéed chicken livers with mâche and radicchio – a reminder to the Foodie of the salade riche of three-star restaurants: warm slices of fresh foie gras, served with a tiny salad of mesclun dressed with fruit vinegar (eg raspberry) and nut oil (eg hazelnut). Or a round of grilled goat's cheese on toast with the same salad. These make the perfect first course for old-hand Foodies, and cause great confusion to beginner Foodies.

Fat animals are dangerous

Foodies were quick to react to the dangers of animal fat. They are connoisseurs of butter, but Foodie tables for at least ten years have featured Flora, Fleischmann's and Fruit d'Or. ('It tastes ghastly,' one Foodie says of Flora, 'but it makes divine sauces. As it already contains an emulsifier, beurre blanc made with it will never separate.') Foodies never admit to liking the taste of these polyunsaturated spreads, but many Foodie households now consume less than a pound of butter a month.

All Foodies sighed with relief when they realised that olive oil was neutral on the saturated/polyunsaturated scale. It remains the Foodies' favourite fat. 'I'd use it to deep *fry*, if only I could afford it.' It's very good for frying, with a much higher 'critical' point, 210°C, than butter, 110°C.

Tasteless safflower and sunflower oil

you might allow a teaspoon of the fat into the potato gratin or, better, into the cassoulet, where Foodies believe its presence is more than compensated for by the fibre-rich beans. (Cassoulet, by the way, is the Foodie baked beans, and is a regular winter meal: 'So good for the children.')

Foodies in general like fart-food; a Martian wandering into a Foodie kitchen would have great trouble distinguishing it from a Wholefoodie's or Veggie's kitchen. They all have storage jars containing pulses. The difference is that, while they all have chick-peas, kidney beans and three kinds of lentils, the Foodie will also have gone to enormous lengths to procure borlotti beans and belles de Soisson.

On the other hand, the Foodie does not eat beans and pulses all that often. ('The family *love* beans; but, my dear, the calories!'). They are simply *too* nutritious, and, as the Foodie is not restricted in his high-

★————— F·O·O·D·I·E·B·O·R·E·S —————★

THE VINEGAR BORE

Worst bore of all is the vinegar bore. Paul Bocuse says: 'Il n'y a point de vinaigre framboise; il n'y a que le vinaigre parfumé de framboise.' Try telling that to the bore, whose larder shelves groan with raspberry, blackcurrant and sherry vinegar. 'I make all my vinegars, of course' – using the slime from the top of the jar, which the bore calls a vinegar 'mother' or,

even more pompously, 'mère' or 'matrix'. It is, in fact, only the effluvium produced when wine becomes vinegar; and only works because of the drops of vinegar that still adhere to the evil substance when one bore gives a piece of it to someone else. And thereby creates a new bore.

★—————————————————————————★

are cherished, too, as they can be blended with olive oil both for cooking and for vinaigrette and mayonnaise, saving purse and arteries alike. And all Foodies know the trick of eking out a few drops of highly flavoured nut oil – walnut, hazel-nut or almond – with one of the unflavoured oils.

Rendered goose and chicken fat are, of course, Foodie prizes. But they are used rarely and with fine discretion, as they are positively atherosclerosis-inducing. Nonetheless, if you have roasted a goose (something no health-conscious Foodie would do more often than twice a year),

grade protein intake (as are Wholefoodies and Veggies), he has no need of extra calories. Indeed, he's probably slimming. So more and more, the mainstay of the Foodie household is fish.

Chefs prefer to cook fish. So do Foodies. For one thing, it's the most difficult food to shop for, as it has to be fresh. More than one Foodie has moved house to be closer to the fishmonger; but most enjoy The Search for Turbot. Fish is high in protein, but low in calories and cholesterol. It is expensive, highly perishable, and many people think it hard to cook.

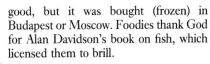

Non-Foodie lovers claim that oysters steam up their spectacles, but Foodie spectacles steam on bream. Foodies adore serving fish at dinner parties – it's so tricky to time, and so easy to convert people who don't think they like it, simply by giving them properly cooked fish for the first time. It is done when there is still a slight trace of pink along the backbone.

All Foodies prefer fish to meat, but you divide fish into three classes.

Show-off fish

These are the great fish – those robust old parties salmon, sea bass, turbot. They can be cooked whole, or cut into tranches and escalopes, or braided like tresses (1980s-style), or sliced Japanesely thinly and eaten raw. They fire the Foodie's imagination. But businessmen muddy the waters. Businessmen like food almost as much as Foodies. Many *are* Foodies, though as a class they are the dreaded *people who like everything flambé*. Like Foodies, they want the best. *If only they knew what it was.* They have turned salmon into businessmen's food, particularly smoked salmon – now rarely up to Foodie specifications. Smoked eel is the smoked salmon of the Foodie.

Odd fish

The second class is the Odd Fish – nobody but a Foodie would think of eating them. But Foodies love to produce a rarity such as a fogash. It's an ugly thing like a large herring, and not all that

good, but it was bought (frozen) in Budapest or Moscow. Foodies thank God for Alan Davidson's book on fish, which licensed them to brill.

Out of your shell

The third class contains the sensitive soles of the fish world – all the shellfish, all flat fish fillets, and escalopes of anything at all. They require split-second timing, so preferably a single guest. If it's a guest you are in love with, the cooking's an act of love, not just sardine-masochism.

While you are preparing the court bouillon, chopping herbs, opening wine, your beloved should be showing worthiness by making a French dressing, or a mayonnaise. (The honeymoon salad, 'lettuce alone without dressing', is not for Foodies.)

You think 'Not now, but *now*' (incidentally the title of Foodie heroine M. F. K. Fisher's only novel). Fish is messy, like love. The bones stick in your teeth – or your throat. Gluey sliced white bread is best to remove fish bones. As you won't have any you will have to try with brown. Reserve the Heimlich manoeuvre, the punch in the paunch, for meat. Eating the fish with its juices, sauces and accompanying pastes, coats the teeth and clouds the wine glasses. If you are already a bit ecstatic, the rest of the wine in which the fish was cooked (two glasses only) may be enough to drink with it. You talk, naturally, about former fish. You boast a bit: you don't want to be weighed in the scales and found wanting. But not too much, because talk of previous meals makes a Foodie very jealous. As green as garfish bones. Or sauce verte.

After the fish, the Foodie lovers have their simple salad and their morsel of cheese (for the red wine). Now comes the hurried washing up (even Quentin Crisp washes a plate once it has been used for fish). Now for the bounce into bed.

But the fish's role in your romance is

TEN RECIPES THAT SHOOK THE WORLD

3 FOODIES EAT IT RAW
GRAVLAX
(SALMON MARINATED WITH DILL)

Once upon a time American and British cooks boiled fish until it fell off the bone and smelled and felt like glue. But the Japanese (who for centuries ate *only* fish – meat-eating is a nasty imported habit) changed all that. In the Seventies, sashimi and sushi chic hit first Manhattan, then London. As far as fish was concerned, Foodies became crudies, and began to eat it raw. This has produced some remarkable micro-organisms in Foodie guts all over the West. None of them are *obviously* dangerous, but unpleasant parasites have been found in the faeces of 40 per cent of the Chinese inhabitants of Hong Kong, and the Cantonese have a habit of eating very under-cooked fish. Ceviche, a Central and Latin American recipe for marinating fish or shellfish in lime juice and chillies, is probably a safer way of keeping up with the (Davy) Joneses. So is the Swedish, slightly cured Gravlax or Gravadlax, the universal restaurant menu cliché of the Eighties.

Alan Davidson's recipe calls for a 1¼ kilo (3 lb) chunk of middle cut, fresh salmon, scaled, boned and cut in half lengthways. In a non-iron dish that just fits the fish, you put one half skin-side down, coat it with 4 tbs of sea salt, 1½ tbs of sugar, 2 tbs of crushed white peppercorns and 'a large bunch' of fresh dill. Make a sandwich with the other half of the fish, skin side up, cover with a plate, place a weight over it, and refrigerate for 36 to 72 hours, turning the fish sandwich over every 12 hours, and basting it with the juices.

Remove the dill and the seasoning and slice thinly like smoked salmon. Serve very small portions with a sweet mustard and dill sauce, made with Dijon mustard, sugar and either yoghurt or oil and vinegar.

not over. Food remains the overriding preoccupation with Foodies. If a saucerful was left, you will both lie awake wondering whether to sneak down and eat it or if the morning will do. As the small hours grow bigger, it is not lust that returns but hunger. You may find yourself beginning to hate that Foodie lying beside you *as still as a pike contemplating a snack.*

Foodie fishes

- monkfish
- little grey shrimps (Britain, Morecambe Bay shrimps; US, Baffin Bay shrimps; France, crevette grise)
- job gris, bourgeois and anything else from the Indian Ocean
- rascasse and red mullet (Foodies love the liver)
- brill and turbot (no American equivalents, but 'New York plaice', a misnomer for the windowpane fish, is similar and good)
- red snapper, pompano (America only)
- omble chevalier (Arctic char), pike, smoked eel and real eel – the only freshwater Foodie fishes
- fresh sardines, anchovies in brine
- oysters (all oysters, especially poached and wrapped in something fiddly)
- scallops, particularly queens (Britain), bay scallops (US), pétoncles (France)
- clams, sea urchins and (US only) soft-shell crabs
- any fish terrine

Fossil fishes

(for dinosaurs who have survived into the Foodie era)

- kippers, finnan haddock, smoked trout
- kedgeree, fish pie, spaghetti alle vongole
- tinned sardines, tinned tuna, smoked oysters
- quenelles made with flour-based panada

Businessman fishes

- big pink shrimps in pink sauce in a cocktail glass
- farmed trout (the only kind served now in restaurants) with almonds all over it
- salmon served whole with a lemon wedge in its mouth, or poached in slices with mayonnaise, or farmed and below the age of consent
- frozen Dover sole (or air-freighted fresh Dover sole in America, where only Businessman can afford it)
- smoked salmon in any helping larger than a canapé

Fish or myth?

- soft-shell lobster

Danger – Foodie at wok

The Foodie kitchen floor is hosable and scrubbable – tiles, flagstones, even lino tiles. There are periodic crashes as the cook's wine glass or a Le Creuset lid falls and shatters.

The kitchen table is deal. The stove is gas. You have to see the height of the flame. To have only electric hobs is non-F. You can have some, if you have gas too. Electric ovens are OK. Agas are Foodie (wonderful slow ovens), but even *you* sometimes forget a stew-pot or stock-pot for 24 hours ... And a Foodie guest cook goes mad when he or she is ready to finish the dish and finds the oven can't be turned up. Eye-level grills are F – better than television. Foodies like a rôtissoire, an electric spit. But the Aga is better for roasting. You have a pair of oven *gauntlets*, protecting your forearm, not oven *gloves*. You bought them in America.

Every Foodie has a Hibachi barbecue. You put it in the fireplace in cold weather. Rich Foodies buy American gas indoor barbecues – a gas grill with volcanic lava, and an extractor fan.

Foodies think about extractor fans all the time. Those and their knives. You dream of having a restaurant extractor fan for proper grilling. You try when feasible to get the restaurant or commercial model of all tools, to prove what a pro you are. You ache to see a smell-extractor hood over the stove as in a three-star restaurant. Foodies object to smelling the last meal at the next: even though they themselves smell of garlic from one continent to the next.

Your masculinity in the right slot

Beside the stove is a wooden slot from which poke the handles of the different knives. It is very, very non-F to have a set of matching stainless steel knives with rosewood handles dangling from a rack. Foodies do allow that a knife could be stainless, but it must be a Foodie brand like the Swiss Victorinox. Sabatiers are lovely, when sharp.

Foodie knives are big restaurant or butcher's knives. Foodie wives are not keen on the 8-inch blades. Non-Foodies looking at the knife slot say 'How can you remember which handle is which knife?' That's like saying 'Could you tell your wife if you only saw her legs?'

The tomato knife marks the true Foodie – the small serrated blade cuts ripe tomatoes without making a mess: you bought it in St Tropez market or somewhere similar.

A Foodie will do anything to get his 8-incher sharper. He buys every new knife-sharpener. He is never satisfied. All Sloane Ranger men can get a perfect edge

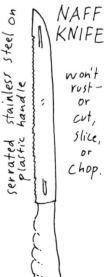

NICE KNIFE

sharp carbon steel (goes black when slices lemon.)

can't go in dishwater

steel extending length of wooden handle

NAFF KNIFE

serrated stainless steel on serrated plastic handle

won't rust – or cut, slice, or chop.

'Ich bin ein Berliner' is a misprint for 'I am a binliner'

FOODIE RUBBISH

Foodies are a civic menace. They cause twice the normal trouble to rubbish-collectors. Instead of putting out a rubbish bag containing a sanitary collection of cardboard packets, polythene wrappings, foil and jars, the Foodie's rubbish bag bulges with smelly bones, mussel shells, crayfish shells, fish heads, chicken feet, rinds, coffee grinds and dabs of creamy slime. (If the Foodie has a garden, some of this can go on the compost heap, but Foodie gardeners have been known to ban the kitchen from contributing: fish eyes are more *grotty* than Grotto, and bones create rats.)

The Christmas agony of the middle classes – how much to tip the rubbish man – is simplified for the Foodie. You know you should find out the average and double it.

THE PROOF OF THE FOODIE IS IN THE
STOCK CUBES

People say in awe, 'Is it true she makes her own stock cubes?' Idiotic question. All Foodies do. You are a fanatic about stock and you only trust one commercial stock cube maker, Poule au Pot – for chicken. (It seems to be the only one in the world made without MSG.) You keep at least seven kinds of home-made in the freezer, seven bags of cloudy squares that look like pale fudge but which are your stock cubes made in the ice tray: game, turbot, chicken, salmon, two beef (one jelly), pigeon. That's what the freezer's for – that and whole tomatoes.

The Foodie has one habit that is indulged behind closed doors – scraping the guests' and family's plates of the chicken bones or fish bones and flinging them into the marmite with nothing but salt and water. You don't need to clarify stock if it's made in an earthenware marmite.

The stock cubes are worth almost as much as gold bars. You always insure the contents of your freezer for £200 ($300, 2300 F, 800 DM, 80,000 yen).

The freezer also contains various carcases you have not yet made into stock but which are haunting you, eg the three-year-old crayfish which is bound to come in handy.

---

on a carving knife, but a Foodie always feels cheated of the ultimate blade.

The Foodie corkscrew is the Screw-Pull. Wall tin openers are non-F, for obvious reasons. You hide the tin opener in a drawer and occasionally lose it. This is agony for your cats.

Many hands make light wok

You have had a wok for *fifteen years*. You feel you should stop wokking now all the young marrieds do it, but you enjoy it too much. You like all-stainless Le Pentole (Italian). To put dirty cutlery in a

saucepan to soak is very non-F – it might damage the metal. You are acutely aware of the cost of the metal, as you spend half your money having your beloved copper pans retinned every year (by somewhere like the Copper Shop, Neal Street, in London). Foodies like utensils that can go on the stove or in the stove and on to the table. Le Creuset is particularly F. You love your Le Creuset gratin dish – the right shape, the right conductivity, and metal. It has the virtues of earthenware but cleans much better. Certain earthenware things are irreplaceable, however, like the marmite for stock.

Hot hands make heavy work

If you make pastry, you have a marble pastry surface. But most Foodies don't enter the pâtisserie game. Foodies tend to have hot hands – your zeal throbbing in your fingers. This makes your pastry heavy. Meanwhile what you call Fossils achieve perfect puff pastry every time. The wise Foodie steers clear of croûte.

Foodies do not display many jars. Rice and so on are kept in the packet, with label showing. 'You wouldn't decant your wine and put it in plain bottles, would you?'

If there is room, the Foodie keeps his or her cookery books in the kitchen.

Hail to the Chef (c'est moi)

The Foodie displays many useful/boastful tea-towels and aprons in the kitchen, either hanging up or on the Foodie's person. These include Foodie trophies or birthday presents such as the Fromages de France tea-towel, and the highly prized apron (displayed in *the kitchen at Jacques Pic's*) announcing the fourteen rules of the chef: '1 Le Chef a raison. 2 Le Chef a toujours raison 3 Même si un subalterne a raison, c'est l'article 1 que s'applique…'

KNOCK KNOCK.
Who's there?
ISLA.
Isla who?
ISLA'VE ANYTHING AS LONG AS IT'S GOT BASIL IN IT.

FOODIE BOOKSHOPS

Shelves groan – staff groan

Businesses specialising in old books on food have *morelled* since Foodies arrived. Nevertheless, the shops dislike the hand that feeds them. The average Foodie speeds in holding a sharpened credit card, asks for a particular title heard about at a Foodie dinner party, and bustles away again – hurrying towards a good long browse in the food shop. The booksellers like customers who *collect* books: Foodies *read, use and stain* books. Many of the food-book businesses are strictly mail order or by appointment so as never to have to see a Foodie.

There are major private collections of cookery books in America, France, Germany and Switzerland – nothing big in Britain. Maxime Rodinson, the French orientalist, has an outstanding collection. From outside New York, collectors Walter and Lucille Fillin send relevant information to serious cookery writers – they deserve a Friends of the Food Scholar award. There *are* British collectors – Alan Davidson, Elizabeth David, Jane Grigson, Anton Mosimann of the Dorchester. Foodie hero Alan Davidson is *not* a cook, but in his publisher's toque he has resurrected several old cookery books, reprinting them in facsimile for Prospect Books.

Worth their weight in truffles

Rare old cookery books are bound to increase in value as more Foodies want the only antiques that matter. A taste of the prices: *Platina*, published in Latin around 1488, published in French in 1515; £4,000 to £5,000 (has earliest known recipe for Welsh Rarebit). *Cuoco Secreto di Papa Pio Quinto* by Scappi, cook to the Pope, 1570; £3,000 to £4,000. First edition of Hanna Glasse's *The Art of Cookery Made Plain and Simple*, 1747, over £1,600 (it fetched that at Sotheby's in 1983). *Mrs Beeton* first edition, 1861, in good condition, £1,000 to £1,500; but battered *Beetons*, around £100. Fifth edition, 1769, of Elizabeth Raffeld's *Experienced English Housekeeper*, £150 to £200. Lebas's sing-along cookbook in verse, *La Cuisine en Musique*, 1738, £350. Recipe books in manuscript form are all over the rare-book market and usually overvalued, but 17th, 18th and 19th-century manuscripts are worth putting in your larder.

Rare food-book sellers

BRITAIN
- Books for Cooks (new, second-hand), 15 Blenheim Crescent, London W11
- Janet Clarke, 3 Woodside Cottages, Freshford, Bath (2 catalogues a year)
- Cook's Books, T. A. McKirdy, 34 Marine Drive, Rottingdean, Sussex
- Culmus Books, 23 St Leonard's Road, Bournemouth, Dorset
- J. S. and G. M. Deith, The Old Bakehouse Bookshop, 16 The Green, West Drayton, Middlesex
- Stephanie Hoppen, The Studio, 17 Walton Street, London SW3
- Kate and Tom Jackson, 22 Parish Ghyll Road, Ilkley, Yorkshire (mail order only)
- John Lyle, Harpford, Sidmouth, Devon
- Piccadilly Rare Books, 30 Sackville Street, London W1

HOLLAND
Titia Bodon, 43 Willemsparkweg, 1071 GR, Amsterdam

USA
- M. M. Einhorn Maxwell Books, At the Sign of the Dancing Bear, 80 East 11th Street, New York, NY 10003
- Marian Gore, Box 433, San Gabriel, California
- Jan Longone, The Wine and Food Library, 1207 W. Madison Ave, Ann Arbor, Michigan
- Nahum J. Waxman, Kitchen Arts and Letters, 1435 Lexington Ave, New York, NY 10128

★★★★★★★★★
A friend visiting Tom admired his expensive food processor. 'Yes isn't it marvellous,' said Tom; 'it was Lettice's.' 'I didn't think you were seeing Lettice any more.' 'I'm not. She's fed up with me for some reason. It's strange, because I thought our last evening together was one of our best.'
'What went wrong?'
'I don't know. She had cooked the magret rare, and the chèvre was perfect. I had brought a bottle of Beaumes de Venise to finish with. We were just sitting there, and she said, "What a magical evening. I have a mind to give you anything you want." I thought: so we really do think as one. And I took the food processor.'
★★★★★★★★★

No Foodie can cook in a power cut

Until the 1950s, mincing involved struggle – feeding meat into a heavy iron mincer you were turning like a mangle, or milling vegetables by hand in a French mouli légumes. You then had to take the machine apart and wash the bits off, which was difficult.

In the Fifties, electric machines arrived that speeded up the grind: mixers/blenders and liquidisers (you had to have both). Every bride asked for a Kenwood mixer or Waring blender, and a Sunbeam or Moulinex liquidiser. But they still had to be taken apart to wash, and they needed different attachments for different jobs. The instrument of the Foodie revolution was still to come. This was the – shazam! – Robot Coupe.

Well done, M Verdun

In 1964, Pierre Verdun, a Frenchman, invented a simplified food processor that revolutionised professional cooking. The Robot Coupe uses a single rotating blade in a bowl, which mixes, blends, kneads, liquidises, purées, minces, chops, slices, shreds and grates. This tool hugely accelerated, and in fact made possible, the spread of nouvelle cuisine. The NC chefs of France all rely on it to do the work the new style demands.

Magimagic and Cuisinart

Robot Coupe then produced a domestic version, the Magimix, launching it in 1971. This French machine entered America (via Carl Sontheimer) in 1972 and Britain (via ICTC Electrical) in 1974. Carl Sontheimer was allowed to call his the Cuisinart – a mistake on the part of the Robot, because in 1978 Carl

Sontheimer got another machine made by Japanese technicians and made on the Sony side of the world. In 1981 Robot Coupe broke off relations with Cuisinart and went into America under their own name to dispute the food-processor market with the upstart Cuisinart.

'In the room the women come and go, torquing about my coup Robot'

Verdun's vital ingredient was torque. Still unique to these machines is the motor – a direct-driven motor with only one moving part. It doesn't have different speed switches (though better models do have a single-revolution pulse switch), and it can take in more power automatically as it is needed, drawing from between 100 and 2000 watts. The direct-drive motor supplies enough torque instantly to do a heavy job – belt-drive motors need time to rev up to achieve torque. In the commercial models that make 60 litres of taramasalata at a time, this is a major consideration.

Switched on in 1955. 'Celebrating contracts to appear on BBC and commercial television and to give demonstrations to audiences throughout the country, food experts John and Fanny Cradock, who write under the joint pen-name of "Bon Viveur", have given themselves a new, fully-equipped kitchen'

Bonjour, M Sorbet

The Gelato-chef is an Italian machine developed, in 1983, from a professional catering model. It churns and freezes simultaneously, producing ice cream in as little as 20 minutes. Unlike previous ice cream machines, which had to use the fridge, this is a worktop machine and can produce 1½ litres at once. Sorbets used to be a choice between a rock-hard filled orange or lemon. Now delicate frozen concoctions can be created from almost any fruit, herb or vegetable. Foodies let their imaginations rip in dreaming up new chilly first courses and palate-cleansers for between courses. The

PUNCTUALITY AND THE FOODIE: GET ME TO THE TABLE ON TIME

It is instructive to ask unpunctual people which they are most often late for: plays, concerts, the office, dinner parties, business appointments? But this is a silly question to a Foodie, who although he may be late for everything else always gets to the table on time. A well-known American Foodie's mother, when someone got her name wrong (in the Forties), used to say 'Call me anything as long as it's not Late For Dinner.' The whole of Foodie etiquette could be boiled down to the commandment 'Thou shalt not imperil thy neighbour's soufflé'. For at their back they always hear someone's spinach soufflé losing air. (A Foodie does not put his own soufflé in until the guests arrive, but as a guest he is always considerate of other cooks.)

Cooking being a matter of clock and countdown, Foodies have a sixth sense for what's going on on the stove and in the oven, and will slip away from a heated discussion in another room at the precise moment when sticking a knife into the potatoes will show they are ready to be drained. Foodies never get carried away enough to forget the pots on the back burner.

Foodies eat late – at the same time as the ruling class in countries where the food habits of the upper classes differ from the lower (America, France, Britain, Germany, the international diplomatic circuit). Six-thirty is very non-F, from 8 until late is F.

Unless it is a cold dish, Foodies eat it in five minutes, then spend ten minutes discussing it. They don't dawdle over the eating, because they want each mouthful to be at the peak of perfection and as the chef intended, whether hot or warm. One woman ate too fast even for a Foodie, and her friends persuaded her to go to a hypnotist to cure it. The hypnotist taught her to put her knife and fork down between mouthfuls, and her glass down between sips. Modern medicine is having to learn to cope with Foodies.

Being a Foodie puts you in the top drawer automatically, although Foodie is not officially in the economists' classification of the AB part of the population (your own business or a job in top management; university degree; title; expensive house; children at private schools; two cars; several televisions.) 'Obsession with food' *should* be there. Fast food is a sure sign of a C$_2$ or a D or an E. Adopting s-l-o-o-o-o-w food is the fast lane upwards. It's not like watching television and owning a computer and going to an exercise class – those *unproductive* leisure activities of non-Foodies.

LAYING THE FOODIE TABLE

Gut thinking

A Foodie is the opposite of Wordsworth's 'plain living and high thinking'. Foodies have achieved gourmand living and gut thinking. Their table is a shrine to this.

The Foodie table is large and strong, to support heavy casseroles. It is never spindly or French-polished. In the middle is a Kremlin of little mills, clear plastic or wood, which contain: rock salt; black peppercorns; black peppercorns and corriander; three colours of peppercorn (black, white and pink) and allspice; coriander alone. (*Not* garlic salt.) These are the original satanic mills. No one but the Foodie understands the system, and a timid twirl of the grinder releases a smutty rain of the wrong thing, so guests dare not season the food. This suits the Foodie chef.

Beside the mills stand bottles, depending on the night's menu and the pretentiousness of the Foodie: for example raspberry vinegar, hazel-nut oil, soy sauce, Worcestershire sauce or tabasco.

TIME TO PLAN THE MEALS

SHAKESPEARE: 'I wasted time and now doth time waste me.'

FOODIE: 'I wasted time so this isn't marinated.'

	Man	Woman	Foodie
Bathroom a.m.	45 min on lav, thinking, reading paper, constipation	5 min	10 min on lav, best place to plan dinner and read cookery books. Foodies do not suffer from constipation; their lav smells of cedar pencils (the wine) and stables (the bran)
Lunch-hour	2 hours in pub or bar	1 hour food shopping	2 hours food shopping
After work	2 hours in pub or bar, or in television torpor	2 hours housework or children work and cooking	3 hours cooking

Service à la Française lasted until the 1840s and '50s – everything on the table, eat what you can reach. Then food hotted up with service à la Russe – separate courses. The Foodie meal now is totally unpredictable – it could be one course or seven. What is inevitable is a tableful of satanic mills

American chilli sauce would be allowed if you could get it. Hellman's mayonnaise *only* – no other Hellman's products.

Beside the mills and bottles, chez *very* pretentious Foodies, stand French jars and tins, eg rouille; mustard (not Meaux, something more recherché like French grocery store mustard, Amora Dijon); and perhaps French butter in its little wooden coffin ('best Normandie unsalted butter').

Glasses are big and strong: half-filled, of course. Foodies snuffle in them for the knowing remark. There are always napkins – cloth if you are lucky, but seldom ironed.

A few Foodies have a sense of presentation: nice tablecloth and flowers, candles, perhaps ivy or vine leaves laid on the table. This is a pleasant change from the usual gastrocentric straight-to-work table.

Foodie cutlery is *no help* to the unfortunate guest. You cannot judge the courses from the silver. You will be told 'Keep your knife and fork' after some courses, in the French manner, and for others, new spoons or knives and forks will be brought by the Foodie host – who feels no bourgeois obligation to have everything ready beforehand, and in his creative fever simply does not understand that you want to know how much else is coming so you can judge whether to have a second helping. Released from the corset of convention, Foodie hosts have become completely relaxed and irresponsible as to what constitutes a meal. 'Dinner is what I say it is' is their opinion. They might serve to dinner party A only salad, cheese and home-made ice cream. Word gets round. The guests at their dinner party B, next week, stuff themselves with bread during the first course, only to find there are four more substantial courses to follow. The Foodie's friends mutter. The Foodie's friends' stomachs growl. The Foodie notices nothing except that the fish was overcooked.

first Foodie basil sorbets ('Don't you *adore* him?') didn't taste of much – freezing diminishes flavour, and an ice-cream mixture has to be much stronger. But eventually Foodies discovered why Basil was so backward.

Pasta posa dilemma

Pasta has become exalted since, in the Seventies, the domestic pasta machine brought fresh spaghetti and all its family to the table at the turn of a handle or the touch of a switch. American Foodies all bought one, but it hasn't been out of the cupboard since 1978.

The difference between fresh and packet pasta provoked a burst of recipes that would astonish a Neapolitan. It has also launched the only fast food Foodies countenance. In the late Seventies (New York) and Eighties (London) shops called Pasta Pasta, Faster Pasta, Parla Pasta, Greener Pasta, Pastas New and Pasta Sauce, Please have spread fasta and fasta from the centa to colonise the country towns and outlying districts of big cities. Expensive little ragoûts of delicate ingredients sit on restrained helpings of pink and green strands of what started life as food for the poor. It's the answer for hostesses, but their guests sneer: 'Pasta with everything.' Pasta is delicious – but it takes pounds off one's reputation.

TEN RECIPES THAT SHOOK THE WORLD

4 TOMATO AND BASIL SORBET

BASIL AND BRIDE IN FROSTY MARRIAGE

This is the recipe for show-offs. When you serve tiny little dollops of this orangey greeny ice as a first course on huge plates garnished with fresh leaves of lettuce-leaved basil, it says to the whole world not only that you own an up-to-date food processor, but that you also have a Gelato-chef or other single-unit ice-cream maker. Basil is of course the darling of nouvelle cuisine, and his alliance with Tomato makes everybody happy.

Quantities are utterly irrelevant to this recipe; tomatoes differ so much in sweetness, flavour and the amount of liquid they contain that measures are useless.

Skin and seed ripe tomatoes, by nicking the skin, dipping them in hot water, cutting them in half lengthwise, and squeezing out the seeds. Liquidise the flesh in the processor, taste for salt, pepper and sugar (it should be slightly sweet), then add torn fresh basil leaves to taste, and, if you like, finely minced garlic. Whizz again, briefly.

At this point you can either add 250 ml (8 fl oz, 1 cup US) whisked double cream for each 1.2 kilos (2½ lb) of tomatoes (weighed before processing) *or* you can add two stiffly whisked egg whites per litre (about one per pint) of the mixture. Churn and freeze for 20 minutes in the automatic sorbetière, or freeze for 3–4 hours in small moulds. Serve half-thawed.

DO YOU REMEMBER THE GARLIC PRESS, MIRANDA?

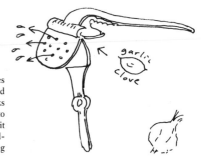

After the war, a garlic press was like an I Love France badge. But by 1975, Foodies had spat them out. Cleaning a garlic press is impossible, involving pins and prods. And a bitter taste always comes through when garlic is pulped against metal. Even tricks like adding a pinch of salt can't disguise the metal. So Foodies have returned to crushing garlic with the flat of a knife, or chopping it finely on a board, or pounding it with a pestle in a mortar. Foodies adore the action of pestle and mortar. It's round-peg-in-a-round-hole, to them. They ask each other eagerly, 'Do you feel like making a pesto?'

PART TWO
THE
FOODIE
EATS OUT

THE FOODIE AT THE RESTAURANT

Foodies are *physically* different

Dining in a good restaurant is to a Foodie what a marvellous party is to a teenager, a big deal to a businessman, a great opera to a buff. Dozens of elements must play their parts faultlessly or the Foodie's hopes will be dashed.

The Foodie enters into a higher state when going into a restaurant. The level of response from your nose, tongue and teeth is raised, so that encountering a scented deodoriser in the restaurant's lavatory, for instance, is like being mugged. Perhaps a physical change takes place in you, as with religious fanatics who can dance on hot coals without getting burnt. It is noticeable that Foodies' tolerance of caffeine is much lower than normal people's. Normal people can drink coffee at night, but you dare not expose your sensitive blood to it after three in the afternoon, and must ask for decaffeinated (made from beans, of course – not instant) after dinner, or a tisane.

As you sit in the restaurant, three of your senses are as vulnerable as an open sea anemone, and your mind is occupied by awe and the wish to worship. Like a believer in church, you do not resent the other people you see there – though they are ordering all the wrong things, and *not paying attention to the food*; you know that a restaurant needs business, even if it's from a swinishly gross palate.

Are you distinguishable to the waiters and the maître d'hôtel? (Foodies don't say metter D – that's Businessman's talk.) You'd better be. If it is a three-star restaurant, you have put aside enough money to cover the most expensive meal, you have probably travelled several thousand miles, and here you are, at the shrine, palpitatingly eager, childishly vulnerable to disappointments or slights.

Do not worry. The waiters spotted you as a Foodie as soon as you walked in. You had that air of expectancy. You treated them with the respect due to their noble

profession. To you they are not minions, but men who can get dozens of people's different food on to their tables at its moment of perfection, and a succession of different wines into their glasses at the correct temperature, meanwhile dressing and redressing the table unobtrusively – all the little services to eating that you try at home and know are fiendishly difficult.

But if you have come a long way to a three-star restaurant, you are secretly hoping for some special mark of favour. And most Foodie pilgrims *are* welcomed at the shrine. Either the head waiter spots you, or more likely, the proprietor was alerted when you booked, by such phrases in your letter as 'Dr Z of Chicago asked to be remembered to you'. The restaurant does not remember Dr Z from Adam, but the keen-bean tone of your letter warned them that another Foodie approaches. They can even recognise you from a telephone booking – the punctilio, the emotion. A Foodie booking at a restaurant is the nearest thing to a sex call.

When you appear in person, they make

you a free apéritif or digestif ('offert' it says on the bill), or a tiny extra course you did not order, or an invitation to go round the kitchens. At the Troisgros, at least three tables of Foodies have to be shown round the kitchens at every meal. But the restaurants are tolerant of the fans. They need a knowledgeable audience. It is not generally recognised that cooking is like acting – the chef has to feel up to the performance, he has to hear rumours of applause through the swing doors – a waiter reports that the people at table nine are overjoyed by the écrevisses, a plate comes back that has been polished to a shine by bread. A great chef is quite capable of marching into the dining-room and asking why you hardly touched a dish. Of course, Foodies have already sent a humble explanation via the waiter.

Behaviour at a restaurant

Booking

Always. Sometimes weeks or even months ahead. But you don't go on Monday – the fish might not be fresh.

Not booking

If by some freak of fate you find yourself strolling along without a reservation, you feel as though walking through a red-light district. You peer through restaurant windows at the *tablecloths*. Must be white linen – or palest pink. The freshness of the cloth hints at the care for the food.

Numbers

Two or four. Six is the maximum. Six has the advantage of only one possible placement for three couples – Foodies don't want to have to bother their heads with social niceties – but the disadvantage that none of the six can reach all the other five plates with a questing fork.

Decor

Doesn't count. Most three-stars are done up hideously in specifically French bad taste. What are invariably handsome are the plates, cutlery and glasses.

Apéritifs

The only spirit you can't resist is a dry martini cocktail, but it would be inappropriate to drink gin before a serious meal. You like to order the apéritif de la maison – usually a Kir Royale (cassis and champagne) or something with framboise or myrtille. Or champagne by itself.

Vodka is a depth charge for the palate. In a horror story told by Foodies, the start of a special menu at a famous London restaurant was caviar with chilled vodka,

A SALAD SUCCESS STORY

Every leaf will be famous for five minutes. (Spinach's turn came between raw mushrooms and radicchio)

The French like their salad fatiguée – so fatiguée that if there is a delay between tossing it and eating it, the lettuce passes out and lies in its oil and vinegar utterly finished. The Americans like their salad energetic, a workout lettuce whose defences no dressing can penetrate and which will flick you in the eye or grease your nose or chin given half a chance. Iceberg is the tip of the aggression pent up in an American salad.

NC chefs tread a middle path: energetic salad, eg radicchio, but in small pieces so as to reduce the annoyance of trying to eat a leaf that is fighting back.

The French have a traditional salad of hot lardons of fat bacon on chicorée frisée, which brutally fatigues the chicory. Americans thought this state of affairs could be improved, and P. J. Clarke's in Manhattan invented a salad of thin lean cooked bacon with raw spinach. The spinach was not easily-tired European spinach, but bouncy springy American spinach. This salad was widely copied, occasionally with the name 'P. J. Clarke's salad'. Spinach salad is a mainstay of Joe Allen's, which took it back to France. The Joe Allens in New York, London and Paris are exactly the same, down to the blackboard menu, brick walls and American waiters. Joe Allen's in Paris is very popular even though the Parisians could easily eat the père of the salad, the so-exhausting lardons on chicory.

Pissenlit (blanched young dandelions) is a French spring salad no one else can be bothered to redesign or even make. To harvest it you need crones with knives in fields – ingredients scarce in America and Britain.

The salad having its five minutes of fame now is mâche (or corn salad or lamb's lettuce). 'Bangers and mâche!' say Foodies as they tuck into their pork-and-fennel sausages and ridiculously refined assemblage of leaves.

and later in the same menu came a vodka sorbet – just to make sure they couldn't taste anything for the rest of the meal. You suck in your breath when you tell this one.

Water

You don't want iced tap water as in America – Foodies travel such a lot they got used to drinking mineral water. Some like Perrier, others consider the bubbles vulgarly big and prefer the discreet bubbles of Badoit. (Foodie children all prefer the Perrier big bubbles and some call the other 'bad water'.)

Children

Foodies take their children to restaurants in France. The baby sits on the annuaire (telephone book) in a pink sling tied to the back of a chair. Most Foodies have been to four three-star restaurants by the age of two. British and American Foodies, like French, Italian, Chinese and Spanish parents, take the children because, one, you consider it is never too young to start. Two, Foodies are 'new' people and you don't believe that 'children should be seen and not heard'. So you push foie gras into the baby's mouth and are shocked that it picks out the chocolate among the friandises although as far as you know it has never tasted chocolate. Is this what is meant by original sin?

Rolls and bread

Yes. You believe the bread of the country is an essential element of most cuisines. Your eye whizzes like a bee over the basket the waiter offers: you take the brown, black or local roll and reject French bread in England (except at the Quat' Saisons – they bake their own in a French oven). You eat the roll with butter or chew even more virtuously because you eschew butter – many Foodies don't eat it because the French don't put it on the table.

Butter

Unsalted, of course.

Amuse gueule (gullet-tickler)

At a three-star restaurant you are keen to see what tiny titbit will be given you first – usually a taste of the region: a weeny onion tart (Georges Blanc), a slice of saucisson de Lyon in brioche (Bocuse), or a mouthful of Welsh rarebit Gruyère (the Dorchester).

Pepper and salt

You can't tell by no salt and pepper whether it's a Foodie paradise or the cook is extremely conceited. The Negresco at Nice has none, for the first reason. If they *are* on the table, the Foodie never, never uses them before tasting the dish, and hates doing it then – quelle insult to the chef.

Time to order

Foodies get down right away to studying the menu. They do not waste the time of that noble person the waiter with a casual 'We're not ready, could you come back?'

What to order

Foodies discuss which of them will order which of the menus of the day. It is made plain who is the subordinate Foodie by who has to have the menu the others didn't choose. You may not be able to resist something from the carte as well, but you don't order a meal from the carte – this would be to disregard the chef's plans. You honour the chef by trying his menu. If it's a famous chef's tasting menu, a menu dégustation, you may all have it, instead of testing different dishes as Foodies are usually honour-bound to do.

Adjectives on the menu

No no no no! 'Small' and 'fresh' are the only ones Foodies allow on a menu. 'Tender' rings the alarm bell hard.

In a nouvelle cuisine restaurant, the real menu is the waiter, who comes and explains the written word. He doesn't let you off a detail of what it is, where from, how cooked, how special.

Wine

Strictly secondary. In France, Foodies order the local wine. You do not want the claims of a great vintage to get in the way of the claims of a great chef. And anyway, if God had not intended the local wine to be drunk with the menu, He would not have placed the restaurant here.

In California, the local Cabernet Sauvignons and Pinot Noirs are too soft and rich to drink with food, and the Chardonnays lack acidity. This complaint also

smoking. But most Foodies have given up cigarettes, in pursuit of the perfect palate. Actually, several famous chefs smoke.

Cigars

Some Foodies do smoke these, but only with brandy and non-vintage port. You wouldn't with vintage port or a delicate eau de vie like Framboise.

Tipping

Foodies don't feel they need add extra if

You are Where you sit

In most European restaurants, it doesn't matter where your table is (except it's downstairs at Langan's Brasserie in London and by a window in the Tour d'Argent in Paris). But New York Foodies must not only eat in the best places, they must be seen at the best tables. Only mid-western tourists sit in the main dining-room of the Four Seasons at lunch, drinking Diet Pepsi with their étouffée of crayfish tails. The smart publishers and power-brokers are in the tastefully panelled and cheaper grill room, drinking Perrier with broiled fish.

Table snobbery began in New York in the Fifties, at Henri Soulé's Le Pavillon, and was carried on by its clones, La Caravelle and La Côte Basque. Lunch is the main test. You're up against what *Women's Wear Daily* calls the Lunch Bunch. The aim is almost always to sit as near the door as possible. Every time

somebody comes in, you get blasted by cold air, but that's the price of table power. At Le Cirque, currently the most fashionable Lunch Bunch place, status is determined by your nearness to the table of Jerry Zipkin, Nancy Reagan's 'walker'. After Dustin Hoffman's first night in *Death of a Salesman* in March 1984, the *New York Times* thought it worth reporting that Hoffman had had a double triumph: he was seated *at the table nearest the door at Sardi's*.

Every New York restaurant has a Siberia, where only pariahs sit. It's much better to leave than to allow yourself to be sent there. One NY Foodie remembers a lunchtime in the Sixties when he and his wife were the only white people in one section of the Caravelle.

Never admit you're booking for yourself. Pretend to be your own secretary and say your boss is on a visit to New York to see someone of proved table power.

applies to some Australian wines. But Foodies have 'discovered' the non-noble grapes like Zinfandel and the light red wines – eg Sancerre Rouge, Beaujolais (crus) and Bouzy Rouge. These will go with fish and can carry on through several of the six or seven courses of a dégustation menu.

Coffee

Small, strong and black, after the meal. Sometimes with sugar – since Foodies seldom get a chance to taste this.

Petits fours and friandises

Another taste treat to postpone your

the service is included (as it is at three-star restaurants, thank God). You are an upholder of the smooth running of a sophisticated system. You don't need to buy acceptance in the restaurant world -- it is your home.

A Foodie Hall of Shame

NAPOLEON – never took more than 20 minutes for a meal

WITTGENSTEIN – didn't mind what he ate as long as it was always the same.

PRESIDENT FORD – always ate the same lunch, and it was cottage cheese, A1 sauce, an onion or tomato, and butter pecan ice cream.

LORD LUCAN – always ate lamb cutlets. In summer he ate them en gelée.

A Foodie view of restaurant guides : knock, knock

There were restaurant guides almost as soon as there were restaurants. In 1789, as cooks left the service of Revolution-chopped aristocrats, the number of restaurants in Paris rose from fewer than a hundred, in the year of the Revolution, to more than 500 in 1804, the year following the publication of the first restaurant guide, the *Almanach des Gourmands*. This annual was the work of Grimod de la Reynière (b 1758), a physically unattractive misogynist, who, according to Quentin Crewe's *Great Chefs of France*, diverted 'his sensual appetites into gastronomy', and whose 'power was enormous, being sufficient to make or break an establishment'. Blanc's *Guide des Dineurs* followed in 1814, and by 1900 the Michelin Tyre company had published its first – and free – motorists' guide to hotels and restaurants in France.

Michelin also sponsored a gastronomic column in several newspapers, and for a time this was written, as 'Bibendum', by Maurice Edmond Sailland (1872–1956), better known under his nom de fourchette, 'Curnonsky'. In a cod plebiscite held in Paris in 1926, Curnonsky was elected 'Prince des gastronomes', and he did not dislike being called Prince Curnonsky. He was such an important part of the Paris restaurant scene that at the time of his death 61 restaurants always kept a table for him. Some Paris restaurants, such as Le Roi Gourmet, still display a plaque over their Curnonsky table.

Michelin introduced their famous star ratings with one star in 1926, then one to three in the 1931 edition. After the war the first three-star ratings were given by their anonymous inspectors in 1951: three such ratings went to Paris restaurants and four to provincial ones. There are now 18 three-star establishments in France. And these are, for the most part, the principal places of pilgrimage on the gastronomic map. However, Michelin can, and does, slip up. They are slow to award three stars – and even slower to remove them. Thus, La Pyramide at Vienne, which Fernand Point's widow has maintained as a memorial to Point, the greatest chef teacher of modern times, retains three stars in Michelin, though it has deserved to lose at least one of them for years. Some feel that even the Baumanière at Les Baux is overrated with three stars.

The Gault-Millau *Guide France*, with its more subtle 20-point four-toque system of ratings (the educated Frenchman marks everything out of 20, as it is the marking system used for the baccalauréat), manages to be up to date.

Gault-Millau give Mme Point's Pyramide what it deserves – on a good day : 16 points (out of 20) and two toques out of four. Her devotion to her chef, Guy Thivard, is admirable; and when he sticks to recreating the dishes M Point made famous – poulet de Bresse en vessie, the chocolate marjolaine – he is successful. But when he gives his own imagination rein, most Foodies feel that they can eat better at home.

Le Père Bise (now demoted to two stars in Michelin) gets exactly the same rating from Gault-Millau, for more or less similar reasons, and so does old M Thuilier's Baumanière. More importantly, all three ratings are printed in black, which, chez Gault-Millau, denotes traditional French cooking.

Red is the desirable colour in the Gault-Millau guide; red toques mean 'cuisine inventive', and Gault-Millau are the people who gave the world the expression 'la Nouvelle Cuisine'. Quick as they are to demote restaurants and to puncture reputations, they are even quicker to discover new talent. For several years now they have given their top award of 19 points (they never award 20) and four red toques to young Jacques Maximin, who is

·F·O·O·D·I·E·B·O·R·E·S·

The FUNGIBORE

Everyone likes mushrooms. The Foodie who likes mushrooms *too much* is a very rare species, but truly, truly boring. 'Do try this,' says the deadly fungibore (the spore bore), forcing a bit of fried bright-red toadstool on you, 'it's one of the few non-toxic amanitas.' Don't hang back – it only tastes of slime and butter. To make the point he shows you the amanita Lesson he keeps in the freezer – a plastic-wrapped lime-green dildo, the Death Cap, Amanita phalloides. 'DESTROY THIS WHENEVER YOU SEE IT.'

The bore can't imagine you don't spend September in damp woods. To him, in the fungus season, it never rains but it spores. He sets out with his pocket Romagnesi and paperback Roger Phillips, scouring the pine and beech-woods of England, Scotland, France, Italy, Poland, Russia and Minnesota, looking for something for nothing. He is funging. He thinks of it as a verb. He fungs like a rattlesnake. Bores keep their mushroom maps to themselves, and passionately hate any other fungus freak they meet in their haunts. All other mushroomers dread the Poles, who hold the Mushroom Olympics title and whose motto is if it lurks, fung it.

Somehow the season gets earlier and longer every year. In June 1984, while restaurants in France were still charging a fortune for the fungus bore's springtime treat, fresh morels, restaurants in Venice were already gouging for autumnal porcini (cèpes). Fungus-bore travellers always buy a pound to take home. When the flight is delayed, the treasure in their paper bag quickly disintegrates into a slimy black mass. The bores control their panic, but the rest of the departure lounge is wondering where the overpowering smell is coming from. Who flung that fung?

In recent years, so many species have been cultivated that Foodies can sometimes buy farmed oyster mushrooms (Pleurotus ostreatus), the Japanese shitake (Lentinus edodes) and matsutake (Tricholoma matsutake), the Chinese straw mushroom (Volvariella volvacea) or mo-er (Auricularia polytricha). Other varieties are picked in the wild, such as the trompettes de la mort (Craterellus cornucopioides), chanterelles (Cantarellus cibarius) or cèpes (Boletus edulis), and find their way to many French markets, or to Robert Bruce in New Covent Garden in London or Dean & DeLuca in New York.

The 1984 Oxford Cookery Symposium produced a thrill for the mushroom bore – a paper by Sarah Bomer on the false chanterelles (Hygrophoropsis aurantiaca) she picks in Berkshire. (Like the true bore, she wouldn't say exactly where.) 'The false are not received with enthusiasm in any book I have read, being described as "worthless", "unpleasant" and even their edibility doubted,' she wrote. But the false chanterelle 'has as much depth of flavour as the true chanterelle, if not more.' She contributed a cold chicken dish with false chanterelle sauce to the lunch, to prove it to the assembled Foodies. Mmmmmm puh puh puh puh. YES! YES! An entirely new food! Orange in colour and not *much* taste, but that thought sprang to no Foodie mind. Foodies have faith in fungi.

Truffles are fungi, but truffle bores are *nowhere*, when it comes to boringness, compared with a toadstool terrier, mushroom maniac or puffball pervert.

chef at the bizarrely decorated Hotel Negresco at Nice. Maximin is one of the cleverest people now working in a kitchen – a real Foodie hero – but has only two stars in the Michelin, and does not expect a third.

You see, the Negresco is a grand hotel, what the French call 'un palace', and the hidebound Michelin people have a rule. They never give three stars to a restaurant in 'a palace', on the spurious grounds that the chef cannot be fully in charge of a hotel kitchen, and that, anyway, the banqueting functions of a hotel prevent true excellence. (This same nonsensical reasoning means that, in the English edition, the universally acknowledged best chef in England, Anton Mosimann of the Dorchester Hotel, has only one star in the Michelin guide.)

Christian Millau and Henri Gault were successful journalists on *Paris-Presse*. Gault was assigned to do a Paris restaurant column, which was edited by Millau. In 1962 they expanded their enterprise and published the *Guide Juillard* to Paris. In 1969 they started their own monthly magazine, *Le Nouveau Guide Gault-Millau*, and from 1972 published their guidebooks themselves. Their detailed reports grabbed Paris by the stomach, and gave Michelin heartburn.

The timing was perfect. Even the revolutionaries of '68 were Foodies at heart – and their affluent parents were just discovering the gastronomic and other pleasures of le weekend when the first guide appeared. Everybody wanted to know more about restaurants than they could learn from Michelin.

In 1973, drowning in cholesterol, swimming in butter and gagging on béchamel, Gault and Millau published a cover story in the October issue of their magazine, 'Vive La Nouvelle Cuisine Française'. This piece did not create a movement – it merely baptised one. The ideas had been born in Fernand Point's kitchens at Vienne; and the new culinary doctrines of lightness and freshness had been promulgated by Point's disciples, especially Paul Bocuse, Michel Guérard, Alain Chapel and the brothers Troisgros. Naturally they were among the first chefs to achieve the top marks in the new Gault-Millau guide – which they have kept ever since (though Bocuse's four toques are now printed in traditional black, instead of nouvelle red).

There are now Gault-Millau guides to practically everywhere – their charm, as always, resides in the racy prose, mostly Christian Millau's. The main ones are *France, Paris, New York, London* and *Italy* (1984). In November 1984, they brought out the first Gault-Millau *Guide du Vin*. They also continue to publish the *Gault-Millau* monthly. It is the success of the magazine that pays the vast expense of research for the guides. Gault and Millau share a weekly radio programme and column in *Le Point*. Henri Gault now devotes most of his time to editing another Foodie magazine, *Ma Maison et la Table*, and Millau does most of the work on the guides.

It is not surprising that real Foodies have deserted Michelin for Gault-Millau. For one thing, the symbols-only format of the Michelin simply does not give enough information – you can't even tell from the standard and cryptic Michelin symbols whether an establishment serves béchamel-thickened traditional stodge or flour-free nouvelle cuisine. For Foodies, this is hopeless. Unfortunately, apart from the French guide, the Gault-Millaus are revised irregularly and published sporadically. This means that some of the information – especially prices – is out of date in *London* and *New York*.

Even so, when the Foodie is in search of local shrines, it is good judgement he wants. Prices, like telephone numbers, can be found elsewhere – for Britain, in Egon Ronay's guides and in the increasingly eccentric and diminishingly authoritative *Good Food Guide*. Foodies are bitchy about the *Good Food Guide*. They pick it over for mistakes, squealing with glee when they find something like 'walnuts' instead of 'pistachio nuts'. 'Can you *imagine* anything more stupid?' Drew Smith the editor has announced that there will be 'no processed food and no Steak Diane restaurants' in the 1985 edition. Foodies are poised to check this, their knives ready.

In China and Hong Kong, Foodies depend on Harry Rolnik's books. For Italy there is *I Ristoranti di Veronelli* by the journalist Luigi Veronelli, which is especially useful for Grapies, the new Gault-Millau and Sheila Hale's *American Express Pocket Guide to Venice* and her second to *Florence and Tuscany*. Outside France, Michelin is unreliable, so Foodies use the less-than-perfect Gault-Millau guides to *Austria, Spain, Switzerland* and *Benelux*.

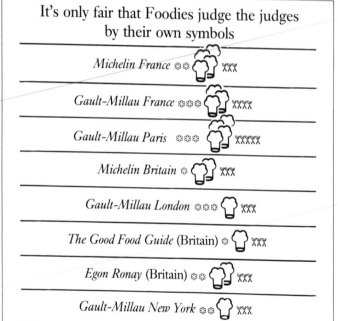

It's only fair that Foodies judge the judges by their own symbols

Michelin France ❀❀

Gault-Millau France ❀❀❀

Gault-Millau Paris ❀❀❀

Michelin Britain ❀

Gault-Millau London ❀❀❀

The Good Food Guide (Britain) ❀

Egon Ronay (Britain) ❀❀

Gault-Millau New York ❀❀

Reliability/judgement: 1-3 Michelin ❀❀❀

Comprehensiveness: 1-4 Gault-Millau

Quantity of information: 1-5 Michelin xxxxx

How to order Foodily in China, Japan and India

Foodies are keen to take the right path through a large foreign menu – the path a Foodie native would follow. We all know *what* the Chinese or Indians eat – but how and in what order? 'There is a form in home cooking, and we must recognise it,' says Hsiang Ju Lin, author of the classic *Chinese Gastronomy*. 'For a plain meal, four dishes and a soup, perhaps as contemptible as the familiar meat-and-two-veg of Britain, but there it is.'

She can afford to offer the word 'contemptible'. No western Foodie would take her up on it. To western Foodies 'admirable' goes with everything the Chinese do in the kitchen. In a Chinese home meal there is little meat, but what there is is only slightly cooked. Fish and fresh vegetables feature more prominently than in the Anglo-American meal, and they have very little done to them to alter their essential character. And in a way that relates ordinary Chinese cooking to nouvelle cuisine, cooking times are short, and both fuel and the cook's energy are conserved.

In a Chinese restaurant

When there is company, the Chinese try to serve one dish per person, plus one extra. Chinese meals very often start with a cold plate. In American and British Chinese restaurants, Foodies almost always order number One or number Two, 'Mixed cold hors d'oeuvres, Imperial Style' or whatever corresponds to that. Soup is, to the Chinese, a drink rather than a solid food dish, and is brought fairly late in the meal so that it can be drunk hot until the meal ends. The very last thing to be brought to the table is usually a fish – the appearance of a whole steamed fish at a banquet signals dinner is about to end.

Chinese table manners are different for family occasions and at banquets, and in the north and south of China. At informal meals, you may help yourself from the serving dishes with your own chopsticks. Not so at a banquet, when this would disgust the Chinese. In the north you will be served by your host at a banquet; in the south, the waiters will serve the meal. The host – and of course the guests of honour at his right and his left – will be seated opposite the door.

Do not turn your fish over when you have eaten one side – southern Chinese think it makes a fishing boat capsize.

In a Japanese restaurant

As in Chinese, the Japanese word for a meal is the word for cooked rice. The first distinction made by Japanese diners-out (who are almost exclusively male) is they never drink sake (rice wine) and eat rice at the same time. Thus, though the tipsy Japanese businessmen at the next table in your local Japanese restaurant will probably eat a great deal more than you, they are not technically having a *meal* at all, but only drinking sake, as they will eat no rice.

Sake etiquette demands one small bottle of hot wine for each person. But you never fill your own cup. If it is empty you replenish the cups of everybody else from your bottle and hope that someone takes the hint. The cup must never be on the table when sake is poured, but held in the hand. Most Japanese drink whisky rather than sake, anyway.

Classical Japanese cuisine, ryōri, is rarely found outside Japan. But Foodies like to know the principles of such a meal even though they may never succeed in eating one. These are not to do with ingredients, but with the methods of cooking. After whatever trifling starters are offered, a typical serious meal will proceed from pickled (sunomo) to raw fish (sashimi), to boiled (clear soup, for example, of salmon

Oldish Chinese joke
The Cantonese will eat anything with four legs except a table and anything that flies except an aeroplane.
Nouvelle Chinese joke
A Cantonese and a Hindu see a creature from Outer Space.
The Hindu begins to worship it.
The Cantonese searches his memory for a suitable recipe.

and seaweed in dashi, the all-important basic stock of kelp and katsuobushi, shavings of dried bonito), to simmered (tofu – bean curd – say, with potato), to grilled (marinated beefsteak, perhaps), to fried (almost certainly the tempura that the Japanese learned to make from the Portuguese), and, as the Japanese eat as few sweets as the Chinese, will finish with fruit (one example is a snow pear, salted and sprinkled with parsley).

The reason for the emphasis on cooking methods, rather than what is cooked, is a chapter of Foodie history. Japan is one of the few countries ever to have been officially vegetarian: there was a mass conversion in the fourteenth century, under the influence of Zen Buddhism. Before that monks as well as ordinary people ate both meat and fish raw, as many of the peoples of South East Asia still do; and as the Chinese, who now eat nothing raw, once did. But this had all been forgotten by the sixteenth century, when the meat-eating Portuguese Jesuits reached Japan. They were astonished to find no recipes and no technology for cooking meat.

In an Indian restaurant

India is not officially a vegetarian country, and many Indians eat meat whenever they can afford it. Nonetheless there is a flourishing vegetarian culture in the south. Indians have no distinctive eating implements – except their fingers. Where the Japanese like slightly glutinous sticky rice that forms balls and is easy to pick up with pointy Japanese chopsticks, Indians eat with fingers – sometimes off banana leaves in the south, and often from a thali, which is the most common way to eat in an Indian home. It is a tray, bearing a complete meal, with the food in little bowls called katori. (Foodies always order the thali in Indian restaurants, because it represents the chef's own choice of what is freshest and best that day – there are usually veggie

Raw fish and silicon chips: a sushi bar in Japan. Customers compose their own combinations and order them on their personal computer keyboard

and non-veggie thalis available.)

Foodies know that the most ignorant error non-Indians make when ordering in restaurants is to neglect the bread, the roti. The often spicy papadam usually comes at the beginning of the meal (though sometimes it is served last, to fill any empty spaces). The abundance of nan, chapati, paratha and puri at every meal, especially in the north of India, is a big feature of the cuisine. Rice, in the north, is often an elaborate preparation of pilau or biryani. In the south it is often made into a flour, to be turned into pancakes such as stuffed dosas or steamed idlis.

'Curry', as every Foodie knows, does not exist at all, except as the name of a leaf used as a condiment. Spices are more common than green herbs in Indian cookery, and are always freshly ground. The level of pepperiness is determined by the quantity and type of chilli used; but it is unusual to encounter the throat-searing brown or yellow stew that is so common in British-Indian restaurants. At lunch, most Indian hotels (proper restaurants are scarce) offer a buffet, and it is rare to come upon anything in the chafing-dishes (which have, after all, been prepared to the local taste) where the food is too hot for even the most sensitive western palate.

All Foodie eater-outers aspire to have eaten in all of these. The only trouble is that so many are around Lyon that you would have to stay a fortnight there, to avoid a crise de foie.

There is an American gastronomic tour that goes to all these French three-stars and to some not rated in this world 18. But Foodies really like to go with a friend or two, on a private trip to excess.

LA MÈRE BLANC, *Georges Blanc*, 01540 Vonnas, France. (74) 50.00.10.

PAUL BOCUSE, 69660 Collonges-au-Mont-d'Or, France. (7) 822.01.40

ALAIN CHAPEL, 01390 Mionnay, France. (7) 891.82.02.

FRÉDY GIRARDET, 1 rue d'Yverdon, Crissier, Switzerland. (21) 34.15.14

LES PRÉS D'EUGÉNIE, *Michel Guérard*, 40320 Eugénie-les-Bains, France. (58) 58.19.01.

AUBERGE DE L'ILL, *Paul* and *Jean-Pierre Haeberlin*, rue de Collonges, 68150 Illhaeusern, France. (89) 71.83.23.

KITCHO, *Teiichi Yuki*, 23–3 Chome Koraibashi, Hi-gashi-Ku, Osaka, Japan. (6) 231 1937.

SONG HE LOU, *Liu Chih*, Guanzhe Road, Suzhou, China.

CHANTECLER, *Jacques Maximin*, Hotel Negresco, 37 Promenade des Anglais, 06000 Nice, France. (93) 88.39.51.

L'ESPÉRANCE, *Marc Meneau*, 89450 St Père-sous-Vézelay, France. (86) 33.20.45.

THE TERRACE ROOM, *Anton Mosimann*, Dorchester Hotel, Park Lane, London W1, England. (01) 629 8888

L'OASIS, *Louis Outhier*, rue Jean-Honoré-Carle, 06210 La Napoule, France. (93) 49.95.52.

L'ARCHESTRATE, *Alain Senderens*, 84 rue de Varenne, Paris 7e, France. (1) 551.47.33.

LES FRÈRES TROISGROS, *Pierre Troisgros*, place de la Gare, 42300 Roanne, France. (77) 71.66.97.

LE MOULIN DE MOUGINS, *Roger Vergé*, 06250 Mougins, France. (93) 75.78.24.

TAILLEVENT, *Jean-Claude Vrinat*, 15 rue Lammenais, Paris 8e, France. (1) 563.39.94.

AUBERGINE, *Eckhart Witzigmann*, Maximiliansplatz 5, Munich 2, Federal Republic of Germany. (089) 59.81.71.

DONG FENG, *Zhou Bai Meng*, Chengdu, Sichuan, China.

TEN RECIPES THAT SHOOK THE WORLD

5 BAIN-MARIE, I LOVE YOU

ANTON MOSIMANN'S

BREAD AND BUTTER PUDDING

To Foodies, English food is a bad joke, a curiosity that ought to be dealt with by anthropologists, not cooks. Even so, English Foodies do have cravings. These are normally for the tastes of the nursery, and are catered for almost exclusively by the dining-rooms of the gentlemen's clubs of London. American and French people can scarcely believe what grown-up, upper-middle class Englishmen will eat for their sweet course – lumpy puddings, steamed to a solid mass with flour and suet, flavoured with commercial jams or treacle, with extraordinary names like 'spotted dick'.

One of the most offensive of these childish dishes used to be bread and butter pudding. *Used* to be, because Anton Mosimann, the Swiss-born chef of the Dorchester Hotel, has refined this baby-talk dish, and made it worthy of a king's table (thank God, as it is the Prince of Wales's favourite).

To serve 4
250 ml (9 fl oz) milk
a pinch of salt
3 eggs
3 small white bread rolls
10 g (½ oz) sultanas or raisins, soaked in water

20 g (¾ oz) apricot jam
250 ml (9 fl oz) double cream
1 vanilla pod
125 g (4½ oz) sugar
30 g (1¼ oz) butter
A little icing (confectioner's) sugar

Bring the milk, cream, salt and vanilla pod to the simmer, and add to the sugar and eggs, mixed together. Sieve the mixture. Slice the rolls thinly, and butter; arrange them in a buttered ovenproof dish, add the raisins, then the custard, sprinkle the remaining butter on top, and poach carefully for 35-40 minutes in a bain-marie. Serve with dribbles of apricot jam, and dust the top with icing sugar.

THE GREAT CHEFS' FAMILY TREE

KING OF THE ANCIENNE CUISINE

GEORGES AUGUSTE ESCOFFIER (1846–1935)

a Foodie hero and the greatest chef of his age, represents the style against which nouvelle cuisine was a reaction. Escoffier worked for César Ritz and ran his hotel kitchens in Monte Carlo, Paris and London. Escoffier rationalised kitchen organisation: each chef de partie was in charge of a department, eg fish, sauces, the larder, but could also work simultaneously with other parties on a dish. The previous method, with no assembly line, was slow, with some chefs working furiously, each on his own dish, while others were idle.

Escoffier also attacked the traditional basic sauces – white and brown – and substituted fumets (reductions of stock) – much lighter and cleaner on the palate. In this he was the ancestor of the nouvelle cuisine chefs. However, Escoffier's practices, recipes (5,000 in his *Guide Culinaire* alone), and dicta (including the nouvellish 'faites simple') assumed the authority of scripture and stifled inventiveness for generations. Chefs were taught that cooking was simply a matter of copying Escoffier. So his culinary progeny are mostly in hotel kitchens rather than serious restaurants.

CATERING COLLEGES AND GRAND-HOTEL KITCHENS

EDOUARD NIGNON (1865–1935)

was chef and later maître d'hôtel at the popular Larue restaurant in Paris. He reacted against the rigidity of Escoffier's followers, saying 'routine in cuisine is a crime'. He taught respect for the character of the ingredients – the main tenet of the nouvelle cuisine – and was the spiritual ancestor of

ANDRÉ PIC (1893–1984)

was one of the three great French chefs outside Paris in the Thirties (the others being Point and Dumaine). He moved his family restaurant, Des Pins, from the hills above Valence into Valence in 1935. By 1939 he had won three Michelin stars; in 1946 he lost a star, and he and the establishment went into a decline. The restaurant was rescued by his son Jacques, who won back the third star in the Sixties.

FERNAND POINT (1897–1955)

the great chef-teacher of our times, taught half the celebrated chefs of France. He trained at the Hotels Bristol and Majestic in Paris, the Imperial at Menton and Royal at Evian-les-Bains. In 1922 his father set him up at La Pyramide, in Vienne, having failed to find a restaurant in Lyon itself. He taught that ingredients should taste of themselves, and never be disguised – therefore they must be of the first quality and freshness. Everything in the kitchen had to be done 'from scratch, with nothing on the stoves' each morning. In 1933, three years after his marriage to a coiffeuse from Vienne in 1930, Point got three Michelin stars.

DIRECT HEIRS OF POINT

RAYMOND THUILIER (b 1897)

Point's great friend, was a life-insurance salesman until he saw the hill village of Les Baux-de-Provence in 1941, and decided to become a chef and restore the building that became the Oustaù de Baumanière. He opened in 1946 and got his third Michelin star in 1954. The cooking is now done by his grandson. Raymond Thuilier is also mayor of Les Baux.

JACQUES PIC (b 1932)

wanted to gain wider experience than his father's kitchen, but was unable to get a place with Point or Dumaine. His training in Geneva, Beaulieu, Deauville and Paris was not, says Quentin Crewe, 'in the mainstream followed by his colleagues of today', but he has won back three stars for his family restaurant. His eight to nine-course menu 'Rabelais' was one of the first 'menus dégustations'.

Indirect heirs of Point

CHARLES BARRIER (b 1916)

has fallen on hard times. He not only lost his third star for his restaurant, Charles Barrier at Tours, but was convicted, in December 1983, of fraud, and sentenced to six months in prison 'for falsifying his tax records'. The oldest of the nouvelle cuisine chefs, Barrier is a wonderful talker, an atheist, Freemason and great cook.

MICHEL GUÉRARD (b 1933)

is the most original of the famous chefs. The son of a butcher, he became a cook only at 17, working first for the caterer Kléber Alix and then for Jean Delavayne of the Camélia in Bougival. Stages followed at Maxim's, Lucas-Carton, the Meurice, the Crillon, and the Normandy at Deauville, before he opened the Pot-au-Feu at Asnières in 1963. He left this to marry Christine Barthélémy, a health-farm heiress. To please her, he lost weight, and invented cuisine minceur. They opened the world's most delicious fat farm at Eugénie-Les-Bains in 1972, and in five years earned three Michelin stars. It remains the only place in the world that serves authentic cuisine minceur.

PAUL HAEBERLIN (b 1923)

chef of L'Auberge de l'Ill at Illhaeusern in Alsace, fought with the Free French Army in the war; his brother, Jean-Pierre, the maître d'hôtel, was conscripted and fought for the Germans. After the war, Paul Haeberlin trained at La Rôtisserie Périgourdine in Paris and with Edouard Weber, who had been chef to the Tsar, to the Kings of Greece and Spain and to the Rothschilds, at La Pépinière at Ribeauvillé in Alsace. He reopened the family auberge in 1950 and it now has three stars.

ROGER VERGÉ (b 1931)

has two restaurants at Mougins, near Cannes. The three-star is Le Moulin de Mougins, which he opened in 1969, after deciding not to be an aeroplane mechanic. He trained at the Tour d'Argent and Plaza Athénée in Paris, then seemed always to be on an aeroplane – he worked at Casablanca, St Moritz, Monte Carlo, and in Jamaica and South Africa before opening his own restaurant. He still enjoys flying down to Rio to do lunch for a couple of hundred people.

GEORGES BLANC (b 1943)

the handsome young chef proprietor of La Mère Blanc at Vonnas. Gault-Millau discovered him (and gave him their highest award – chef of the year – in 1981). He has three Michelin stars. He is firmly in the Lyonnais tradition, and makes wonderful use of the chickens and pigeons of nearby Bresse.

MARC MENEAU (b 1944)

of L'Espérance at St-Père-sous-Vézelay, has at last got three stars in Michelin in 1984. Gault-Millau gave Meneau their highest award – chef of the year – in 1983, and alerted the Michelin inspectors to do their duty.

JACQUES MAXIMIN (b 1948)

of Le Chantecler, in the Hotel Negresco in Nice, trained for two years with Roger Vergé. He may not get a third Michelin star, though he deserves it. Gault-Millau recognised his quality in 1980, the year after he moved to his present post, but Michelin's weird policy is not to give three stars to hotel chefs. Maximin is the only great chef in France to offer a vegetarian menu, and never changes his tasting menu 'because it is technically perfect'.

STARS IN THE EAST

TEIICHI YUKI
the chef of the Restaurant Kitchô in Osaka, is acknowledged universally to be the greatest exponent of traditional Japanese cuisine – ryôri. He is therefore the peer of the other chefs on these pages.

LIU CHIH
is the venerable chef of Song He Lou (the Cranes and Pine Restaurant) in Suzhou, China. The establishment was the favourite of the Ch'ien-lung Emperor (1711–1799). Chef Liu, an official first-class worker and master chef, has lived through the Long March and the Cultural Revolution, doing his

personal best to maintain a standard the Emperor would have recognised. His most famous dish is Mandarin fish in the shape of a squirrel.

ZHOU BOI MENG,
the chef of Dong Feng Restaurant in Chengdu, the capital of Sichuan, worked in the kitchens of several Chinese embassies abroad. He is also an official first-class chef, and his specialities are the fiery dishes of Sichuan province, famous throughout the Chinese-eating world: Governor's chicken, fragrant smoked duck, braised eel with garlic, Ma Pa dofu, Mrs Tsung's dumplings in hot pepper oil, and Sichuan pickled vegetable with chicken stock.

**ALEXANDRE DUMAINE
(1895–1964)**
was born at Digoin, and by 1914 he was working at the Elysée Palace. Curnonsky made his Hotel de la Côte d'Or at Saulieu a gastronomic shrine; but Dumaine, according to Quentin Crewe, 'lacked that ability to teach which might have made him of lasting importance.'

**PAUL BOCUSE
(b 1926)**
is the most famous chef living. Giscard d'Estaing, when President of France, chose Bocuse to organise the lunch cooked by top chefs at the Elysée in 1975 (for which he created his soupe aux truffes) and to receive the Légion d'Honneur. He is the Foodiebiz chef, with his television programmes, his travel, and his interests in restaurants in America and Japan. His own, at Collonges au Mont d'Or, got its third star in 1965; the head cook is Roger Jaloux. Before training for six years with Point (where his father had also been an apprentice), Bocuse did stages at Lucas-Carton in Paris and La Mère Brazier at Lyon.

**JEAN TROISGROS
(1926–1983) and
PIERRE TROISGROS
(b 1928)**
trained at Lucas-Carton at the same time as Bocuse, and also went to La Pyramide. They returned in 1954 to their father's restaurant, opposite the railway station in Roanne, near Lyon. In 1968, they achieved three stars. Their 1975 Elysée lunch dish was escalope of salmon with sorrel, which has become a Nouvelle cliché, as has their terrine de légumes 'Olympe' (named after Pierre's wife).

**FRANÇOIS BISE
(b 1928)**
cooks at and owns L'Auberge du Père Bise at Talloires on Lake Annecy. Confusingly, it was his grandfather who started the business, but his father, Marius, who came to be known as Père Bise; moreover, it was Mère Bise who did the cooking, and who in 1931 was the first woman to win three Michelin stars. After working for Pyramide for three years, François Bise went to Larue in Paris, and came back to take his place beside his mother in 1951. He inherited in 1968.

**LOUIS OUTHIER
(b 1930)**
was one of Point's last disciples. Unlike the others, his father did not own a restaurant, and he found it difficult to establish himself at L'Oasis, at La Napoule near Cannes, which was originally a pension where Outhier cooked two meals a day for the lodgers. Quentin Crewe says that, upon learning of his third Michelin star in 1970, Outhier said only 'Merde': it meant he would have to redecorate his restaurant a third time.

JEAN VIGNARD
was one of Fernand Point's closest associates. His restaurant was Chez Juliette.

**ALAIN CHAPEL
(b 1937)**
is the son of a Lyonnais restaurateur, who acquired his Michelin star in 1957. Too young to have been taught by Point himself, Chapel worked at La Pyramide under Mercier, after his apprenticeship with

**PAUL MERCIER
(d 1962)**
took over as chef at La Pyramide after Point's death in 1955, and maintained Point's menu intact until his own death.

Vignard at Chez Juliette. His father died in 1969 and Chapel took over the business, acquiring three stars and four Gault-Millau toques in 1973. He gets his culinary inspiration from the produce he buys each day, and likes ingredients such as lambs' testicles and calf's ears.

**ALAIN SENDERENS
(b 1941)**
is one of only two Paris chefs of the very highest order. His L'Archestrate may well be the most expensive restaurant in Paris, and thus in France (tomorrow the world . . .), and Senderens is famous for his daring combinations, such as lobster with vanilla. Three stars, four toques.

**JEAN-CLAUDE VRINAT
(b 1936)**
of Taillevent is the other Paris restaurateur about whom Michelin and Gault-Millau can agree: three stars, four toques. He says he prefers 'salmon with mint to cold salmon with mayonnaise, turbot with a cream of leek to turbot Dugléré . . . and our clients do too.' This triumphant proclamation of faith in the nouvelle cuisine is executed by chef Claude Deligne.

**FRÉDY GIRARDET
(b 1937)**
at Crissier, Switzerland, 60 kilometres from Geneva, is said by many to be the world's best chef. His brigade of 17 can turn out some astonishing dishes, including, in season, cassolette de truffes aux cardons, which you can wash down with the world's largest selection of Swiss wines and follow with ditto Swiss cheeses.

**ECKHART WITZIGMANN
(b 1942)**
of the Aubergine in Munich is the only other chef on the Continent of Europe who can or should appear here. His restaurant has only 40 covers, and, like nouvelle cuisine chefs everywhere, he recently discovered a passion for regional dishes, which he lightens and improves out of all recognition.

**ANTON MOSIMANN
(b 1947)**
of the Dorchester Hotel in London is the sole chef in the English-speaking world who belongs in the company of the world's best chefs. The Michelin men, who have only given one miserable star to the Dorchester (and that in 1984), forget that, since Ritz and Escoffier, London has always been different from other capitals in that the best cooking is traditionally done in hotels. Swiss-born Mosimann trained in Switzerland, then in Italy, Canada and – most tellingly – in Japan. He has, of course, done stages in the great nouvelle cuisine kitchens of France. He serves a many-course 'menu surprise' in his Terrace Room restaurant that is the first cousin of the tasting menus of the other nouvelle cuisine chefs; but in his Grill Room, he has done much to rescue English food from the ignominy into which it has sunk.

Why the big influence is little understood

La nouvelle cuisine was christened in October 1973 by Henri Gault and Christian Millau in an article in the *Gault-Millau* magazine called 'Vive La Nouvelle Cuisine Française'. It described a new, lighter, flourless cooking being practised by a group of French chefs, and analysed the principals that govern the new style. The chefs – Paul Bocuse, the two Troisgros brothers, Charles Barrier, Roger Vergé, Michel Guérard and eight others (see p 60–61) – had all been influenced by Fernand Point (d 1955) at La Pyramide in Vienne, or by Alexandre Dumaine at the Côte d'Or at Saulieu. Point is the acknowledged père of nouvelle cuisine, but it had taken twenty years of humble chopping and stirring by his disciples for them to get into positions where his ideas could be recognised.

However, by 1973, they were around 40, confident, owned their own restaurants, and were ready for fame. They could have done without the name of the fame – most don't like 'nouvelle cuisine' and talk about 'cuisine moderne' or something. But the fame itself was very acceptable. Guérard, Vergé and the two Troisgros set about writing books about their methods which made them even more famous.

Foreign journalists hurried to be the first in their country to explain the movement to their readers, but almost all of them got it wrong. Several British journalists thought it was called 'cuisine minceur', the title of Guérard's first book. Cuisine minceur is a variation on NC invented by Guérard for the slimmers at his health farm at Eugénie les Bains. The only places that serve genuine cuisine minceur are Guérard's restaurant at Eugénie and those nearby whose chefs he has trained.

Raymond Sokolov, then of the *New York Times*, had actually written an article for his paper in the spring of 1972 saying that Bocuse and his associates had a new style. He had interviewed Bocuse about it in France, but it still had no name.

Craig Claiborne, the top American food writer, socked nouvelle cuisine to his readers in the same paper after it had been christened – but he gave a Bocuse recipe with flour in 1975, so he obviously hadn't thoroughly absorbed it.

So what *is* it? It's a mixture of Point and pointlessness. The ten commandments Gault and Millau gave, which have been adapted by Anne Willan for her cookery school La Varenne, are:

★ 1 *Avoid unnecessary complication* Use simple methods like poaching, baking and steaming. The exception is puff pastry –

TEN RECIPES THAT SHOOK THE WORLD

6

FRENCH CHEF MINCES WORDS
MICHEL GUÉRARD'S OEUF POULE AU CAVIAR

Almost all non-Foodies confuse cuisine minceur with nouvelle cuisine. This muddle is a left-over from the late 1970s, when food writers and journalists confused the new general trend of French cookery (NC) with Michel Guérard's specialised recipes for slimmers (CM), which he first devised for his own use. This was made easy to do by the simple elegance of CM recipes such as this one, which even the great NC chef Bocuse would occasionally dish up to favoured customers in explicit homage to his CM colleague.

Guérard says to slice the tops of fresh eggs very carefully with a serrated knife about ½ inch (1 cm) above the roundest part of the shell. Then scramble the egg over the lowest possible heat, as slowly as possible, and remove when it is still a light cream. Beat in a half teaspoon of fromage blanc 0% (not butter) per serving, along with salt and pepper, ¼ tbs finely minced onion and ¼ tsp chopped chives. Spoon this into washed and dried eggshells, top each one with 15g (½ oz) best Iranian Sevruga caviar, and replace the top of the egg. *Calories*: not many. *Cost*: plenty.

Nouvelle cuisine food cooked by Anton Mosimann. Note the octagonal plates – helps the chef get the pattern right. The sauce goes underneath – mustn't obscure the view. The truffled chicken liver pâté has roses of tomato peel and chervil. NC is ART – oh yes. The steak is transformed from being Businessman to being Foodie by the criminally under-age carrots and the teeny-weeny portions

the only pastry allowed in NC, and the most complicated to make

★ 2 *Shorten cooking times* The Troisgros brothers' salmon escalopes with sorrel, a nouvelle cuisine classic, are sautéed for *40 seconds* This emphasis on shorter cooking leads inevitably to younger, better ingredients and to:

★ 3 *Shop regularly at the market* Anne Willan points out that when nouvelle cuisine chefs go to market, they buy fish, shellfish, white meats and offal, and avoid red meats except rack of lamb.

★ 4 *Shorten the menu* Barrier and Vergé recommended home cooks to serve only one proper course. However, nouvelle cuisine restaurants may have tasting menus of up to eight courses.

★ 5 *Don't hang or marinate game* Foodies

don't believe the chefs observe this: it would be as tough as vieux boots.

★ 6 *Avoid too rich sauces* The NO FLOUR rule is the chief commandment. Sauces should be made by reducing the cooking liquid and finishing with cream or butter. They go *under* the food, unlike the old sauces, which were poured over it. NC food sits in a lake.

★ 7 *Return to regional cooking* But not to regional fatty casseroles of course. On NC menus, 'Cassoulet', 'pot-au-feu' and 'boudin' usually turn out to be fish. And NC is murder on a region's millers, only allowing flour for bread or puff pastry.

★ 8 *Investigate the latest techniques* Use a food processor.

★ 9 *Consider diet and health* Not much sugar, not much salt, NO FRYING. NC chefs believe their rejection of red meat is good for you.

★ 10 *Invent constantly* This has led bad cooks to bore with kiwi fruit and pink peppercorns, but it is a good idea, if the imagination holds out.

Not in the commandments, but important, is that the chef arranges each plate in the kitchen, you aren't served from a silver platter from which to make your ignorant choice.

So there were the principles, but what did it all *mean?* Almost at once, smart restaurants outside France began adapting their menus to appear NC. In came kiwi fruit, basil, and blackcurrant vinegar, up went prices. Restaurants even bought NC cutlery, French sauce spoons with a straight side for cutting and a bowl for the sauce. The unconvinced amongst the customers said kiwi fruit was the parsley of the new cliché food and that a plate of NC was as pretty as a picture and as filling as a postage stamp.

It looked like a fashion, but something

had happened. Cooking had moved into its next phase. The cooking of the industrial revolution was over. The North had lost. The sunnier Catholic and Eastern countries had won the battle of the estomac. The cooking methods most suited to coal were out. Beef, the top meat of the West, was out. Even veal was out. The animal fats and flour that fuelled you through cold winters were out. The long cooking that softened tough old meat was out. Point said that nothing should be on the stove in the morning – you had to start from scratch.

What had come in were Third World methods of cooking and Third World ingredients like prawns. Oysters, the raw treats of old cuisine, were *cooked* in the new. Out, sacred cows!

Patience and long maturing were over. Farmers didn't have to keep animals or poultry till they grew up, cooks didn't have to spend hours trimming meat for stews. Meat had lost its importance altogether, because it's boring to cook. Fish is the

---

F·O·O·D·I·E B·O·R·E·S

THE CHEESE BORE

The cheese bore may be of any nationality, but what he is boring about is almost always French, Italian or British. Sometimes he goes on about cheese with holes – but most often he dismisses Swiss cheeses as 'cooked' or 'processed', which, technically, Gruyère and Emmenthaler are. To the fromage bore, German and Scandinavian cheeses are poor relations of the real (French) thing. (As American cheese has to be made from pasteurised milk, he considers that it isn't really cheese at all, but a kind of decomposing plastic.)

If the wooden coffer enclosing it doesn't say 'au lait cru', the cheese bore doesn't even bother to open it. He is very keen on funny-shaped cheese, such as the conical Boulette d'Avesnes, which, he tells you, the natives (of Flandre-Hainaut) call 'suppositoire du diable'. He knows that cheese is seasonal, and only eats Roquefort from November through January, and chèvre in spring and summer. He does not realise it yet, but his love affair with the goat is drawing to a close. As chèvre begins to be made in Britain and America, it will be shunned by

the bore. Like all Foodie bores, the cheese bore becomes the cheese bored.

Lately he has got interested in a lot of new-fangled Italian cheeses made in layers with Mascarpone and basil or chillies or pine-nuts, though he knows that nothing compares with a properly-made and aged Parmesan. Italian cheese is definitely a growth area for bores.

So is British cheese. Armed with Patrick Rance's *The Great British Cheese Book,* the bore sets out to explore the smallholdings of the British Isles. Llangloffan, Barac and Single

Gloucester thrill him, though what he likes best is to spend days in Dorset, on the trail of Blue Vinney. This fabled cheese, which is supposed to have died and been resurrected, is still made (by a single farm between Dorchester and Puddletown) from skimmed milk; though the approved method of blueing is no longer drawing a mouldy harness through the vat.

Clutching their copies of Androuët's *Guide du Fromage,* the cheese bores are even now buzzing about the Île-de-France, in search of – what else? – Brie de Nangis. Androuët, in his 1983 edition, declared it EXTINCT. They want to prove him wrong. If they can't, some cheese bores are thinking of moving backwards to the eighteenth century (autres temps, autres bores) and trying cheese with mites. 'Tasteless and inoffensive enough, but the terror of all strict vegetarians,' says André Simon. Mite or myth? the cheese bore asks himself, allowing three different sorts of cheese to mould and moulder in the larder. He hopes to attract some of the tiny creatures to infest them. Then he will hold a mity cheese tasting.

Why do nouvelle cuisine restaurants serve their tiny portions under such big silver covers?
★ They believe in 'Cherchez le faim'.

favourite of all nouvelle cuisine chefs. The food shops' profits shot up when nouvelle cuisine came in – no more converting cheap ingredients into something delicious by care and cooking. The ingredients have to be young and expensive.

Eating nouvelle cuisine *displays one's income.* And think what it means for the home cook when something only needs 40 seconds' cooking. It means your friends can be with you from preparation to table. It turns cooking into theatre. This new movement certainly had everything. At about this point the food lover turned into the Foodie.

Nouvelle cuisine has some of its roots in Japanese and Chinese cooking, which are based on similar principles. Many of the

top French chefs have visited the East. On the ultra-Foodie west coast of America a new 'FrancAsian' cooking was christened in 1984. Everyone wants to obey the tenth commandment and get in on food.

Everyone modern, that is. Some fuddy-duddies still think that nouvelle cuisine is a fad that will be replaced. The chief tip to replace it is historical rediscoveries. But this is head-in-the-sand stuff. Nouvelle cuisine has replaced béchamel and Espagnole with (the older) fumets and coulis, but yesterday's roasts, like yesterday's gravys *cannot* come back while we have central heating and abundant calories. The fats and sugars just don't taste right any more, luckily for the rest of the body. We must learn to love raspberry vinegar.

The slices of baby lamb raying out from a glob of broccoli mousse are so undercooked they look like salmon.

Food can kill

The first misunderstood Foodie hero was Esau, who 'selleth his birthright for a mess of pottage'. The Bible then moves contemptuously on, without putting the case for the defence. What *was* the pottage? Attitudes have certainly changed.

Then there was the Foodie martyr, Henry I of England, who overgorged on lampreys in 1135. Alexander Pope is also thought to have died from eating lampreys, in 1744. Killing those two was the revenge of the lamprey (an eel-like fish) for the way cooks have always treated his kind. Even today, in south-western France, they are bled to death slowly to make the famous sauce thickened with their own blood. André Simon says that the lamprey deserves its reputation for being a dangerous food 'because they each have two filaments in the back which are poisonous and which must be removed before cooking'. But Alan Davidson does not confirm this in his more scientific *North Atlantic Seafood*, which has a long passage on what he calls 'this slimy and antique creature'.

Foodies have usually been their own worst enemies. But Henri Vatel was done to death by Foodism. Vatel began his career as maitre d'hotel to Nicholas Fouquet, Mazarin's ambitious finance minister. Fouquet gave a grand reception for the King at his château Vaux-le-Vicomte in 1661: administration and food by Vatel's men, music by Lully's men, cabaret by Molière's men. When the King saw how regal the arrangements were he cried, 'Fouquet!' His next thought was that dishonesty must have paid for all this. Fouquet was sent to prison, which set Vatel loose. He worked in England and Belgium, then went back to France to work for the Prince de Condé at Chantilly. The King was coming to Chantilly, and the Prince planned to out-Vaux Vaux, nine years later, and with a happy ending.

But everything went wrong. After

Lampreys murdered Henry I

Lampreys later put paid to Alexander Pope

'Why didn't you let me die?' 'I can't work the food processor.'

twelve nights without sleep, Vatel was driven over the top by receiving a delivery of a few fish. He had ordered hundreds of fish. He went to his room and threw himself on his sword (jammed against the door, according to Madame de Sévigné). When the rest of the fish arrived, no one knew how to cook it. After a search they found Vatel's body. They buried him in a field so as not to spoil the party, and later no one could remember where the grave was.

Vatel seems to be the only well-documented Foodie suicide. There are rumours of every new Michelin being greeted by shots as chefs lose their stars, though no one has found a chef's body.

But diets can kill, as the newspapers prove. And they have maimed Foodies. Shortly after the low-carbohydrate Dr Atkins diet was launched in America in the Sixties, a Balliol don brought the book back to Oxford, where High Table stodge has produced centuries of fat fellows. The Atkins diet allowed unlimited fat and protein but no starch or alcohol. The don persuaded two of his don friends, one from Wadham and one from Nuffield, to try the diet for two weeks. The Balliol man lost two stone (28 lb). The Wadham man lost 15 pounds and his gall-bladder. His insides have never been quite right since. The Nuffield man lost seven pounds, but what he had not realised was that his chronic low blood-sugar made the diet dangerous. He passed out and was rushed to the Radcliffe Infirmary in a hypoglycemic swoon. The doctors said that if he had *really* given up drink, he would probably have died. Moral: the Higher the Table, the lower the risk.

Choking on food kills several thousand Foodies a year. Many people have choked to death in restaurants while the other diners thought the Foodie was having a heart attack. In New York, restaurants display instructions for doing the 'Heimlich Maneuver'. Learn this manoeuvre, if you insist on eating like a hoover.

THESE PAGES COULD SAVE YOUR LIFE:
A PUNCH IN THE PAUNCH – THE HEIMLICH MANEUVER FOR CHOKERS

Choking kills, and not only Foodies. The Americans have worked out that choking is the sixth leading cause of accidental death in the population, and the *leading* cause of death in the home for children under a year old. Over 3,000 Americans a year die by choking. However, since 1974 there has been the Heimlich Maneuver, invented by Dr Henry Heimlich – the punch in the paunch. It's a brawn technique depending on *subdiaphragmatic thrust*, and you can read how to do it in many American restaurants. Some British coroners have said they wished it was better known in Britain. Here is the gist, for when the gristle strikes back.

Recognition
Is the person choking? Can't breathe or speak, turning blue, hand clutching throat? (Trained Heimlichers make a V with thumb and index finger at the throat.) Ask 'Are you choking?' and if he nods, you have four minutes to avert unconsciousness, brain damage and death.

Many people waste time wondering if it's a heart attack. If it's in a restaurant, try the Heimlich first, before the kiss of life. In a survey of 56 restaurant deaths, 55 were found to have choked, one to have had a heart attack. (No, it *wasn't* the food.)

Action
● *A standing victim*. Get behind him, put arms round him, make a fist and put it on his stomach, below the tip of the rib cage and above the navel. Grasp your fist with your other hand and thrust it sharply upwards into the victim's abdomen. You may have to do this up to six times, but in over half the cases the obstruction pops out of the mouth after one or two thrusts. (Don't squeeze the ribs. When the HM was new,

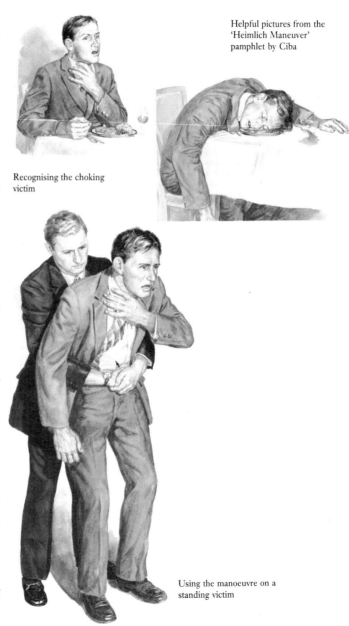

Helpful pictures from the 'Heimlich Maneuver' pamphlet by Ciba

Recognising the choking victim

Using the manoeuvre on a standing victim

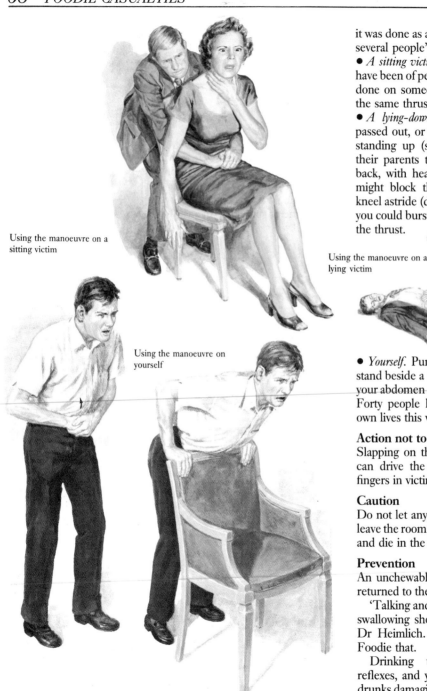

Using the manoeuvre on a
sitting victim

Using the manoeuvre on
yourself

it was done as a 'hug of love', which broke
several people's bones.)

- *A sitting victim.* 82 per cent of rescues
have been of people standing, but it can be
done on someone sitting down. Perform
the same thrust from behind his chair.

- *A lying-down victim.* He might have
passed out, or be too big for you to help
standing up (some children have saved
their parents this way). Put him on his
back, with head straight (head sideways
might block the escape of the object),
kneel astride (don't thrust from the side –
you could burst his liver or spleen) and do
the thrust.

Using the manoeuvre on a
lying victim

- *Yourself.* Punch your own paunch. Or
stand beside a table or other edge and jab
your abdomen against it and think of Vatel.
Forty people have reported saving their
own lives this way.

Action not to take
Slapping on the back. Wastes time, and
can drive the object farther in. Poking
fingers in victim's mouth. Ditto.

Caution
Do not let anyone who might be choking
leave the room alone. They might pass out
and die in the lavatory.

Prevention
An unchewable piece of meat should be
returned to the plate. Politeness is not all.

'Talking and laughing while chewing or
swallowing should also be avoided,' says
Dr Heimlich. You don't need to tell a
Foodie that.

Drinking too much blunts your
reflexes, and you don't want your fellow
drunks damaging your insides with clumsy
Heimlich punches.

Wine has its place (second)

Foodies are careful not to fall into the trap of getting too interested in wine. Wine is too big a subject, too *old* a subject. Literally time-consuming. When a Foodie sees a wine man in his cellar full of dead dead air, gently holding up a cobwebby bottle horizontally to the light to examine the sediment, it somehow sums up for you how far behind you would start if you tried to master that world. 'Grapies' are the wine equivalent of Foodies.

Some Foodies do attempt to straddle both subjects, mugging up little-known Pomerols and the slope that gets most sun. But in your heart, you must be a Foodie *or* a Grapie. Foodies know instinctively that it is *dangerous to food* really to like wine. A Grapie *does not mind what he eats* as long as it doesn't interfere with the wine. Once you start building the meal round a Chambertin 1969, food is betrayed. The Foodie's ideal of six or seven little courses in a tasting menu is the enemy of the Grapie's ideal of four important wines to a meal – good, better, best and dessert. You like unobtrusive wines, that can escort you through the whole programme. You have adopted the light reds. You don't want to be kowtowing to great years and noble vineyards. Anything noble is suspect – the noble varieties of grape like Chardonnay and Cabernet Sauvignon, and even the noble rot of Sauternes and Trockenbeerenauslese. *Food* is noble. Drink goes *with* it.

Foodies are fond of 'country wines'. In a restaurant, you ask for the house wine or some wine discovery you have just made. This does not mean you are insensitive to how wine tastes with the food. You sympathise with the Foodie in the old joke when his neighbour was sick on the table: 'At least the white wine arrived with the fish.' (Though when you last did it, it was Chinon with the salmon.) You *hate* being given the sweet course before cheese – this is *obviously* wrong. If God had intended it, He would not have made red wine robuster than white. The last of the red wine is wrong with the pudding but *necessary* for the cheese.

To you, wine's main purpose is to lift the senses to the precise degree where you will be intoxicated by the food. Foodies seek the eater's high. They are never teetotal. Achieving the right state is very difficult in the Far East, where wine is almost always in poor condition and always expensive. Beer and fruit juice don't elevate you. At first, Foodies won't resort to rice wine or spirits like the natives, but in the end you sink to downing a chota peg before dinner – 90 per cent whisky, 10 per cent water. You would never do it to your palate at home.

The travel and exploration aspect of Foodism can be used for Grapism, and you like finding new wine districts near a toqued restaurant, or a supermarket that has recently taken on a good wine buyer. Those old wine merchants are so snobby and hung up on – well, on *wine*.

Grapies at work. Sniff, swill, snuffle, snuffle, spit. Another day, another tasting

The Grapie world (the Opposition)

Grapies are an energetic modern tribe similar to Foodies, but with its highest concentration in the United States (mostly doctors and dentists). America is the bigger market for wine; but Britain tells Americans what to drink. Britain has the highest concentration of reliable wine journalists, and is used by wine producers as a testing ground. (Britain used to be the important market, and has held on to its reputation for connoisseurship.) Producers are as keen to be praised in the specialist pages of the British *Decanter* as in the more popular pages of the French *Cuisine et Vins de France* and the *Gault-Millau* monthly. Producers would rather see their wines in the *Observer* or the *Sunday Times* than in the much larger-circulation *New York Times* or *Los Angeles Times*. The American wine distributors prefer the views of British wine snobs to their own home-grown wine snobs: *Gourmet* and *Cuisine* both have British wine editors, Gerald Asher and Hugh Johnson.

Foodies are glad that *food* does not have to be channelled through a mere plateful of Brit brains. Food has no bottlenecks. Foodism has representatives all over the world whose reports can be trusted.

Hugh Johnson's certainly gotta lotta bottle

Foodie vintage chart

1976	California
1977	The Loire
1978	Petits châteaux of Bordeaux
1979	Rioja and cava
1980	Rully, Montagny and the Côte Chalonnaise
1981	Wines of the northern Rhône
1982	Washington and Oregon
1983	New Zealand

Foodie discoveries (white)

● Bonnezaux (Loire). Sweetish, good with Roquefort and that smuggled foie gras
● Savennières (opposite bank of the Loire). A fashionable Foodie apéritif
● Château St Jean (Sonoma Valley). Makes a late-harvest Riesling, the Foodie Trockenbeerenauslese

Light reds suitable for a tasting menu

● Beaujolais (but only crus)
● Sancerre rouge
● Bouzy rouge (champagne)
● Chinon
● Bourgeuil
● Tasmanian Cabernet
● Oregon Pinot Noir

After the meal

● Beaumes de Venise. It's the Foodie's Château d'Yquem (the *meanie's* Château d'Yquem, Hugh Johnson says)

In the garden

● Any of the above. The flowery German wines like the Mosels and Rheingaus that Grapies drink in the garden, because they are best by themselves not with food, seem dangerous, even mad, to you. What if this habit caught on? (Foodies are anti-German even if they are too young to remember the war. It's the Schweinebraten and Schinken that appals them.)

Anytime, anywhere

★★★★★ Champagne

PART THREE
THE GLOBAL FOODIE

FOODISM ON THE MOVE

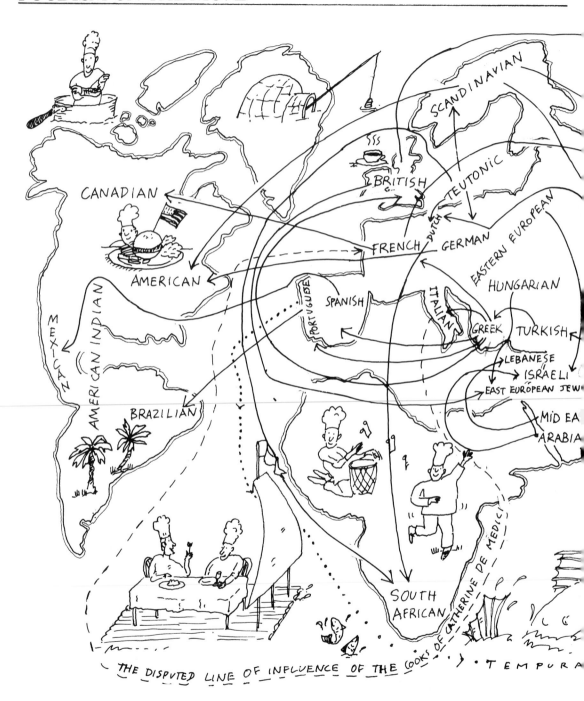

THE DISPUTED LINE OF INFLUENCE OF THE COOKS OF CATHERINE DE MEDICI · TEMPURA

THE THREE HOLY LANDS OF FOODISM

The big F, the big C, the big J – and why you can't eat out decently anywhere else

Like all other religions, Foodism has its shrines – places where Foodies go to worship. These sacred places are called *restaurants*. Some are so important that serious Foodies will not let anything stand between them and their object. Distance – what's that? Lack of money can't stop you for long. The only drawback is that there are so *many* shrines. Other religions have one, or at most two – Mecca, Jerusalem, the Ganges, Santiago de Compostela. But every Foodie wishes to visit the dozen best restaurants in France and the three great culinary addresses of Chengdu, Suzhou and Osaka (see p 59).

It is lucky for zealots that there are only three great restaurant cultures in the world: France, China and Japan. In these countries, people are brought up from infancy to take part in the ritual of Eating Out. (True, they are brought up the same way in Italy and Spain. However, those countries are not Holy to Foodies: many are called, but few are chosen.) In France, in all social classes, the entire family eats out together once a week. This is a little like going to the theatre: one of the goals is to be entertained. Even quite young children develop a critical attitude to food and service, as they would to actors or acrobats.

Chinese children are trained the same way, though standards have slipped a bit in China itself; to see how things used to be, look at rich Hong Kong.

In Japan, the men eat out – women seldom do. Mr Foodiyama either 'eats rice' or 'drinks', but never both at the same time; though he does have a constant supply of delicious titbits offered to him as he 'drinks'. Nonetheless, Japan is a restaurant culture, unlike Italy. Marcella Hazan, author of *The Classic Italian Cookbook*, says: 'The best cooking in Italy is not … to be found in restaurants, but in the home. One of the reasons that Italian restaurants outside Italy are often so poor is that they do not have Italian home cooking with which to compete.'

It's the difference between going to church and building cathedrals.

It has recently been suggested by some writers that the French cooking in Japan is as good as the best in France. Most French have naturally pooh poohed this, but they allow that as with cars and electronics, it could happen – and point out that there is a Japanese working in almost every good restaurant in France. There is also the indomitable Professor Tsuji, turning out 2,500 students a year from his school at Osaka, all perfectly trained as French chefs.

Few countries of the Middle East have a restaurant culture. Southern Europe has coffee-houses and tavernas, but no Foodie goes to such places to eat seriously. India not only has no restaurant culture but, apart from the grand hotels, has hardly any restaurants. Germany and Austria have restaurants, but nothing to eat in them, say horrid Foodies: German and Austrian food is too gross and unrefined for the devotee's palate – though Das Neue Küche (nouvelle cuisine) may change that. England and America are beginning to develop a restaurant culture, but the food served in the restaurants is seldom British or American. So there remain France, China, Japan, these three; but the greatest of these is France. (From the gospel according to Foodies.)

Foodie heaven – all the dumplings you can eat. Chinese Foodies at the Xinfeng in Peking

Underdone is Well Done:
THE CRISPY FOODIE

The Foodies of the West were the first to notice what everyone in the East has known for ever – vegetables and meat should be *almost* cooked. They should be crisp, or al dente as it is known in the ancestral homeland of Al Capone.

The Chinese and Japanese actually cook everything very quickly over a fire because they are short of wood. Wood is good, coal is crime, in Foodie eyes. Coal countries have terrible cuisines – Britain, Germany, Belgium, Pennsylvania – ugggh. Coal leads to ovens and hobs, and ovens and hobs lead to overdone roasts, stodgy puddings and flabby vegetables that are boiled for hours. Shorter vegetable cooking times were one of the post-war miracles. Foodies stand at the stove poking with a fork at the haricots verts, their faces flushed but stern, tiny blood vessels popping in their cheeks and noses, their hair sopping up steam and smells, waiting for the precise second when the young vegetable is à point.

'Primavera' is today's menu name-drop. Foodies love to sink their teeth into *youth*. The western youth mania embraces food. The Romans had their primitiae, 'the firsts', but those were the exception in their diet. The French NC chefs cook practically nothing *but* primeurs. The taste of experienced flesh or an ancient sow of a marrow is an affront to modern palates. Foodies are *namby-pamby*. In the Fifties, people joked that French restaurants piped the smell of the lavatories into the dining room to give customers the authentic smell of France. Customers today

Contrast of textures is essential. Two Tokyo cooks contrast poisonous snakes with undercooked shredded veg

would send for the public health inspector.

When Foodies chew the chicken of France and China, they forget the hidden ingredient is maturity. (Maturity – ugggh!) American and British chickens are killed at eight weeks, French at thirteen, and a high-class French chicken has a label, telling its age, eg 91 days. The extra 35 days are supposed to give taste. But for real taste find a two-year-old boiler.

Mutton is another victim of fast farming. MacFoodie has murdered sheep. Sometimes a Foodie does manage to buy a leg of the older animal in an obscure part of Britain, France or Kentucky (the lamb bastion of the USA). It ages another week while you hunt for a recipe. Eventually you invite several Foodie friends and dish up your boiled mutton with caper sauce, and you all taste it and – long faces. Baaah! No, no, *no*. It is rank and horrible. Back to steamed fish.

It's the same with pork. Western Foodies consider fresh pork both gross and uninteresting and it is fast fading out of western diets. The Chinese still believe you can make a silk purse out of a sow's ear, and always kill and eat the pig the same day.

Foodies approve of game, in theory, but Americans haven't much wild game left and British cooks hang theirs to let decomposition soften it – which brings that strong old taste again. NC cooks are flying in the face of nature by their principle of not hanging game – if it's young enough, yes, but how are they going to get it young enough? The answer of course is farming. Namby-*pamby*.

Time, Crime and the FOODIE

	1950 cooking time	1984 Foodie cooking time
lamb	35 min a lb	15 min a lb
beef	30 min a lb in a slow oven	15 min a lb in a hot oven (unless you're NC and have given up beef)
courgettes/ zucchini	20 min	5 min
rice pudding, hotpot, Irish stew	various long cooking times	Foodies don't make them
mutton	45 min a lb	Foodies have made it extinct
pork	45 min a lb	Foodies are about to make it extinct

Foodie take their whining bad-tempered standards everywhere (and their Foodie addresses – see p 80)

While no Foodie would volunteer to go to certain countries, there are occasions when you might find yourself in Russia or even Israel. The world's worst food is, of course, found in Britain and America, the giants of junk food, but Canada, New Zealand and Australia deserve dishonourable mention. However, there is always something delicious to be had in all these countries, and the standard of food is nothing like so low as in genuinely non-F countries such as Nepal and Peru.

A is for advanced

Australia and New Zealand are the California of the eastern hemisphere. Foodism is the second religion, after exercise, and they are developing their own branch of nouvelle cuisine – Franco-Oz? New Zealand gave NC kiwis, which became so much a trademark that they are now taboo among fashion-victim Foodies. Chefs know the kiwi's worth and it will soon be back, in all its tanginess and beauty (those eyes!).

There are good restaurants in New Zealand and Australia but they lag behind the general aspirations of home cooking and behind the native wines, which now have a finesse equal to Europe's – again, like California.

B is for belly

Belgium is a country of native Foodies and Common Marketeer Foodies. Too bad they have to cross the border for many of their best meals. However, they have Comme Chez Soi in Brussels, credited with playing a part in Common Market history. When a Foodie British Minister was negotiating Britain's entry, he is said to have cut short a vital meeting so as not to lose his table at Comme Chez Soi. The French and Belgians understood.

C is for caught between cultures

Canadian food used to be Escoffier-British, Parisian French or fast-food American. But several *Canadian* consciousnesses found their feet about 1967, not because of Expo but as a result of books and new museums and a general rehabilitation of the past – British, French (Jean Pallardy's book on French-Canadian furniture was a time bombe surprise), and German (in Nova Scotia). Canadians find it very difficult to give themselves physically, but they are certainly *trying* to be Foodie.

G is for gross

For the Foodie traveller in Germany: Würst is best.

G is for grease

Though there are Greek restaurants the world over, there is scarcely any edible food in Greece itself. You are glad you are expected to go into the kitchen at the taverna to choose the least lethal-looking stew. In general, it's as well to stick to fish.

H is for hoi polloi pollution

It is sad that Hungary, once so proud of her cooking, has become a Foodie desert. Goulash (gulyás) isn't what you think it is (what you think it is is called pörkölt) but a soupy mess over-seasoned with paprika that the natives only eat at holiday time. Only tourists eat it every day. The use of paprika in Hungary is recent: Columbus introduced it from America into Spain in the late fifteenth century but it didn't reach Hungarian saucepans until the late nineteenth century. Pity it doesn't move on somewhere and get lost.

Unkind lapel badge.

The food is degraded in even the best restaurants – the famous Gundel's of Budapest is no exception. Hungarian emigrés on return visits say the decline is the fault of a shortage of chefs. Hungary is a popular tourist country, especially for East Germans, and too few cooks spoil the broth. There is good Hungarian cooking in London, at the Gay Hussar, and Chicago, at Louis Szathmáry's The Bakery restaurant. Foodies should forego fogas and paprikás by Lake Balaton and fly the other way.

I is for indigenous dishes

The food in India can be good. But Foodies know that there is no restaurant tradition: as in English and American Indian restaurants, the restaurants are run almost exclusively by Punjabis. As Indian food is very regional, eating in Punjabi-run restaurants outside the Punjab guarantees that the food is not authentic.

You can avoid this by eating in the posh restaurants of the posh hotels – both the Taj group and the Wellcom group emphasise regional cuisine, and some of their cooks are excellent. Or you can eat in the very clean Woodlands chain of vegetarian restaurants (branches in London and New York). South Indian vegetarian food is fit for the gods (especially for the Foodie one, Ganesh, the pudding-tummied elephant god).

I is for inedible

There is an *Israel Good Food Guide* by Evelyn Rose. It really is one of the shortest books ever published. Mrs Rose's advice boils down to a recommendation to eat in Arab and Middle Eastern restaurants, unless you enjoy Jewish heartburn.

I is for I

Culinarily, Italy is still a collection of city states, all Medici-proud, competitive and ready to poison (you against) rivals. *Don't* tell a Tuscan you had a good meal in Taormina – they know the only cooking worth the name in Sicily is their sardine sauce for pasta. Italians boast all the time about their latest great meal – 'Nobody knows the truffles I've seen.' Intelligent Italians visit France but all agree the food is disgusting. They believe the French got their cooking from them, and got it wrong. They believe the Chinese sent pasta via Marco Polo to be perfected.

Delicious things do come from their forests and fields – wild salads, wild asparagus, little birds, big wild hogs and an endless series of wild mushrooms. Shrewd Foodies visit the market to see what is in season, then ask for it in restaurants. If the restaurant cannot provide it, you win the respect of the waiter.

The most sophisticated gastronomic regions are Piedmont, Emilia-Romagna and Lombardy. South of Rome the food is pretty crude and sometimes poisonous.

F·O·O·D·I·E·B·O·R·E·S

THE OFFAL BORE

Knows that in London, Bellamy's in Earl's Court Road have the best brains, Curnick's have the best sweetbreads, Randall & Aubin's tripe is unbeatable. In New York, he haunts Les 3 Petits Cochons. The last time he was in Lyon he had tripe six different ways. He will devote an entire evening to explaining the difference between gras double and tripes, will draw diagrams on napkins showing the stomachs of ruminants. Caen, Lyon (for tablier de sapeur) and Provence (for pieds et pacquets) are names that make his piggy eyes light up. He refuses to look at the cathedral in Sienna because he has heard that there is a restaurant which does tripe with basil and fennel and he has to find it. He thinks Spain is wonderful. He has a strong second suit as a sausage bore – Camisa and Le Cochon Rose are the places he haunts, and, of course Randall & Aubin for andouillettes and boudins. Once upon a time in Ceuta he missed a ferry to Algeciras because he just had to have another lot of deep-fried brains. He is actually not very keen on liver, though devours platesful of kidneys – his hero is Leopold Bloom. Unfashionably he likes pigs' kidneys. The prize he pursues, so far unsuccessfully, is animelles – fry – testicles – balls.

He despises English sausages and the fondness of Graham Greene and Anthony Burgess for those bread-filled tubes. His favourite restaurant in England is almost too refined for him – the Manoir aux Quat' Saisons, where Raymond Blanc is trying to get the British to eat 'the less noble offal'. In Blanc's médaillon de veau et ses béatilles, the veal fillets are served with sweetbreads, brains and amourette – spinal column.

The offal bore is lonely; he finds few people with whom he can share his passion. His wife cannot bear the smell of tripe and complains that the sight of a bloody animal's brain in the refrigerator is off-putting first thing in the morning.

Venetian food is a disappointment mag-giore. Elsewhere, especially in the country and in rich cities like Milan and Turin, the standard is more reliable and pleasurable than in any other European country except France.

It is very unchic to order pasta as a main course in Italy; and any pasta dish with smoked salmon is for tourists only.

M is for macho

You can eat perfectly well in Mexico – if you dare – and Tex-Mex cooking is a current fad in America, even with Foodies. As for the rest of Central America, Foodies report finding delicious enchiladas in unusual places, but on the whole you prefer to spend your Yankee dollars drinking non-dysentery-making rum and Coca Cola (*without* ice).

N is for No, No, No

In today's Nepal there is no food at all. (Foodies shun Tibet too, except yak-milk addicts.) Russian Boris, who formerly owned the Yak and Yeti, got generations of Foodie tourists over their Everest of deprivation, but Katmandu is now better left to the nine-year-old living goddess or the blond boy lama found as a baby in Boston. A stomach has to be caught early to be trained to be able to deal with real gastronomic misery.

R is for room self-service

In Moscow and Leningrad in winter there is almost no food in the shops except pickled cucumbers and salt cabbage, both invariably delicious, if not nutritious. 'Meat' is sold generically, without naming the kind of animal or which part. It is scarce, except in the great tourist hotels, where tons of it are wasted. Fresh fruit or vegetables from Georgia appear occa-sionally, causing long queues in shops and free markets. Visitors to Russia are often offered caviar by English-speaking

TEN RECIPES THAT SHOOK THE WORLD

1 CHILLI CON CARNE TEX-MEX REX OR SEX AID?

Chilli con carne is a Foodie indulgence, as it's the Philistine-Foodie's favourite: gross, meaty and full of beans. When properly made it is redolent of cumin, and smells of armpits. The reason all American rednecks are addicted to it, steal each other's recipes, and have chilli festivals involving entire towns, is that they subconsciously *think* it's aphrodisiac. The reason for this, in turn, is pheromones. A good chilli con carne emits sex signals.

Most recipes for it are ridiculous. James Beard even gives one (with suitable apologies for its authenticity) involving *green olives*. Yuck! Of course chilli is a bastard dish, but there's no need to rub it in. In her recipes from the *Regional Cooks of Mexico*, Diana Kennedy gives two that obviously have something to do with its parentage. One is 'carne con chilli verde' and the other 'chamberete de res en chille morita'. Both use *un*ground beef, garlic, onion, tomatoes and chillies, but only one of them has the essential cumin.

Most American cooks will use a prepared spice and herb mixture. The best is Spice Islands, but Old El Paso has its partisans. It is, though, much better, much cheaper and *much more Foodie*, to do it from scratch. Quantities don't matter – you have to taste constantly anyway. What matters is that at least some of the meat (all beef, or ⅔ beef, ⅓ pork) should not be ground, but should be cut in bite sized cubes. It must therefore come from a tender cut or the chilli must simmer longtemps.

In a very heavy saucepan you brown at least 125 g (¼ lb) meat per person in a tasteless vegetable oil, then add one small minced onion and a minced clove of garlic per person, plus any other members of the onion family you have to hand, treated the same way. Then add half each diced small green and red peppers per person, and half mild green chilli per person, also minced, and without seeds. When these are transparent, add the freshly ground seasonings to the casserole – *before* adding any liquid: large quantities of ground coriander seeds, cumin seeds and dried oregano, plus cayenne pepper if you think you need it, and mild or hot paprika. This last will thicken the eventual sauce and give it a good colour, so use the best Hungarian. Now add one coarsely chopped small tomato per person, skin, pips and all. (At this point real Foodies resort to the freezer, and simply pop in whole frozen tomatoes.) When these have pulped down, and provided some liquid, add the beans. You will have previously cooked 60 g (2 oz) red kidney or pinto beans per person, with bacon rinds, a few sprigs of thyme and a bay leaf or two, and a clove of garlic, but NO SALT until the cooking is finished.

After you have added the beans and some of their cooking liquid, taste for salt and seasoning. There is still time to adjust the spices, though they must simmer until they no longer taste raw. It is perfectly OK to add more oregano any time before serving the dish, and a handful of chopped fresh coriander added just before bringing it to the table creates excitement.

Now serve it – in bowls – and watch the bewildered Brits and Frogs, who can't decide whether to eat it with a fork or a spoon. (Tex-Mex Rex uses a spoon.)

hustlers. Only fools buy from these be-jeaned, gum-chewing salesmen, who are either in the black market or the KGB. You can buy good-quality caviar in blue tins marked ИКРА from the berioshkas – hard-currency shops – or from the trolley that is regularly wheeled through the hotel lobby.

Usually, you book and pay for your meal in advance through Intourist. It can be difficult to get a table in a restaurant (they are occupied by swanking, privileged members of the Nomenklatura) and sometimes not worth the effort, especially in winter. If you have a Russian-speaker in your party, you can bribe everyone in the restaurant chain of command, starting with the doorman and ending with the maître d'hôtel, to give you a table. How-ever, the smoked sturgeon sandwiches sold at the bar at nearly every hotel are probably better than the food at any but the Georgian or Azerbaijani restaurants of Moscow or Leningrad. Many Foodies sup in their hotel rooms on open sandwiches and pepper vodka.

S is for short stay

Foodies beef about Argentine food, and Brazilian feojada fills the stomach without thrilling the senses. There are authenti-cated cases of cannibalism in the Andes. The bitchy Foodie shouts: 'South America, take it away!'

S is for snacks

In Spain, the fish can be splendid, though very expensive. Foodies don't go to the Costa Fortune for their holidays, but hang around Seville, Cordoba, Madrid and Barcelona. Catalonia is F. In all these it is possible to eat well by eating only tapas, which are officially snacks to be nibbled with drinks, but which can be wonderfully various: raw ham, cuttlefish in its own ink, sausages, bits of Manchego cheese, tiny deep-fried mullet, grilled sardines.

S is for stay in your hotel

It is tempting to say that tourism has ruined the cuisine of Sri Lanka – but probably false. Even the Chinese restaurants, normally oases in gastro-nomic deserts, are awful. 'What though the spicy breezes/Blow soft o'er Ceylon's isle;/Though every prospect pleases' – the food is exceeding vile. There is the odd edible South Indian speciality, such as idlis – steamed rice pancakes – and the similar Dutch-influenced hoppers, but it is far better to eat in your hotel and stick to 'rice and curry', the generic expression for non-European food. Sunday tiffin at the Mount Lavinia Hotel near Colombo is a traditional treat, with a magnificent seafood buffet. And the food in private houses can be very good. But no Foodie, under any circumstances, should eat a 'European' meal anywhere in Sri Lanka, unless you are very fond of very old goat, which is what is meant by the word 'mut-ton' on the menu.

T is for Toll Gate

Foodies adore Thai food – in Britain and America. Thai food in Thailand is another matter. It *looks* wonderful; but is often so hot with chillis that you burn your mouth. The burningest is street food, abundant all over South-East Asia, but the food is ferocious in most non-tourist restaurants, and sometimes in private houses. The big hotels of Bangkok are safe – but Foodies seek out Mom Taw.

ML Taw Kritikara (a member of the royal family – 'ML' is the abbreviation of her title) runs the Toll Gate restaurant and advised the Thai restaurant at the new Peninsula Hotel in Bangkok. If you are lucky you will get her onion and basil-seed soup, crab cake, stuffed chicken wings, her 'basket of fruit and vegetable', or her beef and tongue curry. Nam prik is the Thai national dish, but be prepared – even Mom Taw's version can be tongue-twistingly chilly-willy-shrivelling.

You do not believe in travelling hopefully

The Italian writer Italo Calvino understands you. He wrote in his story 'The Jaguar Sun', 'the true journey ... implies a complete change of nutrition, a digesting of the visited country – its fauna and flora and its culture (not only the different culinary practices and condiments but the different implements used to grind the flour or stir the pot) – making it pass between the lips and down the oesophagus. This is the only kind of travel that has a meaning nowadays, when everything visible you can see on television without rising from your easy chair. (And you mustn't rebut that the same result can be achieved by visiting the exotic restaurants of our big cities; they so counterfeit the reality of the cuisine they claim to follow that, as far as our deriving real knowledge is concerned, they are the equivalent not of an actual locality but of a scene reconstructed and shot in a studio.)'

Exactamente! This is why Foodies, above all people, love travel.

Your Foodie parents went on the *Normandie*, or the *Twentieth Century* express between California and New York. The silver and crystal were wobbly but the food was fine. *You* are offered the second-hand steak obviously cooked in a kitchen owned jointly by all the airlines. You refuse. You Take a Picnic. The really finicky Foodie, on the way to Heathrow or Kennedy or Charles de Gaulle, fills a basket at the Rosslyn Deli or Zabar's or Fauchon. Ditto if you are driving there in your Foodiemobile. Since you grew up, you have never entered a British motorway restaurant or a Howard Johnson's or a French autoroute restaurant except Quatre Pentes – you might roule up there to refuel.

You are heading for the nearest Foodie touring address. One of the following will certainly be on your list.

The Foodie touring address book

Australia

ADELAIDE
● NEDDY'S (Franco-Australian cuisine), 170 Hutt Street. (08) 223 2618.
BRISBANE
● MILANO, 78 Queen Street. (07) 229 3917/ 221 5972.
MELBOURNE
● FLEURIE, 40 Ross Street, Toorak. (03) 241 5792.
● CLICHY, 9 Peel Street, Collingwood. (03) 417 6404.
● TWO FACES, 149 Toorak Road, South Yarra. (03) 261 547.
PERTH
● ORD STREET CAFE, West Perth. (09) 321 602.
SYDNEY
● BEROWRA WATERS INN, Berowra Waters. (02) 456 027. (The best restaurant Down Under.)
● BAGATELLE, 117 Riley Street, Palm Beach. (02) 357 5675.
● BARRENJOEY HOUSE, 1108 Barrenjoey Road, Palm Beach. (02) 919 4001.
● YOU AND ME, 143 King Street. (02) 232 6670.

Austria

Foodies Take A Picnic – TAP

Belgium

BRUSSELS
● COMME CHEZ SOI (*Pierre Wynants*), 23 place Rouppe. (02) 512 2921. Closed Sun, Mon, all July, Christmas–1 Jan. Gault-Millau's 'Chef of the Year' for 1984, the only one outside France except Girardet.
● LA CRAVACHE D'OR (*Abel Bernard*), 10 place Albert-Leemans, 1050 Ixelles. (02) 538 3746. Closed Aug.
● LA VILLA LORRAINE (*Marcel Kreusch*), 75 avenue du Vivier-d'Oie, 1180 Uccle. (02) 374 3163. Closed Sun, 3 weeks in July.

Canada

MONTREAL
● LES HALLES (*Jean-Pierre Monnet*), 1450 Crescent Street. (514) 844 2328. Closed Sun and all July.
● LA MARÉE (*Jacques Ducasse*), 404 Place Jacques Cartier. (514) 861 8126. Closed Sat and Sun lunch, Christmas, New Year.
● LA SILA (*Antonio*), 2040 Saint-Denis Street. (514) 844 5083. Dinner only. Closed Sun, all July.
● AU TOURNANT DE LA RIVIÈRE (*Jacques Robert*), 5070 Salaberry, Carignan, Chambly. (514) 658 7372. Closed Mon, Tues.

TORONTO
● FENTON'S (*Werner Bassen*), 2 Gloucester Street. (416) 961 8485. Closed Christmas and New Year's Day.
VANCOUVER
● UMBERTO'S (*Douglas Leask*), 1380 Hornby Street. (604) 687 6316. Closed Sun, Mon, public holidays.

Eire

SHANAGARRY, nr Midleton, Co Cork
● BALLYMALOE HOUSE (*Myrtle Allen*). (021) 652531. Closed 3 days Christmas.

England

LONDON
● LA TANTE CLAIRE (*Pierre Koffmann*), 68 Royal Hospital Road, SW3. (01) 352 6045. Closed Sat, Sun, 10 days Easter, 3 weeks Aug/Sept, Christmas, New Year, Bank Holidays.
● MIJANOU (*Sonia Blech*), 143 Ebury Street, SW1. (01) 730 4099. Closed Sat, Sun, 1 week Easter, 3 weeks Aug, 24–31 Dec, Bank Holidays.
● CHEZ NICO (*Nico Ladenis*), 129 Queenstown Road, SW8. (01) 720 6960. Closed Sat lunch, Sun, Mon, 4 days Easter, 3 weeks July/Aug, 10 days Christmas.
● INTERLUDE DE TABAILLAU (*Jean-Louis Taillebaud*), 7 Bow Street, WC2. (01) 379 6473. Closed Sat lunch, Sun, 1 week Easter, 3 weeks summer, 1 week Christmas, Bank Holidays.
● HILAIRE (*Simon Hopkinson*), 68 Old Brompton Road, SW7. (01) 584 8993. Closed Sat lunch, Sun, 1 week Christmas, Bank Holidays.
● L'ESCARGOT (*Martin Lam*), 48 Greek Street, W1. (01) 437 2679. Closed Sat lunch, Sun, 25–26 Dec, Bank Holidays.
● BOMBAY BRASSERIE (*Sandeep Chatterjee*), 140 Gloucester Road, SW7. (01) 370 4040. Never closes. The best and most chic of the new-style Indian restaurants. Owned by the Taj Hotel group.
● THE RED FORT (*N. P. Pittal*), 77 Dean Street, W1. (01) 437 2115. Closed Christmas, Boxing Day. North Indian.
● THE GRILL, DORCHESTER HOTEL (*Anton Mosimann*), Park Lane, W1. (01) 629 8888. Closed Christmas night. The best English food.
GREAT MILTON, Oxford
● LE MANOIR AUX QUAT' SAISONS (*Raymond Blanc*). (084 46) 230. Closed 23 Dec–end Jan, and Sun dinner and Mon to non-residents. *The* restaurant outside London. Food: three stars. Ambiance: also starry.
CHAGFORD, Devon
● GIDLEIGH PARK HOTEL (*Kay Henderson*). (06473) 2367.
DARTMOUTH, Devon
● THE CARVED ANGEL (*Joyce Molyneux*), 2 South Embankment. (08043) 2465. Closed Sun dinner,

Mon, 24–26 Dec.
GULWORTHY, nr Tavistock, Devon
● THE HORN OF PLENTY (*Sonia Stevenson*). (0822) 832528. Closed Thurs, Fri lunch, Christmas.
NEW MILTON, Hampshire
● CHEWTON GLEN (*Pierre Cheviallard*). (042 52) 5341. Never closes.
OAKHAM, Leicestershire
● HAMBLETON HALL (*Nicholas Gill*). (0572) 56991. Never closes.
WINDERMERE, Cumbria
● MILLER HOWE HOTEL (*John Tovey*). (09662) 2536. Closed 5 Dec–mid-March. Too much cinema, but somewhere for Foodies to eat in the North.

France

PARIS
● JAMIN (*Joël Robuchon*), 32 rue Longchamp, 16ᵉ. (1) 727 1227. Closed Sat, Sun, all July. Discovered long ago by Gault-Millau and given third Michelin star in 1984.
● GUY SAVOY, 28 rue Duret, 16ᵉ. (1) 500 1767. Closed Sat, Sun, 1–15 Jan, 15–31 July. Large dogs banned.
● AU TROU GASCON (*Alain Dutournier*), 40 rue Taine, 12ᵉ. (1) 344 3426. Closed Sat, Sun, all Sept.
● PIERRE VEDEL, 50 rue des Morillons, 15ᵉ. (1) 828 0437. Closed Sat, Sun, 7 July–5 Aug, Christmas–New Year.
AIX-EN-PROVENCE
● LES CAVES HENRI IV (*Jean-Marc Banzo*), 32 rue Espariat. (42) 278639. Closed Sun, 11 June–2 July, 24 Feb–10 March, Mon lunch in July.
AUCH
● FRANCE (*André Daguin*), place Libération, 32000 Gers. (62) 050044. Closed Sun dinner and Mon out of season, all Jan. Must book Sun.
BORDEAUX
● RESTAURANT CLAVEL (*Francis Garcia*), 44 rue Charles Domercq. (56) 929152. Closed Sun, Mon, 10–31 July, school holidays Feb.
● RESTAURANT RAMET (*Jean Ramet*), 7 place Jean Jaurès. (56) 441251. Closed Sat, Sun, 24 Mar–8 Apr, 13–25 Aug.
DIGOIN
● LA GARE (*Jean-Pierre Billoux*), 79 avenue Générale-de-Gaulle, 71160. (85) 530304. Closed Jan, 20–28 June, Wed lunch, July–12 Sept.
JOIGNY
● A LA CÔTE ST-JACQUES (*Michel Lorain*), 14 faubourg de Paris, 89300. (86) 620970. Closed 1 Jan–mid-Feb.
LYON
● LA TOUR ROSE (*Philippe Chavent*), 16 rue du Boeuf, 5ᵉ. (7) 837 2590. Closed Sun.
● LÉON DE LYON (*Jean-Paul Lacombe*), 1 rue Pléney, 1ᵉʳ. (7) 828 1133. Closed 23 Dec–8 Jan, Sun, Mon lunch, public holidays.

REIMS
- LES CRAYÈRES (*Gérard Boyer*), 64 boulevard Vasnier. (26) 828080. Closed Mon, Tues lunch, 24 Dec–15 Jan.

SAULIEU
- LA CÔTE D'OR (*Bernard Loiseau*), 2 rue Argentine, 21210. (80) 640766. Closed 20 Nov–20 Dec, Tues 1 Nov–30 Apr. Alexandre Dumaine's restaurant now revived.

STRASBOURG
- RESTAURANT BUEREHIESEL (*Antoine Westermann*), 4 parc de l'Orangerie, 67000. (88) 616224. Closed Tues nights, Wed, 8–23 Aug, 24 Dec–4 Jan, school holidays in Feb.

VALENCE
- PIC (*Jacques Pic*), 285 avenue Victor-Hugo, 26000. (75) 441532. Closed Sun night, Wed, 1–25 Aug, school holidays in Feb.

VERSAILLES
- LES TROIS MARCHES (*Gérard Vié*), 3 rue Colbert, 78000. (3) 950 1321. Closed Sun, Mon.

Germany

BERLIN
- RESTAURANT MAÎTRE (*Henry Lévy*), Meinekstrasse 10, 1000 W Berlin 15. (030) 883 8485. Closed Sun, Mon, Tues lunch, mid-July–mid-Aug. Run by a Frenchman using imported French foodstuffs.

COLOGNE
- GOLDENER PFLUG (*Ludwig Robertz*), Olpener Strasse 421, 5000 Köln (at Cologne 91-Merheim by Deutzer Brücke). (0221) 895509. Closed Sat, Sun, Bank Holidays, 3 weeks July/Aug.

FRANKFURT
- STEIGENBERGER AIRPORTHOTEL, Flughafenstrasse 300, 6000 Frankfurt 75. Pergola Restaurant (069) 69851. But ring (069) 692503 to book at
- WALDRESTAURANT UNTERSCHWEINSTIEGE, a rustic country-house restaurant, astonishingly located in the hotel grounds.
- DIE ENTE VOM LEHEL (*Hans-Peter Wodarz*), Kaiser-Friedrich-Platz 3, 6200 Wiesbaden. (06121) 301516. Closed Sun, Mon, public holidays, end June.

MUNICH
- See the 18 Best Restaurants, p 59.

Greece

TAP

Holland

TAP

Hong Kong

- RIVERSIDE RESTAURANT (Cantonese), Food Street, Causeway Bay. 5-779733.
- KING HEUNG PEKING RESTAURANT, Paterson Street, next to Food Street, Causeway Bay. 5-771035.
- UNITED RESTAURANT (dim sum, reservations accepted), 5th/6th floors, United Centre, 95 Queensway, HK. 5-295010.
- SICHUAN GARDEN, 3rd floor, Gloucester Tower, Central, HK. 5-214433.

KOWLOON
- SUN TUNG LOK SHARK'S FIN RESTAURANT, Phase 3, Harbour City, 25–27 Canton Road, ground floor, Kowloon. 3-7220288. *The* place for expensive and unusual southern Chinese food.
- CITY CHIUCHOW RESTAURANT, 1st floor, East Ocean Centre, 98 Granville Road, Tsim Sha Tsui East, Kowloon. 3-7245383.

NEW TERRITORIES
- FUNG LUM RESTAURANT, 45–47 Tsuen Nam Road, Taiwai, Shatin, NT, HK. 0-621175. For pigeon-fanciers.
- OI MAN RESTAURANT, 4 Ching Street, Lau Fau Shan, NT, HK. 0-721504. In the middle of a crowded market. Live fish and shellfish for the hardy Foodie.

Italy

FLORENCE
- ENOTECA PINCHIORRI (*Annie Feolde*), via Ghibellina 87, Firenze 50122. (055) 242777. Closed Sun, Mon lunch, Aug, 25–27 Dec.

MILAN
- ANTICA OSTERIA DEL PONTE (*Ezio Santin*), cassinetta di Lugagnano, near Abbiategrasso, Milano 20081. (02) 942 0034. Closed Sun, Mon, 1–15 Jan, Aug.
- SCALETTA (*Ernesto Maestri*), piazzale stazione Porta Genove, Milano 20144. (02) 835 0290. Closed Sun, Mon, 20–30 Apr, Aug, 24 Dec–7 Jan. For Design Foodies – done by Gian Franco Frattini.
- ALFREDO GRAN SAN BERNARDO (*Alfredo Valli*), via Borgese 14 Milano 20154. (02) 389000. Closed Sun, all Aug, 21 Dec–19 Jan.
- RISTORANTE DON LISANDER CUCINA NUOVA (*Daniel Drouadaine*), via Manzoni 12a. (02) 790130. Closed Sun, Mon, 19 Dec–9 Jan.
- GUALTIERO MARCHESI, via Bonvesin de la Riva 9, 20129 Milano. (02) 741246. Closed Sun, Mon lunch, all Aug.

TURIN
- RISTORANTE VILLA SASSI (*Antonio Ibba*), strada al Traforo del Pino 47, Torino 10132. (011) 890556. Closed Sun, all Aug.
- RISTORANTE MONTECARLO (*Domenico Moccia*), via San Francesco da Paola 37, Torino. (011) 541234. Closed Sat, Sun, all Aug.

VENICE
- HARRY'S BAR (*Alfredo Del Peschio*), San Marco 1323, calle Vallaresso, Venezia 30124. (041) 36797. Closed Mon, 3 Jan–13 Feb.
- CORTE SCONTA, calle del Pestrin 3886, Venezia

KNOCK KNOCK.
Who's there?
CLEM.
Clem who?
CLEM FLAICHE FLOM THE HONG KONG HILTON.

30122. (041) 27024. Closed Mon, Tues, 8 Jan–6 Feb, 15 June–15 July. Seafood only.

New Zealand

AUCKLAND
- HARLEY'S, Anzac Avenue. Unlicensed.
- FRENCH CAFÉ (*David Hartley*), Symonds Court, Symonds Street (09) 771911. Unlicensed. Book a week ahead. Tues–Sat dinner, weekdays lunch.
- ORLEANS, 106 Symonds Street. (09) 773155. Unlicensed. Tues–Sat dinner.
- WHEELERS RESTAURANT, 43 Ponsonby Road (Ponsonby Road is the restaurant capital of NZ). (09) 763185. Tues–Sat dinner.

WELLINGTON
- LA NORMANDIE, 116 Cuba Street. (04) 845000.
- THE BOMBAY BICYCLE BAR AND BISTRO, at Upper Hutt, 15 miles from Wellington.

Portugal

TAP on TAP Air Portugal

Scotland

GULLANE, Lothian
- LA POTINIÈRE (*Hilary Brown*). (0620) 843214. Closed Wed, lunch Sat – only open for dinner Sat at 8. 1–2 Jan, 25–26 Dec, 1 week June, Oct. But where else is a Foodie to eat in Scotland?

Spain

MADRID
- LOS SIETE SARDINES (*Alicia Rios Ivars*), San Vicente Ferrer 86 (1) 232 2519. Closed Sun. Otherwise TAP or tapas

Switzerland

BASLE
- BRUDERHOLZ 'STUCKI' (*Hans Stucki*), Bruderholzallee 42, Basle 4059. (061) 358222. Closed Sun, Mon, 16 July–6 Aug. Gault-Millau say this is the 'best table of Switzerland after Girardet'.
GENEVA (Also see the 18 Best Restaurants, p 59)
- LE DUC (*the brothers Michelli*), 7 quai du Mont-Blanc. (22) 317330. Closed Sun, Mon.
- LE VIEUX MOULIN (*Gérard Bouilloux*), 89 route d'Annecy at Troinex 1254, 5 km S of Geneva on the route de St-Julien. (22) 422956. Closed Sun dinner, Mon, 24 March–9 April, 1–17 Sept.
ZURICH
- CHEZ MAX (*Max Kehl*), Seestrasse 53, at Zollikon 8702, 5 km S of Zurich. (1) 391 8877. Closed Sun, Monday lunch, 8–29 July.

Thailand

BANGKOK
- TOLL GATE RESTAURANT (*ML Taw Kritikara*), 245/2 Soi 31, Sukhumvit Road. 391 3947.

USA

NEW YORK
- AN AMERICAN PLACE (*Larry Forgione*), 969 Lexington Avenue (between 70th and 71st). (212) 517 7660. Closed Sun, public holidays. American chauvinist cuisine.
- FOUR SEASONS (*Seppi Renggli*), 99 E 52nd Street. (212) 754 9494. Closed Sat lunch, Sun.
- HUBERT'S (*Leonard Allison*), 102 E 22nd Street. (212) 673 3711. Closed Sat lunch, Sun.
- LA TULIPE (*Sally Darr*), 104 W 13th Street (212) 691 8860. Dinner only, closed Mon.
- THE QUILTED GIRAFFE (*Barry Wine*), 955 Second Avenue, between 50th and 51st. (212) 753 5355. Dinner only., Mon–Fri.
- THE RIVER CAFÉ (*Charles Palmer*), 1 Water Street, Brooklyn (Cadman Plaza West). (212) 522 5200. Closes Christmas Day.
CINCINNATI, Ohio
- MAISONETTE (*George Haidon*), 114 E Sixth Street. (513) 721 2260. Closed Sun, lunch Sat, public holidays, first 2 weeks July.
WHEELING (nr Chicago), Illinois
- LE FRANÇAIS, 269 S Milwaukee Avenue. (312) 541 7470. Closed Mon, major holidays.
NEW ORLEANS, Louisiana
- PAUL'S LOUISIANA KITCHEN (*Paul Prudhomme*), 416 Chartres Street. (504) 524 7394. Closed Sat, Sun, public holidays.
BERKELEY, California
- CHEZ PANISSE (*Alice Waters*), 1517 Shalluck Avenue. (415) 548 5525. Closed Sun, Mon, public holidays.
- FOURTH STREET GRILL (*Mark Miller*), 1820 Fourth Street. (415) 849 0526. Closed public holidays.
- SANTA FE BAR AND GRILL (*Jeremiah Tower*), 1310 University. (415) 548 5525. Closed 4 July, Labour Day, Thanksgiving, Christmas Eve and Day. Jeremiah Tower also has a new (July 1984) restaurant, STARS, 150 Redwood Street, San Francisco. (415) 861 7827.
SANTA MONICA, California
- MICHAEL'S (*Brian Netter*), 1147 Third Street. (213) 451 0843. Owned by Michael McCarty. Closed Sat and Sun lunch, Mon, public holidays. One of the most expensive restaurants in the world. Cheaper to fly to France for lunch.

Wales

LLANDEWI SKIRRID, nr Abergavenny, Gwent
- THE WALNUT TREE INN (*Franco Taruschio*). (0873) 2797. Closed Sun, 25–26 Dec.

The big O again and again

Foodies love shopping. It is an emotional as well as an artistic experience to face vegetable shelves or a cheese counter. You adore bread shops (you're an abject fan of Poilâne) and behave like a child in delicatessens, wanting to try all the joints of smoked meat and colours of peppercorn. You pursue delicious food with *no conscience* – you do not worry about political-climate-of-country-of-origin, or the big supermarkets driving the little man out. You are not interested in big or little men, merely big mushrooms and little broad beans. There's a lot of Mae West in most Foodies.

The exception is fish shops, which have been given a shot in the prawn by the Foodie love of fish. Foodies are friends of the ocean, if for personal reasons.

Foodies like supermarkets because after all, supermarkets are cannily catering for the Foodie market. They employ Foodies as advisers and to write those food-chain cookbooks. Supermarkets *adore* Foodie shoppers. They're such suckers. The Foodie rolls up in the Foodiemobile, always large, usually a station wagon – to carry the charcoal briquettes and all that food. The shop is designed with high light so you will buy. Foodie men in particular break down completely under this 'never again' torture, and spend at least £20 too much trying to postpone the next visit. But at by-Foodies-for-Foodies shops like Dean & DeLuca in Manhattan and Hobbs in London, they insist on shopping every day. Buying two days' supply would be unthinkable.

A city can't be a modern city without at least one space the size of the town hall or cathedral devoted to food. Boston led the way with Faneuil Hall, the old market converted into a compound of food boutiques. The Sainsbury's which opened in 1983 in the former Cromwell Road air terminal in London has been thronged ever since with a far smarter clientele than Harrods – a *concentrate* of Foodies. The same sort of temple to food was opened in New York in 1983, in the old Fulton Street fish market.

Foodies also seek out unreconstructed local markets. You ogle the fish slabs at a market like St Raphael, eyeball to eyeball with the loups de mer, and come away with soaking shoes: the slabs have to drain somewhere.

Shopping together can ruin a Foodie friendship, let alone a romance. You enter your first shop together nervously, conscious it is a test. You may leave it estranged by estragon, or by any number of other little things. Your prospect might have asked for kiwi fruit (a Foodie cliché), or chutney (Foodies don't *have* cold meat), or bought a jar of Instant. Instant-drinkers are rough trade, the roughest.

Foodie shopping in Paris

Wondering if a French person is a Foodie is like wondering if an alcoholic ever takes a drink. Because foodisme of the Anglo-Saxon lemming variety is nouveau in France, you rarely find Parisians among the pilgrims to Foodie meccas like Fauchon. Parisians prefer to shop locally: all have their own neighbourhood sources for the best fruit and greenstuffs, the best beef, the best baguette. Sometimes, particularly when it comes to a mythical substance like bread (Parisians are foremost among subscribers to the Foodie legend that French bread is the world's best), they should make more effort.

To begin, then, with the basics:

PAIN GLOSS
Parisians still line up outside *Poilâne* (8 rue du Cherche Midi, 6e) for sour pain de campagne and apple tarts. But a Foodie backlash has set in now that pain Poilâne is delivered to shops all over town: Foodies

The symbolic baguette (the word also means chopsticks and wand in French). This is not Poilâne, but any good Paris boulanger has the dozen or so breads shown here

claim it's boring, it isn't what it used to be, and trek to out-of-the way boulangers like *Ganachaud* (150 rue de Ménilmontant, 20e), where traditional breads are shovelled in and out of wood-fired ovens.

FROMAGE À TROIS

Every Foodie who was anybody used to go to *Barthélémy* (51 rue de Grenelle, 7e); many still do. But there are now so many celebrities among this shop's custom that lesser known Foodies are often made to feel like intruders. You are more cordially served, with absolutely no loss of Foodie face, at *La Ferme Saint-Hubert* (21 rue Vignon, 8e) or *Cantin* (père, 2 rue de Lourmel, 15e; fille, 12 rue du Champ de Mars, 7e).

ALCOOL

Not many Paris Foodies buy wine from a merchant: most spend weekends stocking up chez their favourite growers. But resident Anglo-Saxon Foodies tend to seek security with a bargain vin de terroir from Steven Spurrier's *Caves de la Madeleine* (Cité Berryer, 8e) or Fiona Beeston's *Lucien Legrand* (1 rue de la Banque, 2e). The English connection enhances the snob value for the native Parisians who shop at both. The fruit liqueurs for the Foodie apéritif come from *Petit Bacchus*, 13 rue du Cherche Midi: crème de cassis, framboise, myrtille, cherry de Bourgogne.

MEALS ON HUILES

At the tourist end of the Ile St Louis, but patronised by Parisians: *A l'Olivier* (77 rue Saint-Louis-en-l'Ile, 4e).

CAVIAR EMPTOR

Petrossian (18 boulevard Latour Maubourg, 73), of course; the holiday queues are composed of Parisians. They flock there for smoked salmon, too.

A FOIE, FOIE BETTER THING

If a Paris Foodie can't get foie gras from a Périgord grandmother, he buys it from a restaurant – like *Gérard Besson* (5 rue Coq

A Parisian Foodie indulges her favourite pastime, lèche-vitrine (literally, licking glass) – window-shopping. For charcuterie, see Jaws IV, p 88

Show me your packets and I will tell you where you are

Foodies are interested in food shops, though all too few (the Façade Foodies) are able to lift their thoughts above the contents to realise that conservation has neglected shops while saving houses and factories. Mahogany counters, marble slabs, bacon slicers and French lettering were ripped out in the Sixties and replaced by plastic shop fittings, often to be replaced in the Seventies and Eighties by mahogany counters, marble slabs, bacon slicers and French lettering – Foodie *theme shops*.

Foodies like to display tokens of their shopping in their kitchen. It's your equivalent of designer labels.

Labels that impress everyone

All Foodies like plain hand-written labels and packets tied with string or ribbon.
- ИКРА blue tins (caviar from Moscow)
- Clément Fougier's Crème de Marrons de l'Ardèche, in brown, green and gold art nouveau tins. A favourite for 80 years – such reassurance
- Bornibus moutarde de Dijon
- Strings of odd peppers (shows you've been to Hungary)
- Cèpes. Three grades of Foodie smartness:
1 cèpes threaded on strings (you dried your own)
2 paper-thin slices in a big flat packet called porcini (from Italy)
3 a string with big cèpes at the bottom, tapering up (from Georgia via Moscow market)
- Trenel Fils liqueurs, to mix with champagne for the Foodie apéritifs: Crème de Cassis, Crème de Framboise or Crème de Myrtille (from Petit Bacchus, rue du Cherche Midi, Paris)
- Poilâne flat round pain de campagne. (Poilâne, also rue du Cherche Midi. The 5 kilos of it will have been your 5 kilos overweight baggage)
- Le Nôtre polystyrene insulation for

sorbets (from Le Nôtre, Paris. This is the ultimate status symbol in London and New York – how did you get the sorbet home? It's against the laws of nature)

Labels that impress London

- Anything from Fauchon
- La Baleine sea salt with the whale (comes to the table)
- Own-label supermarket wine from Sainsbury's or Tesco (inverted chic)
- Chocolat Meñier
- Loose wild rice from America
- French or Italian coffee, 100 per cent dark roasted arabica
- Teuscher's champagne truffle chocolates – highly perishable (from Zurich or New York)
- Zabar's labels (New York)
- Dean & DeLuca labels (New York)
- Badoit mineral water
- Beurre d'Isigny in its wooden coffin (to table)

Labels that impress New York

- Anything from Fauchon
- Jackson's tea
- Twining's tea
- Badoit mineral water
- Fortnum & Mason labels
- Harrods labels
- Italian labels

Labels that impress Paris

- British biscuits in tins, eg McVitie's, Rowntree Creamola
- A l'Olivier olive oil (from the Ile St Louis. Not all that superior to Félix Potin's in the Handi-Grip shape, except for the bottle and label)
- Côte d'Or chocolates
- American riz sauvage
- Hédiard labels (the French think Fauchon is for tourists)
- Chinese things (unlike almost all other cities and countries, the only Chinese goods obtainable in France and Paris are *Indo*-Chinese). Tianjin cabbage. Sichuan preserved vegetable
- Indian lemon and lime pickle
- Fresh ginger root
- Teuscher's chocolates (as London)
- Sherry (so expensive in France, it shows you've been through the duty-free)
- St Michael labels (the Countess de la Rochefoucauld gives pounds of Marks & Spencer chocolates in their plastic boxes every Christmas)
- Twining's tea
- Jackson's tea
- Tiptree's jam
- Crabtree & Evelyn labels (pastiche packaging)
- Marmite jars
- Old El Paso Chile

Héron, 1er) or *Lamazère* (23 rue de Ponthieu, 8e).

TRUFFLES NEVER COME SINGLY
This arch-Foodie staple, to be eaten fresh or not at all, is bought from the *Maison de la Truffe* (19 place de la Madeleine, 8e), where prices adhere to the market average. When he can, though, the arch-Foodie secures his black gold from a Périgord market.

VIANDE THE PALE
So French: your roast comes from a shop classified as an historical monument. But the cuts available at *Bell Viandier* (25 rue du Vieux Colombier, 6e) are a match for the décor. *Lamartine* (172 avenue Victor Hugo, 16e) also maintains a satisfactory décor/quality ratio, with the added Foodie fillip of a London branch at 229 Ebury Street. More Formica, inox, and plate glass than charm at *Boucheries Nivernaises* (99 rue du Faubourg St Honoré, 8e), but the quality of the meat attracts Foodies – restaurateurs and home cooks – from all over Paris. In general, Paris Foodies cultivate (sometimes with tips) a local butcher.

PARFAIT DE FRUITS (& VEGETABLES)
The frilly-cupped grape cluster and tissue-wrapped peach, available in plenty (see *Leave me in épiceries*, p 89), are spurned by true Paris Foodies, who patronise local markets exclusively. These might include the *rue Mouffetard* or the *rue de Buci* – if you live nearby. Otherwise, tourist (or package) Foodies impede the shopping rite and shove prices up. Tourist-free local colour with appeal to the Foodie branché is better sought in the *rue Daguerre*, the *rue du Faubourg St Denis*, or the *rue Montorgueil*. Nor should beau-quartier markets, like *Passy*, be overlooked: the ménagère bourgeoise (a practising but non-ideological Foodie) keeps shrewd watch on the quality-price ratio.

JAWS IV
Cold cuts with cachet are found in all the big Foodie emporia, but more reliable are specialists like *Provost* (128 avenue Général Leclerc, 14e), where everything is fait maison. *Coesnon* (30 rue Dauphine, 6e) purveys 18 varieties of house boudin. Both establishments are Paris Foodie meccas.

POISSON IVY LEAGUE
Parisians tend to rely on neighbourhood fishmongers, though for oysters and shellfish some (especially outside shop hours) are always ready to jump into the car for a dash to the seafood banc outside a favourite restaurant: typically, one of the two *Charlots* (81 and 128bis boulevard de Clichy, 9e and 18e) or *Le Divellec* (107 rue de l'Université, 7e). Otherwise, *Poissonnerie Jeannette* (55 avenue d'Italie, 13e) is worth a déplacement: variety vast, prices right. But as in other domains, any Paris Foodie worth his sel has his own highly reliable and relatively obscure source.

POULET VOUS? (& GAME)
Au Poulet de Bresse (30 rue des Belles Feuilles, 16e) provides chicken comme autrefois and game in season to the 16th and several other arrondissements. Even French consumer magazines, frequently as preoccupied by bacteria-count as by flavour, admit that a poulet de Bresse (available from most butchers) is actually better. The *Que Choisir?* and *50 Million de Consommateurs* approach capitulates, in fact, one French Foodie ethnic: they put tested quality before bonnes addresses.

CAFÉ OLÉ (& TEA)
Nearly every quartier has a decent brûlerie, but a trip across town to *Verlet* (256 rue Saint Honoré, 1er) is worth a Foodie's while: you can sit down to taste one of the cafés du jour before choosing from Verlet's sophisticated range. None of Verlet's teas has been trafiqué (vanilla, geranium, cinnamon), but Paris pseudie Foodies are avid drinkers of these atrocities, available in too many pseud-Foodie shops.

Iam forte

Confitures offer another fertile ground for pseud-Foodie trafiquants, and even houses with artisanale traditions and over-whelming Foodie charm (premises and acceuil) like *Tanrade* (18 rue Vignon, 9e), falter badly. Flawless, luxurious, pricey: *Fouquet* (22 rue François ler, 8e; 36 rue Lafitte, 9e).

Take the honey and run

It shouldn't be, but is, another prime pseud-Foodie comestible. *La Maison du Miel* (24 rue Vignon, 9e) lets you taste and is a guarantee of authenticity at prices no higher than those in many grandes sur-faces and about a third lower than in health-food shops.

Choc of your life

Now only one address, among many assez bonnes: Robert Linxe's *La Maison du Chocolat* (225 rue du Faubourg St Honoré, 8e). There are Foodies who seek out Belgian *Godiva* and *Léonidas* imports, but Linxe's truffes au chocolat are sought after by le tout Belgique.

Glacé-eyed

Paris Foodies are less likely these days to want to queue outside *Berthillon* (31 rue St Louis en l'Ile, 4e), the top bonne addresse, along with le tout Thomas Cook. And, like pain Poilâne, glaces Berthillon have become a restaurant cliché (get bread from Poilâne, ice cream from Berthillon, and what comes between doesn't matter). Parisians who haven't located a glacière of quality in their coin may, however, travel to *Christian Constant* (26 rue du Bac, 7e), who turns out exquisitely refined sorbets and ice creams.

Bliss, glaces and pâtisseries in the Marais

Pastry case

A Paris Foodie often buys ices and pastries from the same shop: *Christian Constant*, of course, but also *Dalloyau* (101 rue du Faubourg St Honoré, 8e, and branches), whose complicated ingredients seem to impress Foodies; *Millet* (103 rue Saint Dominique, 7e), simpler, fresher, lighter, cheaper, in short more prestige- than li-queur-laden; or *Le Nôtre* (shops all over town), BCBG dependable (bon chic bon genre – French Sloane). Since it rarely crosses the mind of a Paris Foodie to make his own dessert, pâtisseries are in any case two to a block: as Marie Antoinette foresaw, an acceptable cake is a lot easier to come by than a decent loaf.

Leave me in épiceries

The Paris counterpart to Fortnum's or Harrods or Zabar's or Dean & DeLuca is *Fauchon* (26 place de la Madeleine, 8e). Foreign Foodies flock there. But Paris Foodies (unless they're Anglo-American residents looking for tinned chilli con carne or Marmite) prefer the bon ton and leisurely, almost colonial, atmosphere of *Paul Corcellet* (46 rue des Petits Champs, 2e) or *Hédiard* (21 place de la Madeleine, 8e, and branches) – though the latter has begun to diversify alarmingly. The Anglo-Saxon colony *and* the Parisians crowd into *Marks & Spencer* (35 boulevard Haussmann, 9e): any food from here is a Foodie item. Foodie exotica ranging from Aunt Jemima pancake mix to chutney are found picturesquely and cheaply at *L'Épicérie du Monde* (20 rue François Miron, 4e), where Françoise Izraël keeps her oriental bazaar; the Platonic ideals on which health-food shop products are

based can actually be purchased, with Foodie cachet, from *La Petite Marquise* (3 place Victor Hugo, 16e). (Health-foods – produits de régime – are the Paris Foodie's carefully hidden, but widely pre-valent, vice, indulged – for a price – mainly at the sinister *La Vie Claire* boutiques.)

BATTERIE DE CUISINE

Paris Foodies shop at the grands magasins, straying only rarely into tourist-Foodie suppliers like *Dehillerin* (18 rue Coquillière, ler). More often they'll venture into *A. Simon* (36 rue Etienne Marcel, 2e) or *M.O.R.A.* (13 rue Montmartre, ler), both suppliers to the trade, for specialist Foodie utensils.

Foodie shopping in London

L ong ago, when pterodactyls still flew around Kensington, and there was still a Jackson's in Piccadilly, Ur-Foodies could *only* shop at *Harrods Food Halls* and *Fortnum & Mason*. Harrods is better than ever, but Foodies can shop locally since London began turning Foodie five years ago. There are those who claim that north London is still the only place for a Foodie. The large Jewish populations left Foodie footprints as they made the historic trek northwards to Golders Green from the East End, and marked each resting-place with a good delicatessen shop.

TELL ME WHERE IS FANCY BREAD

The best bakery in the country is not in London, but in Oxford. *La Maison Blanc* (3 Woodstock Road, with a branch in Oxford Market) makes the nearest thing to a real baguette, and the best croissants, in England. Several top London restaurants have their bread baked by Raymond Blanc and delivered. It is avail-able to the public in London only at the Roux Brothers' *Boucherie Lamartine* (229 Ebury Street, SW1). *Rumbold's* (2 Heath Hurst Road, NW3; 4 Flask Walk NW3; 279 West End Lane, NW6) are old-

TEN RECIPES THAT SHOOK THE WORLD

8 JEWISH MOTHERS' MONOPOLY ENDED:

ADA GAIL'S AUTHENTIC JEWISH PICKLED CUCUMBER

The only place in the world you can *buy* a real dill pickle is New York. Foodies have cravings like everybody else, but until this recipe was published in the Conran/Habitat *Cook's Diary* for 1980, non-NY Foodies were unable to achieve satisfaction. (The *Diary* was a sell-out in England, France, Belgium and America; copies of it changed hands on the black market and fetched inflated prices in second-hand bookshops; the recipe was bought and anthologised by Time-Life in *The Good Cook* series.)

A misprint in the Habitat French translation resulted in too much salt. For months after its publication hundreds of Belgians and Frenchmen were seen walking around with puckered lips. This is the correct version.

3 kilos (6 lb) pickling cucumbers, about 8cm (3 in) long, scrubbed
18 sprigs of fresh dill
18 peeled cloves of garlic
6 mild chilli peppers
36 black peppercorns
1 tbsp mixed pickling spice
6 vine leaves (optional)

1½ tsp alum (available from the chemist or pharmacist, important for keeping the pickle crisp)
8.5 litres (14.4 pints, 9 US quarts) water
350g (12 oz, 1½ US cups) coarse salt
12.5 cl (4 fl oz, ½ US cup) cider or white wine vinegar

Into each of six sterilised jars put three sprigs of dill, three cloves of garlic, one chilli, six peppercorns, a pinch of pickling spice and of alum. Tightly pack the cucumbers into the jars.

Make the brine by boiling the water with the salt and vinegar, and pour the *hot* brine over the cucumbers, reserving the remaining brine. Cover each jar with a vine leaf and seal. After two or three days bubbles will appear, indicating fermentation. Top up the jars with the reserved brine, brought to the boil, and seal the jars again. When the brine clears, fermentation has stopped, and you can eat the pickle four or five days after this. In any case, eat it all up within a couple of months.

Green tomatoes, beans and other vegetables can be pickled in the same way.

fashioned bakers; *Justin de Blank Hygienic Bakery* (46 Walton Street, SW3; 115 Randall Road, SE11) is newer-fangled.

THE CRUELL'ST CHEESE ALIVE

Harrods, of course. But *greatly* improved is the old shop *Paxton & Whitfield* (93 Jer-

Lovely and extravagant – the caviar counter in Harrods' fabled food halls

KNOCK KNOCK.
Who's there?
EEL.
Eel who?
EEL BE SORRY HE SMOKED.

also larger *Waitrose* supermarkets (and *Sainsbury's*, ditto, but Foodies say the butchery is not as good). Trad butchers, poulterers and game merchants are *R. Allen* (117 Mount Street, W1), *W. Fenn* (27 Frith Street, W1; 6 The Market, Covent Garden, WC2), *Randall & Aubin* (16 Brewer Street, W1); *Rudds*, 17 Kensington Court Place, W8; *Hicks & Rudds*, 97 Old Brompton Road, SW7 and *Wainwright & Daughter* (95 Marylebone High Street, W1; 359 Fulham Road, SW1; 275 Kensington High Street, W8). In a category of its own for customer-loyalty is *Lidgate's* (110 Holland Park Avenue, W11) – the reason many Foodies refuse to move away from Notting Hill Gate. Most of these shops sell game, and the little yellow French maize-fed chickens which are the only ones that do not taste of fish.

BY THE PICKING OF MY PLUMS
London Foodies use the supermarkets. The larger stores – branches of *Waitrose*, *Sainsbury's* and even *Tesco* – stock every imaginable fruit and veg (with the exception of smelly durian), even if they don't always know what they are or how to eat or cook them. With the high turnover of supermarkets, their veg are usually crisper than those of traditional greengrocers. But for wild mushrooms and black truffles, and a large selection of ordinary things such as salads and potatoes, Foodies go to restaurant supplier *Robert Bruce* (C5/C6 New Covent Garden Market, Nine Elms Lane, SW8); they deliver. There is no London equivalent of the New York Korean greengrocer, but the Cypriot *Michael's* (Rosslyn Hill, NW3) or *L. Booth* (St Andrew's Hill, EC4), greengrocers to the City and Fleet Street, have very high-quality things with a good deal of choice. South-of-the-River Foodies sometimes venture to *Brixton Market* (near Brixton tube, SW9) for West Indian produce, and to Gerrard Street, Soho's Chinatown, where *Loon Fung* (39 Gerrard Street, W1) is a reliable source of Chinese vegetables.

myn Street, SW1), and some locals swear by *Justin de Blank* (42 Elizabeth Street, SW1). The biggest selection apart from Harrods (and owing to high turnover, the best-condition cheese) is at the *Rosslyn Delicatessen* (56 Rosslyn Hill, NW3).

SHALL I COMPARE THEE TO A BUFFET TRAY? THOU ART MORE LOVELY AND EXTRAVAGANT
Harrods, Fortnum's. In north London, M Bellier's *Rosslyn Delicatessen* is the chief stockist of most such items of luxe; Zyw olive oil, nut oils from Berry, cav and foie gras en bloc are almost always available, and he'll order anything he hasn't got. Mayfair Mercs get theirs at *Hobbs & Co* (29 South Audley Street, W1), where Romilly Hobbs even has the odd (fresh) white truffle in season.

WHEN SHALL WE TRY MEAT AGAIN?
Foodies patronise a French butcher, whenever one is available: smaller portions, but no waste and less lethal animal fat, as the French butcher removes the animal's own fat and replaces it with a paper-thin pork fat bard. There is French butchering at *Harrods*, the Roux Brothers'-owned *Boucherie Lamartine*, and

HARRY PORKY, CALLED CHUTZPAH
Harrods, the *Rosslyn Deli, Camisa & Son* (61 Old Compton Street, Soho, W1).

PERCHANCE TO BREAM
Harrods. John Blagden (64 Paddington Street, W1). *Richards (Soho)* (11 Brewer Street, W1). *R. Rowe & Son* (243 Camden High Street, NW1). *D. T. Foster* (Hampstead Community Market, Hampstead High Street, NW3; 824 High Road, N12). *Steve Hatt* (80 Essex Road, N1). *R. E. Wright & Sons* (10a Warwick Way, SW1). *La Marée* (76 Sloane Avenue, SW3). *J. Mist & Sons* (254 Battersea Park Road, SW11). *Bob White* (1 Kennington Lane, SE11). *Ashdown* (Leadenhall Market, EC3). *Chalmers & Gray* (67 Notting Hill Gate, W11). *Treadwell's* (97 Chippenham Road, W9) sell nostalgic pre-Foodie cockles, winkles and jellied eels. *The J.A. Centre* (348–356 Regent's Park Road, N3) has a Japanese fishmonger who slices fish for sushi at weekends. Fish is Foodie, Foodie is fish; that is all ye know on earth, and all ye need to know.

TEA'S DONE
Fortnum's. And *The Drury Tea & Coffee Co* (3 New Row, WC2; 37 Drury Lane, WC2, 3 Mepham Street, SE1) has a very big selection. *Monmouth Coffee House* (27 Monmouth Street, WC2) sells Kenyan, Colombian and Mocha, roasted on the premises, along with the usual mixtures. *Higgins* (42 South Molton Street, W1) will roast coffee to your own specifications. *Whittards* (111 Fulham Road, SW7) is one of the last great tea merchants – over 60 varieties, as well as tisanes and coffee.

SORBET OR NOT SORBET
London Foodies make their own. But *La Maison des Sorbets* (140 Battersea Park Road, SW11) has several delicious flavours, though the tomato is too sweet. *Lorier Sorbet* (35 Drayton Gardens, SW10) import ices from Valence, and supply Harrods, Justin de Blank and some Foodie restaurants.

OUT, DAMNED CHOC!
Chantal Cody's Rococo (321 King's Road, SW3), where Helge Rubinstein also sells Ben's chocolate chip cookies, was a greater revelation to Foodie Brits when it opened in 1983 than were the real hamburgers and Chicago pizzas of the Seventies. *Hobbs* (29 South Audley Street, W1) always has a deeply wicked selection of chocs. *Clare's* (3 Park Road, NW1) makes chocolates on the premises, and specialises in truffles. So does *Prestat* (40 South Molton Street, W1), whose truffles – no matter which of the many flavours they choose – are the Foodie's favourite.

Foodie shopping in New York

I t's no joke being a Foodie in New York. The standard is skyscraper-high and the fashions glide in and out like subway trains, signalled by the *New York Times*. This year the taste is baked garlic, with cactus leaf and hazel-nut coming up as a starter. In 1983 it was goat's cheese. In 1982 it was tortellini salad. Pink peppercorns were the spice at the beginning of the Eighties. In 1983–1984 it was coriander – there was practically coriander pudding.

YOU ARE MY REASON FOR LIVING
The famous Foodie shops (*Balducci's, Bloomie's, Dean & DeLuca, E.A.T., Jefferson Market, Zabar's*) do specialise, but more or less sell the same things. At seven in the morning the makers of these Foodie things are scurrying about delivering them. *Zabar's* (2245 Broadway) was one of the first Foodie paradises. It's rough-and-tumble – Yuppies and exHart voters. *E.A.T.* (1064 Madison Avenue) is run by Eli Zabar, son of Z, and is 25 per cent more expensive than Z for the convenience of being on the Upper East Side. *Balducci's* (424 6th Avenue) has Lauren Bacall and Ed Koch as customers, and showed the way to *Dean & DeLuca* (121 Prince Street). *D&D*, in SoHo, is a sort of

Fair stands the wind for food – the old Fulton Street downtown fish market is now a bunch of Foodie boutiques

April 30, 1984   THE   Price $1.50

NEW YORKER

food gallery. They introduced track lighting for cheese, then were trumped by the *DDL Food Show*, who introduced spot lighting for cheese – until the Food Show closed. *Jefferson Market* (6th Avenue between 10th and 11th Streets) looks like an English grocer in the Fifties, except that it stocks everything. *Bloomingdale's* ground floor (1000 3rd Avenue) has much of the best of Europe, including the Michel Guérard comptoirs.

DON'T KNOW WHEN I'LL BE BACK AGAIN
Foodies also make pilgrimages. To Brooklyn for olives; it is unthinkable to buy them anywhere except Atlantic Avenue. To Chinatown (below Canal and Mott Streets) for fish – the shrimps are not tasteless from freezing. To Yorkville, the old German area on the Upper East Side, for chocolates. To the strip on 10th Avenue around 42nd Street for Caribbean and African stuff, from egussi to smoke-dried Haitian shrimps. To Little Italy for Italian food.

I'D HAVE BAKED A LOAF
Lithuanian bread is the hottest thing at the moment, from the *Silver Bell Baking Co*, 4304 Junction Boulevard, Queens, Wednesday, Friday or Saturday; Foodies also buy it at *Balducci's* etc but pretend they trekked to Queens.

CHEESE MY BABY
New York Foodies are eating less cheese. Many of you go to the gym four times a week and you know that cheese is rich in FAT AND SODIUM. But you attend *Murray's Cheese Store* (42 Cornelia Street). The queue is 25 to 50 on a Saturday. *Murray's* have everything at three-quarters or half the price; even Argentinian Parmesan, if you are too mean to buy Italian.

YOU ARE MY CAVIAR
Foodies watch and wait for the annual price war between *Zabar's and Macy's* (W 34th Street and Broadway) in March or April, when beluga sometimes comes down to $140 a lb. The world's seas seethe so that New York can have every sort of caviar (except Iranian?). American caviar from the North Atlantic is said to be wonderful but spoiled by the processing. (Like American olives.)

YOU SAY TOMATO AND I SAY TOMATO
The *Korean fruit and vegetable stores* with their wonderful displays cornucopia-ing on to the sidewalk have beautified New York in the last five or six years. Even the old-money stretch of Park Avenue has one, although the old money fought it. Lilies, lilac, oranges, plums, melons and cherries entice, and – vital to Foodies – they always have sorrel. NY Foodies like fava (broad) beans and samphire, in season. They visit the so-called *green markets*, eg in Union Square on Wednesday and Saturday: farmers from New Jersey selling their produce.

SMOKE GETS IN YOUR STIES
The headquarters of French charcuterie is *Les 3 Petits Cochons* (17 E 13th Street), which supplies several other shops. There

are also *Demarchelier Charcuterie* (1460 Lexington Avenue), *Élysées Pastries* (939 1st Avenue) (good charc department) and *Macy's* Cellar. Dean & DeLuca does a good saucisson à l'ail among its charc. *Faicco* (260 Bleeker Street) is the Foodie source of Italian sausage of all kinds.

GONE FISHING

The Foodie fish are monkfish (lotte) and skate. You can get them, though not everywhere. 'In Europe,' said the man at *Captain Ben's Fish Dock* (319 Woodcleft Avenue, Freeport, Long Island), who sells it, 'skate is a delicacy, but here it's insulting.' Sea robin, conger eels and dogfish are other fish Foodies want but which most uptown branches of fish shops don't stock. They are sometimes available at the *Central Fish Market* (527 9th Avenue), *Sea Breeze Market* (541 9th Avenue), *DeMartino's* (132 8th Avenue) and *Grillo's* (19 Newkirk Plaza, Brooklyn). What you can't get is scallops with coral. American fishermen cut it off. Intact scallops turn up seasonally, imported from France (*Balducci's*).

RUN RABBIT, RUN RABBIT, RUN RUN RUN

It is illegal to sell local game in New York State. Quail comes in deep frozen, and noticeably overkilled, from Canada or California. Frozen hares come from Australia. You can get fresh pheasants and partridges, from New Jersey. All NY Foodies insist on the free-range chickens they buy having been reared by *Bell & Evans*.

THE TICK TICK TOCK OF THE STATELY CHOC

Li-Lac Chocolates (120 Christopher Street) have amusing shapes in superb chocolate – Lacoste alligators and so on. Foodies hunt for chocs in Yorkville. The *Elk Candy Co* (240 E 86th Street) make the best truffles in New York. The European chocolate firms have outposts in New York: *Godiva* of Belgium – now owned by Campbell's Soups (701 5th Avenue),

---

1984's
Tough Little Bully
THE FLAVOUR OF THE YEAR

In 1984 it's hazel-nuts for Foodies. It's surprising the world's hazel trees can cope. Some Foodies have them at every meal, starting with breakfast, in muesli. Waitrose muesli has whole hazel-nuts, so you can see the little husked balls, like something glimpsed in the Smaller Mammal House. This may be the point to mention that hazel-nuts have a very strong, masculine flavour. They're fighters. The jaded Foodie palate needs that.

At lunchtime, Foodies have salad, with hazel-nut oil dressing. The hazel-nut fights with the salad. It doesn't taste fresh and green, it tastes gamy and red, like protein – the equivalent of beef or cheese. Hazel-nut flavour is definitely ballsy.

At dinner, the Foodie will again indulge in hazel-nuts, perhaps as praline ice cream. Chèvre will probably also be on the menu. Chèvre is another bully that's hanging in there. But hazel-nut sees off the rank goat. Hazel-nut is teethier and has staying power, working away in the stomach manufacturing turbulence.

If the Foodie is eating at an expensive restaurant, chocolates will be brought at the end of the meal. They are crunchy with hazel-nuts, of course.

Shouldn't a Foodie diet be varied? Don't you mind living all day under the domination of one powerful flavour? You haven't even noticed. In 1982, you happily ate chèvre at every course. In 1983, you happily ate basil at every course. In 1985, you will happily eat ??? at every course. Foodies do what it is *Foodie* to do. Foodies are fashion victims. Foodies are a breed of nut.

Perugina of Italy (636 Lexington Avenue), *Dalloyau* of Paris (Bloomingdale's), *Corne de la Toison d'Or* of Brussels (Trump Tower). *Teuscher* (25 E 61st Street; 620 5th Avenue) get their chocs weekly from Zürich, and are the big name in champagne truffles. Chocolate truffles are made daily at *Le Chocolatier* (843 Lexington Avenue, upstairs). *The Chocolate Garden* (1390 3rd Avenue) hand-dips its own chocolates, also makes jelly beans; over 40 varieties of choc. Maimie Lee from Shanghai also hand-dips at *Chocolates by M* (61 W 62nd Street): she was taught by a Viennese chocolatier. *Plumbridge Confections and Gifts* (33 E 61st Street, upstairs) has *American* candies and has been owned by the same family since 1883.

ICES HELLO

Foodies are eating proper sorbets again rather than ice cream (the gym strikes again). Le Sorbet is the Foodie brand. The mango is lovely.

PUDDING ON THE STYLE

New York flutters with light hands turning out puddings, pies and confections. *E.A.T.*'s look a bit lopsided, therefore homemade, and *E.A.T.* gets specially thick cream from Pennsylvania cows to pour on them. *Flourings* (340 E 11th Street) specialise in small things – tiny pumpkin pies, gingerbread houses and cookies designed by an illustrator. *Pierrot* (108 Montague Street, Brooklyn Heights)

The Silver Palate delicatessen at 274 Columbus Avenue published their own cookbook in 1981. It sold zillions

make a croquembouche among other things. *Lanciani* (271 W 4th Street) is a wonderful shop with the best Sacher Torte in town. *Country Host* (1435 Lexington Avenue) makes honest lemon loaves and so on. The *Leonard Baking Co* (1412 3rd Avenue) makes 'a superb apple cake', raved the *New Yorker*'s Foodie, who also fell joyfully on Michel Guérard's apple Tarte Tatin *(Bloomingdale's)*. *Bonté*

(1316 3rd Avenue) is New York's best French pastry shop, say Gault-Millau, and Maurice Bonté has won the Best Pastrycook award in France and the US. *Délices la Côte Basque* (1032 Lexington Avenue; Olympic Tower Arcade, 635 5th Avenue) is the second best. *Dumas* (116 E 60th Street) is another good French one. *Sarabeth's Kitchen* (412 Amsterdam Avenue, 1295 Madison Avenue) is American and healthy: everything made with natural products, no artificials, colouring or preservatives.

THE GOOD SHOP COOKING-POT

There are kitchenware departments at *Zabar's, Dean & DeLuca, Bloomingdale's, Macy's* Cellar, and the classic French shop on W Broadway. The American Foodie's wish-book is the Williams-Sonoma *Catalog for Cooks*, PO Box 3792, San Francisco, CA 94119.

C-C-C-C-C-C-CATERERS

A lot of people don't even try to cook for their own dinner parties any more. Canapes are always ordered. (Canapes are an art form in New York – it's OhWow.) *E.A.T.* is the Foodiest caterer. *Délices la Cote Basque* is trad French. *Glorious Foods* (172 E 75th Street) does an American version of French nouvelle: good presention. *Remember Basil* (11 Cadman Plaza W, Brooklyn Heights) is neck and neck with *Glorious Foods*: theatrical presentation – they invented the walking buffet (like cigarette girls) and filled the Guggenheim with food for a ball. *Les 3 Petits Cochons* are French rustic cooks. *Madame Germaine* (38–09 33rd Street) is a very good French classical cook. *Jean Pierre Briand* (440 E 56th Street) caters for a maximum of 50 diners and 300 cocktail-drinkers – for the drinkers, he miniaturises French dishes to bite-size. Cecile Arnett of *La Table du Roi* (675 Water Street) also does canapés that are like inch-square French masterpieces; her dinner cooking mixes nouvelle and trad French.

THE GREAT TRUFFLE SCANDAL

Keep your nose clean, Foodie

In February 1984, two British newspapers, the *Observer* and the *Sunday Telegraph*, had the same story planted on them: there was a world truffle shortage, and prices were rising out of sight. Each of these stories was illustrated by a photograph of a wizened Frenchman with a long white beard. He owned a truffle-canning factory in Périgord, and his public relations people were obviously very efficient. Black truffles did cost £180 ($270) a kilo that winter, but in January 1980, one of the same newspapers reported that they were £134 ($200) a kilo, and in 1983 they were reported to have reached £200, while the rare white Italian truffle was selling at Hobbs in London for £19 an ounce, or £678 a kilo. So this story seems to come up every year.

It is true that the black or Périgord *Tuber melanosporum* and the white *Tuber magnata* are the most precious substances known to Foodies. The strongly perfumed black truffle can be cooked whole, but is usually used in tiny slivers to flavour other food. In the great truffle shortage of 1984, people joked that Foodies were adding shavings of rubber tyres to the truffles. Truffles *attract* myths and lies.

The even more strongly scented white truffle is never cooked, but shaved over your risotto with a razor device to keep the slices paper-thin. The white truffle attracts even bigger stories among Foodies, like the one about Principessa X, who said, 'Once when I was asked to luncheon in the country,' (she lived in Venice and anything on dry land was 'the country') 'everyone was raving about some funghi. So I bought one that weighed a kilo. I carried it back to Venice, but I do not trust these funghi so I took it to my greengrocer and said, "What do you think of this fungo?" "Ah," he said, "that is a *wonderful* fungo." (It ought to have been – a white truffle weighing a kilo, worth £300

even in Italy.) 'Well,' she said, 'I still was not sure so I took it back to my maid and said to her, "What do you think of this fungo?" and she said "I would not eat such rubbish." So I threw it in the canal.'

Everyone knows the reason these king funghi are expensive is that they grow underground and can only be detected by specially trained dogs (pigs are seldom used any more) handled by clued-up peasants who know where to look. What everybody doesn't know is that the reason the peasants know where to look is that, for a long time now, the black truffle has been *cultivated*.

All through the winter, at Aups in the Haut Var, French peasants sell their truffles to the wholesaler every Saturday. They conceal their 'black diamonds' in plastic bags in their Citroëns and Peugeots, until the dealer comes along with his hand-held scales. Then the peasants whip out their booty (black dia-

Knock knock.
Who's there?
Gianni.
Gianni who?
Gianni addresses in Alba where we can buy truffles?

Black gold changing hands in Périgord. Truffles are sold by weight, including the earth that clings to them

TEN RECIPES THAT SHOOK THE WORLD

❾ RISOTTO WITH WHITE TRUFFLE

FOODIE DISCOVERS ITALY, MORTGAGES HOUSE

Risotto is a turning-point in every Foodie's life. It has to be served immediately after being made. As it cannot wait or be reheated, it is not a restaurant dish. The moment of truth is when a Foodie learns to make it herself. Only then does she discover what the fuss is about – soft, creamy but separate grains of rice, each one exquisitely flavoured, bound in just the right amount of sauce.

The principle of making risotto is to coat special rice – Arborio – and aromatics, such as onion or shallot, with oil and butter, then adding small amounts of a hot, flavoured liquid, and stirring constantly until the rice has exactly the correct degree of chewiness and the right amount of sauce. The risotto is finished with freshly grated Parmesan cheese and more butter, and the white truffle is sliced razor-thin over the top with the special instrument pictured here.

This recipe is adapted from Marcella Hazan's *Classic Italian Cookbook*, and makes four servings as a first course.

In a heavy-bottomed saucepan sweat 2 tbs finely chopped shallots in 25 g (1 oz) unsalted butter and 2 tbs of good oil. Do not brown. Add 300 g (10½ oz, 1½ US cups) Arborio rice, and stir until coated with the fat. Stirring constantly, add 150 ml (¼ pint, ⅔ US cup) hot chicken stock. When this liquid is absorbed, add another 150 ml, until you have used up 1¼ l (2 pints, 5 US cups) of stock, adding hot water if more liquid is required, and slowing down the rate at which liquid is added as you near the end of the cooking. Marcella Hazan says it should be 'creamy but not runny'. Taste for salt and stir in 60 g (2 oz) fresh grated Parmesan, and, if you like, 15 g (½oz) more butter.

Shave as much white truffle over the top as you can afford. This recipe is *quite* good without the truffle.

monds are a churl's best friend), weigh it, take the money and drive off – fast.

In Italy, around Alba in Piedmont, where the best white truffles come from, the folklore is even greater. There is a Truffle King, Signor Morra, who has a perfectly legal monopoly in dealing in white truffles – he is the only person qualified to issue Value Added Tax receipts, so he sets the prices. If the peasant doesn't like Signor Morra's offer, he can take his chances and sell his tartufi at the Saturday market in Alba.

But the fungus really hit the fan in November 1982, when two journalists from Britain [Jane Grigson and Paul Levy] discovered that even the *white* truffle could be cultivated. Giusto Giovannetti, Professor of Mycology at the University of Turin, made the revelation. He was backed up by Francesco Tagliaferro, whose Turin firm specialises in mycorrhising the roots of young trees – infecting them with truffle spores that will give rise to mycellium (the mass of underground white threads that is the business part of a fungus) – when the tree is planted, which will produce, in about five years, the actual fruiting body of the truffle.

Professor Giovannetti reported that Signor Tagliaferro had collected some black truffles the same morning; and that it could be done on an economic scale: 'the production of the black truffle is now 100 kilograms per hectare. Quite satisfactory.' Production of white truffles has not yet reached commercial proportions, but both men expected that it would soon.

Hard-boiled ego

So why is the truffle industry conducted as a black market and coccooned in folklore like a truffle wrapped in tissue and stored in a jar of Arborio rice? Because in France at present, truffles are considered windfall, and are not taxed. Once it becomes established in law that they have been cultivated and not just stumbled upon by a peasant taking his pig for a walk, they will be taxed like any other crop.

Here is the good news. In September 1983, a summer truffle, Tuber aestivum, was found in Wiltshire. It strongly resembles the white Italian truffle and is highly perfumed. It was stumbled upon by a young man taking his bicycle for a walk.

Will modern marketing bring rewards in an underrewarded profession?

There are two sorts of Foodiebiz. One is lending your name. The other is standing over a hot stove feeding it £20 notes with one hand while peddling a fashion bicycle and trying to hide £5 notes from the income tax in your ear.

Lending your name – 'le business'

When the famous French chefs talk about 'le business', they mean endorsing. In Foodie countries like France and America, the top professionals are like film stars. They are pestered to lend their names and faces to products in return for large sums of money. Most of them are fat, middle-aged, bald, bespectacled or all four – but these faces sell things to Foodies.

There would be a difference – if any of the chefs did it – between selling their own home-made products, such as, say, pâtés and jams, and lending their names to products made by other people. Favoured clients of the great chefs may get the odd home-made terrine in a Christmas hamper, but such things seem never to be for sale.

What *is* for sale is Paul Bocuse's selection of beaujolais for Georges Duboeuf or Piat's Beaujolais-Villages Cuvée Georges Blanc. From Michel Guérard's 'Comptoirs' in Paris and at Bloomingdale's in New York, you can buy fresh (not canned) food prepared to the master's specifications – if not quite fait by his own main – and in supermarkets there are frozen foods blessed by Guérard. At another counter you will find Roger Vergé's clever range: herbes fortes pour poissons et crustacés, le mélange du diable, radicelles

The archbishop of Foodiebiz. Paul Bocuse with own brands, own bottles and own portraits

de crosnes d'hiver au vinaigre, la moutarde forte aux olives noires, to name but four.

Having your name (and often face) on a product, though, does not *necessarily* mean that you know exactly what's inside the carton, can or sausage skin. Industrial products are all too often mistakable for the more desirable artisanale edibles – this is how Guérard got bitten by a sausage. In December 1983 he was found guilty of 'false advertising in connection with the sale of food products bearing his name'. The charge was that the labels implied the products were 'artisanale', prepared by rural craftsmen in the Landes district near Eugénie, whereas they were made in a factory. Guérard maintains staunchly that they were all good products, and says of the case and the fine, 'It was not for nothing that it took place in Lyon' (the Lyons den of Foodiebiz).

Foodiebiz is big biz. James Beard and Robert Carrier selling their names and fame

Blessing a new line of food is different again from lending your name to already existing products. James Beard, claim John and Karen Hess, 'has toiled for such clients as Planters peanut oil, Green Giant, Nestlé, Restaurant Associates, and Pillsbury, the owner of the Burger King chain'. Craig Claiborne does not endorse products commercially, but the Hesses damn him for his too-kind attitude to brand names: praising, for instance, Medaglia d'Oro coffee, Howard Johnson's canned beef gravy, Seabrook's 'inspired beef à la bourguignonne', Betty Crocker's instant meringue, Borden's Instant Starlac and Instant Whipped Potatoes, Carnation Golden Fudge and Campbell's frozen fruit pies. Claiborne's collaborator Pierre Franey works for Howard Johnson. Foodies shudder.

However, in Britain only the irrepressible Robert Carrier touts for Foodie trade on television – on behalf of Tesco supermarkets. Clement Freud, MP, author of

several cookery books and food columnist for *Punch*, has made dog-food commercials. But perhaps that doesn't count.

You won't find Alain Chapel's blackcurrant vinegar in a supermarket. And you won't find Pierre Troisgros' vinaigre de vin vieux aromatisé à la groseille extrait naturel de fruit, Sélection Troisgros. For those you will have to go to Mionnay or Roanne. Even though the TG bottle admits it's actually made by 'Ets Fallot et Cie 21200 Beaunes'.

Le souvenir business

Restaurants used to give menus to customers who asked for one, and the customers stole their own souvenir ashtrays. But nowadays, the three-star restaurants of France have shopettes where they sell their menus, their ashtrays, the chef's books, and little mementoes such as their own vinegar or eggcups. It makes a fine souvenir for the kitchen of 'the old lady in Dubuque', who the *New Yorker* used to say they did *not* edit for. In the 1980s, the old lady's dream is to eat a meal cooked by Paul Bocuse.

Restaurant economics

It's very hard to make money running a restaurant. You can only charge so much for a meal, and profits are nibbled away by the staff from below and the income tax from above. It's traditional that: the staff steal food; the cook gets a backhander of 8 to 10 per cent from the food supplier; the food supplier invoices the restaurant for supplies he has not supplied, and he and the cook share the money. César Ritz and his chef the great Escoffier were sacked from the Savoy Hotel in 1898 for operating a racket like this (see *Escoffier* and *Ritz* in the Who's Who).

The unkind credit card

The spread of the charge card (Diners Club launched theirs in 1950, American Express in 1958) robbed waiters and also proprietors of money they had relied on. Waiters are traditionally paid the legal minimum wage and expected to get most of their income from tips – which they used to minimise in their tax returns. But with the service charge included in a prix fixe menu and paid in plastic, waiters are caught. A tip paid by credit card is subject to VAT (15 per cent off, in Britain). The Inland Revenue will then deduct 35 to 40 per cent from the waiter for income tax. The proprietor also hates the plastiques: the credit firm wants its commission (average 5 per cent of the bill; as much as 10 per cent of a restaurant's takings can go on credit-card commission), and the plastic pirates don't have to pay him for 30 days. But most restaurants dare not refuse to handle credit cards – 80 to 90 per cent of their customers normally pay that way. It is chefs' common gossip that the Roux Brothers' restaurants in Britain take around £35,000 a week in American Express business. A restaurant that feeds the credit companies exceptionally well can ask for and get exceptional terms – low commission and rapid

Famous chefs used to give menus to favoured customers. Now they sell them. Menus add their mite to Foodiebiz

★★★★★★★★★★★★★★★★★

CARDINAL TO POPE: 'I'm awfully sorry, your Holiness, but I have to report nine cases of herpes in the Vatican.'
POPE: 'I'm rather relieved actually. I was getting very tired of Frascati.'

★★★★★★★★★★★★★★★★★

Notre Carte

LE FOIE GRAS FRAIS DES LANDES FAIT A LA MAISON
LE SAUMON FUMÉ DANOIS
LE CAVIAR BELUGA D'IRAN AVEC LES BLINIS, les 100 grs
* LA DODINE DE CANETON AU FOIE GRAS AVEC LES GRIOTTES EN AIGRE DOUX
* LE PATÉ DE SOLE EN CROUTE, SAUCE GRELETTE
* LE JAMBON DE PARME
LA SALADE MIKADO
* LE GATEAU DE LAPIN SANS LE GÈNE, AU CHABLIS
* L'OMELETTE A LA TOMATE FRAICHE A LA FACON DU MOULIN
* LA TERRINE DE RASCASSE AU CITRON AVEC LES CONCOMBRES A LA CRÈME

* LA LANGOUSTE ROYALE GRILLÉE AU BEURRE DE BASILIC
* LA LANGOUSTE ROYALE AU POIVRE ROSE

Roger Vergé aujourd'hui vous suggère...

LE CONSOMMÉ D'HUITRES AU CITRON VERT
LA SALADE DE TRUFFE DU VAUCLUSE AU VINAIGRE DE JEREZ
LE BOUQUET DE SALADES GOURMANDES AUX QUEUES D'ECREVISSES
LA PETITE SOUPE DE GRENOUILLE AUX FEUILLES DE MENTHE
LE GRATIN D'HUITRES DE BELON AUX EPINARDS
LA FRICASSÉE DE St PIERRE DU PAYS AUX PETITS LÉGUMES
LE CIVET DE HOMARD AU VIEUX BOURGOGNE
LA DAURADE ROYALE DU PAYS ROTIE AU LAURIER, AVEC LA FONDUE D'ORANGE ET DE CITRON
LE BISCUIT DE LOUP AUX ASPERGES SAUVAGES, SAUCE LÉGÈRE
LA COMPOTE DE GIGOT D'AGNEAU A LA SARRIGETTE ET AUX AUBERGINES AVEC LES TARTINES DE PUREE D'AIL
LE SUPRÊME DE VOLAILLE DE L'ALLIER ETUVE AUX HERBES VERTES DU JARDIN
LA TRUFFE DE GRILLON CUITE SOUS LA CROUTE AU SEL
LA FAISSELLE DE FROMAGE BLANC A LA CRÈME
LES FROMAGES DE LA FERME SAUVAGÉ, AVEC LE PAIN DE SEIGLE AUX NOIX ET AUX RAISINS

Jacques Pic vous propose

Salade des Pêcheurs au Xérès 150
Damier de Rouget au Foie Gras 100
Salade de Saint-Jacques aux Huitres 95
Terrine de Foie d'Oie 95
Salade d'Aiguillettes et Foie de Canard 85
Millefeuille au Ris de Veau et Ecrevisses 85
Truffe de la Drôme entiere aux Navets 240
Cassolette d'Huitres aux Powrons 120

Filet de Loup au Caviar 150
Escalope de Turbot aux Morilles 100
Assiette des Quatre Poissons 150
Copeaux de Saint-Pierre aux Ecrevisses 85
Julienne de Sole au Safran 85
Tresse de Loup aux Huitres
   sauce Champignons 100
Noix de St-Jacques et Rougets aux Endives 90
Médaillons de Langouste aux Truffes 250
Blanquette de Homard
   aux Artichauts 250

Pigeon de Bresse Fourré aux Morilles 95
Ris de Veau Braisé aux Echalotes 90
Cervelles d'Agneau au Cornas 70
Rognon de Veau escalope au vieux vinaigre 80
Filet d'Agneau a la Gousse d'Ail 80
Tournedos de Charolais a la Creme de Basilic 80
Canneton Rouennais Lie de Vin
   (a partir de 2 personnes) 180
Foie de Canard entier aux Raisins
   au Marc de l'Hermitage (a partir de 2 personnes) 280

Choix de Fromages
Desserts de Saison

* Sur Commande
Ragoût Princesse
   Poularde de Bresse en Vessie "André Pic"
Notre Champagne Brut illustré par "Peynet"

Service compris 15%

---

payment. But it's not as good as before the cards came, when the restaurants relied on a fair proportion of the cash getting lost on its way to the bank.

The taxman attacketh

In the Sixties, when 'affluence' and 'the steak-eating classes' were young, a typical apportioning of a restaurant's takings was: one third to costs, one third to overheads, one third profit. Restaurant-owners flourished. Luigi's shiny red pepper mill grew to a foot long. Then envious governments devised ways to shorten it. Britain introduced SET (selective employment tax), followed in 1972 by the hated VAT (France invented it in 1949 – it spreads like phylloxera). The British customer was obliged to pay at least 10 per cent more for the same meal, and the restaurateur to become a part-time unpaid tax collector. About the same time, the increasing use of 'service included' raised the average bill a compulsory 10 to 15 per cent. Businessmen liked the fact that the bill was all in, and could be passed back to their firm with their expenses claim. Business entertaining was tax-deductible. Restaurants became dangerously dependent on expense-account customers. Then the lobster-rosy times (fairly rosy, despite credit cards and VAT) were turned black in France by President Mitterrand's imposition in 1981 of a 30 per cent tax on business entertaining. The new tax has had a marked effect on takings, and nowadays, profit is down to about 20 per cent of the breakdown anyway – costs and overheads account for 80 per cent. Wholesale food prices are particularly vulnerable to inflation (they rose by 35 per cent in 1975, for example), while such necessities as cleaning materials and Clingfilm climb close behind them. Will the old lady from Dubuque be able to fill the financial hole left by Businessman? Her heart's certainly in the right place.

Close your pies and think of money

With Foodism such big business, a food photographer's the thing to be: £1,000 ($1,400) a day for advertising photographs, £400 ($640) for editorial. 'Is it a sloop or a ketchup?' said someone when a food photographer bought a yacht. The client reckons he might get four different shots from a day's shoot. On top of the photographer's fee, there is the home economist's £100 (she buys and 'cooks' the food) and the stylist's £80 (she borrows and brings the tablecloth, candlesticks, spoons, flowers, things that add *atmosphere*.)

So when they all gather in the studio with its kitchen, the atmosphere is as tense as the set of *Ben Hur.* When the photographer's assistant eats something before it's been photographed, or the home economist's assistant trips over a cable and douses the lights, no one laughs.

The Sixties was the start of Foodie food photography, with advertisements and colour supplements voracious for it. They wanted it bright, clean ('Cleanliness is definitely next to godliness for food companies,' said an advertising art director), filling (spaghetti spilling over the edge of the plate) and *atmospheric* (foreign). Some photographers, eg Jack Nisberg and Robert Freson, actually went on the food photographer's Grand Tour to photograph French restaurants. Daylight and real surroundings do look better than the orange-marmalade landscape and beige food that is apt to come out of the studio.

In those early days, even Foodies didn't know much about eastern food, and some gaffes were committed – such as the picture in *The World of Robert Carrier* in which a bamboo whisk sits in a wok: only it wasn't a whisk, it was a Chinese washing-up brush. In another Carrier faux pas, there are chopsticks with a Thai dish: Thais eat Thai food with a fork and spoon. Mistakes like these are chewed over pleasurably by Foodies for years.

Pontius Palate

Advertising art directors can be a bugger in the foodpile if they don't understand food. They confidently draw a 'visualisation' for the client containing a bloomer: say, Neapolitan ice cream slices layered vertically. Once it's approved, the photographer has to produce that, even though the food photographers' Madame Tussaud has made the wax Neapolitan

A spiced peanut cutlet caught at the psychological moment by Robert Golden for 'Good Housekeeping' in 1984. Note the magnetised insect – artifice or luck?

Joceline Dimbleby did not mind the accusations of gastroporn – she admits food rouses the physical in her

★ Fish fingers, hamburgers and so on look bigger if made by hand – they are, in fact, bigger.
★ Orange rind lies better if peeled anti-clockwise.
★ Bread is always glazed.
★ Dumplings look lighter if floating, with corks inside.
★ Tiny glass bubbles are floated on drinks and soup.
★ Sauces look realler with unnatural colouring.
★ Drinks, sauces and other bottled liquids are poured through bottomless bottles attached to a clamp.

The Americans were the pioneers in most food photography techniques. Robert Golden, one of the leading food photographers in England, is American. Despite their work, many food photographers still love food: Jhon Kevern, Bryce Attwell, Michael Boys and Christine Hanscomb are Foodies.

Tessa Traeger, who has photographed food for British *Vogue* since 1975, was one of the harbingers of the nouvelle non-obscene look: natural colours, pleasing patterns, unfilling food. The spaghetti has retreated to the middle of the plate. (Pasta with a hole in it is hell to photograph: either all the holes gape blackly at you, or they all turn away and it looks contrived, or the sauce collects in the cracks like coagulated blood.)

Nouvelle cuisine *needs* photographers. Some Foodies take their cameras to the restaurant and snap their plates before tucking in. Such artistry must not go unrecorded! The food photographer Anthony Blake travelled with the writer Quentin Crewe to do *Great Chefs of France*, and the book is 'by' them both. One of the best British food photographers, Paul Kemp, who works with his food stylist wife, thinks food photography is about to move out of boring tidiness. Some of the gastroporn artists are experimenting with half-eaten platefuls, crumby tablecloths, the cigarette that bears a Foodie's traces.

slices the right way, layered horizontally.

Some purists, such as the *Observer* colour magazine, don't use artificial aids. But the others delight in their mastery of the artifice. For example:

★ A half-cooked chicken covered in French polish doesn't wrinkle like a cooked chicken.
★ Fruit, vegetables, ice-cream and ice cubes photograph better if made in wax; a British woman makes these: £10 to £20 for a pod of peas.
★ Pies are filled with tissue paper.
★ Ammonia or spirits of salt look like steam.

It's very hot in this kitchen

The difference between the amateur and the professional Foodie is like the difference between an ordinary exhibition-goer and an art dealer. There are more camps at the top level of Foodism than on the night before Waterloo. Foodie X *loathes* Foodie Y. And if anyone defends Y, X will say 'He's *no good*!' No good? After spending 30 years, approximately 20,000 meals, studying food? 'The food he likes is *disgusting*. He has set the course of cooking back 40 years. He's a *fossil*.' So *he's* out, in the eyes of X's camp.

The ordinary person who simply is *interested in food*, the 'I know what I like' Foodie, does not realise what is happening in the higher echelons. Your palate is the *least* of it. Even wankers have palates. All those evenings spent pinpointing the exact pale scented olive oil, from between Livorno and Pisa, that won't overpower a Dutch lettuce – it's just massaging your own palate.

Foodism is at this point like a business empire. To get anywhere, you have to be a sort of Blake Carrington in a striped apron. You have to work (equals eat) desperately hard: two memorable meals a day. And you'd better remember them. You already have your talent (your wanker's palate). But you need luck (equals timing, equals knowing the right Foodies). Craig Claiborne and James Beard and some other senior Foodies are kind about pushing young Foodies' careers. But if you do get up there, you still aren't safe. You must fight not to become yesterday's Foodie. A leftover. You can't rest on your sorrels when all the other Foodies want to dislodge you like a fish bone in the throat. They are dying to christen you Fossil.

And there is yet another danger. You may have got into the wrong *camp*. Like any other profession at a certain stage, Foodism is becoming established. The ambitious Foodies are introducing rules and associations and international links, to raise the status of their subject. (And of themselves. They usually end up President or something of whatever group it is.) They want Foodies to be like doctors. D. dill. Or perhaps Bachelor of Edibles. *They*'ll be the Professors of Edibles.

Sabatier in the back

This bid for influence takes Foodism through the swing doors to the big hot kitchen where money and power are being slammed around. But many Foodies of great taste and reputation, such as Elizabeth David, do not want to work there. They prefer to remain scholarly and quiet. They are not keen on judging competitions, doing demonstrations and accompanying gastronomic tours of Foodie hangers-on. Which leaves the public arena to those who like it. To the Foodie fighters.

The success of Foodism has attracted some pretty sharp people. The Bachelors of Edibles have had to swallow a few unedifying things.

Foodie associations have turned out to be a problem. It was predictable. Where there are 40 Foodies there are bound to be at least three camps and one bad egg. 'A governing body' sounds all right when Mr Ambitious Foodie suggests it, but quis custodiet the custardies?

The International Association of Cooking Schools, based in Washington, was horrified when a past president, Richard Nelson, was sued for $1,050,000 by Richard Olney for plagiarism, in 1984. A cribber in the foodpile! (See p 108.) Nelson was also on the advisory board of the Foodie body, the American Institute of Wine & Food, which has been urgently fermenting since it was founded in 1982.

Most of the associations are not dramatically bad, they are merely dramatically mediocre, because spurned by the top Foodies. At their dinners it is the people

F·O·O·D·I·E·B·O·R·E·S

THE PEPPERBORE

She is an endangered species, besieged by the common herd. Now *everyone* knows that you don't serve white pepper but very coarsely ground black peppercorns. Steak pepper from Sainsbury's is the right sized bits – so what's the point of being a pepper bore any more? Real Foodies grind their own, and have at least two kinds in mills on the table. Paul Levy struck a blow for élitism in 1981 by publicising the green and pink peppercorns sold by Fauchon and his local Rosslyn Delicatessen in Hampstead, but then Alan Davidson, a *bit* of a mischief, published in his *Petits Propos Culinaires* in March 1982 an article by Alexandra Hicks saying that pink peppercorns had been found to cause symptoms of drunkenness in birds ...

who *aren't* there, the Banquos, who are really significant.

Every male French Foodie has his eating group, not *quite* called Les Cronies du Cochon, but nearly: Les Gais Gentilhommes Gastronomes, L'Académie du Lapin ('Secrète et Gourmande'), the Ordre Mondial des Barbus Gastronomiques, the Mousquetaires de Lyon: 11 academies, 16 associations, 12 clubs and 52 confréries. (This is the number in *Le Grand Livre des Sociétés et Confréries Gastronomique de France* by Fernand Woutaz, published in 1973, but more must have appeared.) Several were founded in the nineteenth century.

The Académie des Gastronomes, based in Paris, considers itself of international importance (it sends out publicity material in English). It was started by 'Prince' Curnonsky in 1930. He was such fun, and Foodie politics so young, that many real Foodies came to dinner – Guérot (whose recipes Bocuse used), Vrinat, and a couple of Cointreaus. Curnonsky presided over the dinners and meetings until 1948. He was succeeded by Paul Gaultier, who was succeeded in 1956 by Vincent Bourrel, who was succeeded in 1980 by Jean Laurens-Frings, the present president. The press handout says: 'The aim of the Academy is first of all to allow its members to practise the art of gastronomy as a hobby by inviting them to meals where each person in turn can reveal to his colleagues his knowledge of and familiarity with the classical, the original and the new.' Testifying to the scrumptious palate of Me! It sounds deliciously pseud, and even more so when you realise that although the Academy has 40 'chairs', none is occupied by any of France's three best food journalists, Robert Courtine, Christian Millau and Henri Gault. Those banquets score Banq000. There are no women, either. (Banq♀ ♀ ♀ ♀ ♀ ♀ ♀ ♀ ♀ ♀ ♀ ♀ ♀ ♀ ♀.)

A Spanish academy, the Academia Espanola de Gastronomia, was started in 1973, with 52 members. Some international Foodies scoffed and said there's nothing edible in Spain except the tapas. None of the names of the academicians is known to international Foodiedom, but Foodies recognise two Miembros correspondientes, Don Claude Jolly and Don Egon Ronay.

Don Egon Ronay runs the Egon Ronay Organization's hotel and restaurant guides in Britain. Egon is a Hungarian name, loved by the more frivolous British food journalists, who delight in egging Ronay on in and out of print: poaching Egon, making omelettes without breaking Egon, deciding that Egon is good or cracked or coming out of his shell, noticing Egon toast, Egon top or Egon his face. Ronay doesn't like it.

Foodiebiz is Big Biz

In 1983, Ronay founded the British Academy of Gastronomes, with 52 members. The nuisance for him is that there are three other Foodie guides to Britain, now that Foodiebiz is such big biz – Michelin, Gault-Millau (London only) and the *Good Food Guide*. But no one from the editorial staffs of these rivals are members of the 'British Academy', unless you count Peter Goldman, director of the Consumers' Association, which publishes the *GFG*. So the

*A STRAIGHT
ANSWER TO
THE AWKWARD
QUESTIONS*

Must a Foodie be able to cook?

No. It may be a disadvantage. People will say 'But have you eaten anything X has *cooked*?' or 'We were sick all night after the last meal we had there' or 'If she's giving you lunch, be sure to have a sandwich on the way.' Foodism is sustained by food-in-the-head. Try to get it there and keep it there.

Or have a good palate?

A successful Foodie must have a *tolerant* palate. The Foodie with a purist palate is almost certainly unable to see the wood for the walnuts. He or she is the 'This is your palate speaking' Foodie. As Foodism marches on they are *held back* by their palate.

Here is a simple exercise to rid yourself of domination by your palate.

1 Go to the mirror. Open your mouth and FACE YOUR TONGUE. Stick it out and look at it. Isn't it a slob? You will thank nature that this organ is usually hidden in the privacy of your mouth.

2 To make your cure complete, stick your tongue up to your top teeth. Aaaaaaargh! Lolling like some Alien on your lower teeth is an engorged red lump with purple blood vessels trailing in skeins across it. The tip is suggestive and horribly alive. The rest of it looks more like liver, or worse. Honestly, Portnoy's experiment begins to look suspicious.

It's all right, you can put your tongue back. You've given this thing asylum in your mouth and that's all you need do for it. Never let it lead you astray again. Good food is what you *think* it is.

British Academy's banquets score Banq000.

Many of its members are either titled, flash or foreign. Of the foreigners, there is R. W. 'Johnny' Apple, London bureau chief of the *New York Times*, Tony Clifton, who does the same job for *Newsweek*, and Claude Jolly (who, curiously, is not a member of the French academy, only the British and Spanish).

But the big names of British gastronomy are absent: the lack of Elizabeth David, Alan Davidson, Jane Grigson, Fay Maschler and Claudia Roden, for five, brings the British Academy's score to Banqu00000000. Some of the top Foodies were asked, but a few refused to join, and others resigned after the first meeting, when they saw who their fellow 'academicians' were going to be. Others were not even invited.

More than half a dozen British Foodies and Grapies of repute *have* joined the Academy. Foodies in opposing camps are waiting to see.

America, naturally, has also been organising its Foodism. But Americans think BIG, and did not want to get bogged down in little self-elected 'Academies'. Instead, they invented a large self-elected Institute.

Enter David Segal.

In 1981 a group of Californian Foodies heard that the rump of the André Simon-Eleanor Lowenstein collection of historical cookery books had been sold by Mrs L's widower to David Segal, an enterprising academic economist, for a sum said to be $120,000. Segal did not actually have the cash, and he finessed the debt brilliantly, so that the collection ended up stored in a San Francisco bookshop, and the debt ended up with Napa Valley winemaker Lila Jaeger.

Enter Richard Graff, dynamic president of the excellent Chalone Vineyard of Monterey, who acted on behalf of Julia Child, and a British-educated Foodie in California called Jeremiah Tower, with

KNOCK KNOCK.
Who's there?
JUANITA.
Juanita who?
JUANITA TIME, DARLING,
JUANITA TIME.

strong promises of financial support from Danny Kaye – and, hey presto! a large debt was magicked into the grand-sounding American Institute of Wine & Food: acting president, Richard H. Graff.

'Wine' came first, because that's where the money – apart from Julia Child's and Danny Kaye's – was expected to come from. Then the Foodie Chancellor of the University of California at Santa Barbara, Robert Huttenback, was roped in. And before anyone knew it, the 'Institute' had been promised premises at Santa Barbara. But SB is a short aeroplane flight from San Fran, and the SF Foodies got hopping mad about the Institute being moved from the centre of civilisation. They want the address to remain 655 Sutter Street, San Francisco (415 474 0407).

The move to make the Institute international (and change its name) failed. British Foodie Alan Davidson was one of its

Four Dollars

The Journal of
GASTRONOMY

Published Quarterly by The American Institute of Wine & Food   *Vol. 1 Summer 1984*

Bacchus to the tune of $2 m. First issue of the American Institute of Wine & Food's quarterly, 1984. They have other grand plans

directors, and there was a long and international list of advisers, but the AIWF got more and more inward-looking. Gerald Asher left over the Santa Barbara issue, for example; and disillusion has struck most of the foreign advisers.

Finally, a professional administrator was hired to be President, at a reported salary of $100,000 a year. George Trescher, who came up with this particular plum, had already done a similar job for Radcliffe College, where he flopped thrillingly. AIWF publishes a handsomely-printed monthly newsletter, edited by James Beard's assistant, Jackie Mallorca. The parts of it that are not lifted from old cookery books and the like are written entirely in baby-talk ('To our rescue has come Mnemosyne (Ni-mos'e-ne), goddess of memory.... She whispered into the ear of Rosemary Manell, who passed it along to Julia Child, who announced it at our Annual Meeting in Santa Barbara, the simple mnemonic EIPPR [Education, Information, Publication, Preservation & Research]. Certainly, anyone can commit these five letters to memory') or American business jargon ('... affirms my belief that many professionals and dedicated amateurs ... the same interests and concerns that motivate the American Institute of Wine & Food, and it is my hope ... membership will quintuple ... considerable impetus to realizing that goal ... first phase goal of $2 million in hand by September of 1985.') Two million dollars! That cake certainly rose. But if you keep your eye on this kitchen, you will see more cooking like that in the next few years.

In 1984 the AIWF distributed a bit of the cake by publishing the first number of its scholarly journal, *Gastronomy*. Alan Davidson and M. F. K. Fisher were in the first issue – delicious! The rates of pay are equally appetising. Foodie writers passed the word around that for a long piece, *Gastronomy* pays the equivalent of 40 four-toque dinners.

PLAGIARISM PAYS – USUALLY

'Journalistic ethics are to real ethics what Velveeta is to cheese'

Non-Foodies think that the authors of most cookbooks spend all day plagiarising, dishing up basic recipes in a slightly new way. So it came as a surprise to them when high-up Foodie Richard Olney, from his home on a hill in France, slapped a lawsuit on high-up Foodie Richard Nelson (past president of the International Association of Cooking Schools, on the advisory board of the American Institute of Wine & Food, food columnist for the Portland *Oregonian*) in New York in February 1984, asking for $50,000 for infringement of copyright and $1 million in punitive damages, because he said Nelson had used 39 of Olney's recipes from *Simple French Food* in his new book, *Richard Nelson's American Cooking.*

It came as much more of a surprise to Foodies, who had got used to writers saying they had been plagiarised but acting as passive as bread sauce. As Foodie historian and stirrer Karen Hess had written in *Harper's*: 'Short of hard-core pornography there is no branch of publishing more cynical than that concerned with food – so much so that honest writing about it (and there is some) seems unprofessional to the trade. If I may steal the old joke about the Hungarian recipe that begins, "First, you steal a chicken …", then the first direction for writing a cookbook is, first you steal a lot of recipes.'

Purloin of beef

Authors whose recipes were plagiarised had beefed, but not gone to court since 1943, in America. In Britain, *Handbook of Copyright in British Publishing Practice* has only fourteen lines on reference works, including cookbooks. You cannot actually sue for plagiarism, only for breach of copyright. Cookery writers had not had the money to take on the multimillion-pound/dollar cookbook publishers. And the publishers themselves did not want to sue another publisher on behalf of one author: what if the horrible smell of grilled crumbs was in their own kitchen next time? Also, the top Foodie author-journalists stick together. Don't poke at the upper crust. 'They can wreck you,' Karen Hess told the Orlando *Sentinel*. 'All they have to do is just raise an eyebrow and say "Oh, *her*", or give a lousy review …' 'An odious old-boy system,' said another woman food writer.

But how *can* you copyright a recipe? There aren't a million ways to make an omelette. And that the directions for making a French region's traditional casserole should turn out to be owned by a Manhattan scribbler seems mad as well as unenforceable.

It is a problem the Foodie world is divided on. The women recipe-writers are on the whole less possessive than the men, if Julia Child and Jane Grigson are representative ('Because it's not women's only creation,' said another woman). Foodies are delighted there is to be a legal ruling, when the Olney case comes to court. Lawyers differ as to who will win. But they agree that the result will have an important bearing on the copyrighting of computer programmes. This leaves Foodies cold of course.

What the law seems to say is that ingredients and method are not copyrightable (unless they are so unusual as to be provably the property of one inventor who wrote them down). What is copyrightable is the words of the writer, and perhaps the shape or sequence of a book. The law treats cookery books like literature.

The words of the writer, the shape of the book! It had taken Eliza Acton and Mrs Beeton and Fannie Farmer years to get *rid* of vague poetic words from recipes and the odd arrangement of books, and to standardise the way of stating ingredients

Exhibit A M'lud, the plagiarised potato ✓

TEN RECIPES THAT SHOOK THE WORLD

10

RICHARD OLNEY'S

SPROUTS GRATIN

THE DISH
THAT LAUNCHED

A
$1,050,000
SUIT

This was the recipe that set off alarm bells in the head of Robert Shoffner, wine and food editor of *The Washingtonian*, when he read how to make the same dish in 1983 in a review copy of *Richard Nelson's American Cooking*. Shoffner is fond of Brussels sprouts, and he thought he saw similarities in Nelson's recipe to his favourite Richard Olney recipe from *Simple French Food*. The recipe is reproduced here by the kind and *explicit* permission of Richard Olney, whose breach of copyright suit values it at $26,923.07.

60 g (2 oz) lean bacon, cut into ½-in widths
30 g (1 oz) butter
500 g (1 lb) small, compact Brussels sprouts, outer leaves removed, parboiled 12 minutes, drained and coarsely chopped
salt, pepper
150 ml (¼ pt, ½ US cup) double cream
handful (⅓ US cup) breadcrumbs
butter (for gratin dish and surface)

Cook the bacon gently in butter until limp but not crisp, add the sprouts, season and toss over a medium-high flame for a minute. Spread into a buttered gratin dish, spoon the cream over the surface, sprinkle with breadcrumbs, and distribute paper-thin shavings of butter here and there. Cook for about 25 minutes in a 400 F, 200 C gas 6 oven.

and method. And this did give housewives the idea that recipes were a set of index cards, information you bought in books or copied from somewhere, and modified and gave away copies of – something serviceable and basic and your own.

Elizabeth David was the first post-war cook to set out her recipes differently, and she stamped her personality on them too strongly for anyone else to think they owned them. Perhaps this is why she has not been effectively plagiarised, though restaurateur Peter Langan wrote, 'She has had many imitators with a lot of gall and little talent who have lifted her recipes, pasting them into blank pages and changing a word or two here and there.' Elizabeth David's books encouraged cooking literacy and individuality. *The words of the writer* … Richard Olney acknowledges being inspired by her.

Richard Olney has a very individual way with words. They certainly seem to have stuck in Richard Nelson's mind. For instance, Richard Olney said in *Simple French Food*, 1974, that for Onion Pudding you bake the onions 'until swelled up and well browned.' *Richard Nelson's American Cooking*, 1983, says 'until puffed up and well browned'. In Creamed Broad Beans and Bacon, Richard O wrote 'turn the flame high for a few seconds to launch the cooking'; Richard N wrote 'turn the heat to high for a few seconds to launch the cooking'. In Sprouts Gratin, Richard O wrote 'cook the bacon gently in butter until limp but not crisp, add the sprouts, season, and toss over a medium-high flame for a minute'; Richard N wrote 'Cook the bacon lightly in butter until limp but not crisp. Add the sprouts, season, and toss over medium heat for a minute'. The ingredients and method were the same too. Oh, those copyrightable, individual *turns of phrase*.

W̲hat does 'Foodies' mean on a shopping list?
★ Dog meat.

Poached recipes

Robert Shoffner, scholarly wine and food editor of *The Washingtonian* magazine, was the first to notice the similarities between the two books in November 1983. Once alerted to the likeness to Olney's recipes, he looked up other books in his library. He found in Nelson's book 74 other recipes he thought he could trace the source of: 40 from *North Italian Cooking* by Francesco Ghedini, published posthumously in 1973, eight from three James Beard books (James Beard had written the introduction to Nelson's book, which raises the question: do Foodies just endorse books, or do they read them first?), five from two Craig Claiborne books, and 21 others from sources he thought he recognised – making in all almost a quarter of Richard Nelson's book. Robert Shoffner told Richard Olney of his discoveries in November 1983, and the fat was in the fire.

Richard Olney's publishers, Atheneum, would not sue, so his own lawyer Joseph Santora did, naming Nelson and Nelson's publishers, New American Library. Nelson says NAL offered Olney an out-of-court settlement of a percentage of the royalties from the book, but Olney refused.

Of course he refused! He's not a whore, he's Richard Olney, the Big O of the Foodie world. And apart from the principle, there is a lot of money at stake here for all Foodie writers. A famous cookery author can get a book contract worth six figures, but one of the standard clauses is that all the material is original. And once it's published as your copyright, royalties will come rolling in for as long as the copyright lasts (50 years, in Britain). To accept a measly mess of pottage for undermining the system would be suicide.

Richard Nelson still couldn't see what all the fuss was about. He was 58, and had been a cookery teacher for 35 years, using recipes transferred to sheets of paper. It was the index-card syndrome. 'To think that that man thinks I sat down and copied recipes out of his book is absolutely absurd,' he said. 'All cooks get recipes the same way. They're passed around.' His feelings towards James Beard, who had written praisingly in the introduction but later admitted that he felt the book contained borrowings, seemed to have been that the shit had hit the fan. 'That snake.'

See you later, tasty data

A really successful recipe goes through four stages: **1** originator; **2** data; **3** dissemination; **4** 'Do you like me in this new jacket?'

Richard Olney is unusual in being an inventor of recipes, an *originator*, rather than compiling anthologies of other people's recipes. Elizabeth David and Claudia Roden are not originators or anthologists – they are anthropologists.

For *A Book of Middle Eastern Food*, 1968, Claudia Roden stood beside the stoves of women from Egypt, Syria, Lebanon, Turkey, Iran, Morocco and Tunisia and noted faithfully how they cooked. But it is inevitable that when a field-worker publishes a book, a typing ocean of cookery writers, journalists, teachers and

F·O·O·D·I·E·B·O·R·E·S

THE OLIVE OIL BORE

The olive oil bore actually smells of the stuff. Someone taught him years ago in a little mountain village in Italy that the right way to buy oil is to rub some into the palm of your hand, then cup your hands and inhale deeply. Now his pores, his pans and his kitchen all ooze olives. Mmmmmmm puh puh puh puh. He loves olive oil – the only oil that is extracted purely by mechanical means, without chemicals and without heat – if it is virgin.

'Extra virgin' says the bore's tin. Isn't that like being more dead? But the bore understands that 'virgin oil' has up to 4 per cent oleic acid content, whereas 'extra virgin' has no more than 1 per cent acid. Acid is the criterion the professionals use to buy olive oil – the less, the finer.

Virgin olive oil has character – too much character, think some. There are British supermarket chains that do not even stock virgin oil but have only 'pure' olive oil on their shelves. In oil, pure is definitely not virgin. Pure olive oil is a BLEND of cold-pressed virgin oil and REFINED olive oil, that has been treated with an alkali to neutralise the acids, then heated and filtered through charcoal or earths to remove its colour (too vivid) and then steam-stripped in a vacuum to remove its taste (too strong).

The French and the Italians use most of their own virgin oil. A tiny amount makes its way to Britain and America. Spain is a much bigger exporter of olive oil, but no longer to Britain and the US, though they are trying to get their oil through the door again. Spanish virgin used to be rank, but no longer seems to have the old kick. This is because, though all oil is made from ripe olives (the yield from unripe ones is at least 20 per cent smaller), the Spanish no longer leave their ripe olives to fall on the ground and rot before collecting them, and they now spray the trees to remove the taste of insect pests from the finished oil. Namby-*pamby*.

Nicoise olive oil has its partisans. But Foodies know (because Elizabeth David has told them so) that the best olive oil comes from the estate of Mrs Leslie Zyw at Poggio Lamentano, Castagneto Carducci (Livorno), Italy. It can be from Haynes, Hanson & Clark, wine merchants, 17 Lettice Street, London SW6 and from Adam Zyw, 1 Hawthornbank Lane, Dean Village, Edinburgh EH4 3BH. American bores get their oil from Mrs Zyw on location and bring it back in their suitcases.

The oil bore suffered a blow to his pride when it was proved that olive oil does not differ from year to year. In 1935, Vyvyan Holland, Oscar Wilde's son, had started a club in London for tasting vintage tinned sardines. Its members believed, until some damn chemist's report, that olive oil like wine has good years, which makes the sardines tinned in that year better. *F**** chemists.

But olive oil is still romantic, because it's in danger. In countries like Greece, wizened peasants prepared to do the work are literally dying out, which leads to the dreaded commercial processes.

The oil bore is enraged when a restaurant serves less than virgin oil, and has been known to bring a vial of his own to avoid their vile stuff when dressing a salad. He has recently become a walnut or hazel-nut oil bore – wonderful in vinaigrette. He claims to be able to distinguish Berry's huile de noix from Bergerac's huile de noix. He says he can tell the approximate provenance of any nut oil (he's just acquired some almond oil) by its colour, perfume, taste. Puh puh puh puh.

---

housewives copy the recipes on to their index cards. They are now the right size to be *data*, and part of the information explosion.

One typical American newspaper of the sex-'n'-sports type has two eight-page colour sections a week devoted to food. The demand for recipes is literally insatiable. So as for agonising over who *wrote* the recipe before it became data – who has the time?

Within a few years, the recipe is *disseminated* all over the Foodie world. Then, some writer, journalist, teacher or housewife publishes her own anthology, using the data 'discovered' in the course of her work – though in a smarter, shinier jacket than the anthropologist's book.

Anthologists are a lot more worldly than anthropologists, who still believe you have to spend months finding out how people actually cook in the place the recipe comes from.

The cash-in cookery writer is more highly motivated (in the words of the market) than the ordinary anthologist to *change* traditional recipes. If a book, say *The Cookery of Anonybia*, sells well, other publishers commission quick cash-in books on the same country, usually cooked up from a dozen of X's Anonybian recipes, a handful of Y's Anonybian recipes, a sprinkling of Z's Anonybian recipes – all with *little changes* to evade copyright. After Claudia Roden wakened interest in Middle Eastern food, several books and articles on the region appeared, in which traditional recipes had undergone *little changes*.

Claudia Roden says that she is happy to see her records of recipes which belong to a particular country, town, village or community, passed around, and she thinks it is fine if cooks experiment and change them to suit their taste. 'But although there are no *standard* recipes in countries where they don't use cookery books and where dishes are passed down in the family – and although there are many versions of a dish – there are just so many and no more. When people from a different culture make up their own original version without bothering to find out, it usually has nothing to do with reality. With so many recipes now lifted from one book to another each with "one small change", nobody will know what the truth is any more.'

As well as the danger to the truth, Claudia Roden is hurt and angry that Arto der Haroutunian, in his books *Middle Eastern Cookery* (1982) and *Complete Arab Cookery* (1982) has a great many of the same recipes as hers (some of which had never been in print before), similarly described and including some of the mistakes – even to leaving out an essential ingredient – that she corrected in her second edition. He also included some of the same poems, background material and historical observations. As a writer who gathered her material physically, Mrs Roden feels 'He has stolen my shadow.'

Paula Wolfert, an American scholar, cookery teacher and writer, has had a similar dispiriting experience. Some of her pupils took down her recipes and put seven of them unacknowledged in a book, *Connecticut à la Carte*. This won the American cookery book Oscar, a Taste-maker Award, for 1982. Paula Wolfert said: 'I wouldn't have cared except those women won the Tastemaker Award – we (professional cookery writers) don't have any other awards.'

Cooks of other people's books – food journalist

Food journalists have often cried 'Thief!' about recipes. The only unusual aspect of Richard Olney's thinking Richard Nelson has copied 39 of his recipes is that Olney is suing. All the cookery writers here are alleged by reputable journalists to have had a book or books robbed by other cookery writers – not just Nelson – of a number of recipes. The reaction of the 'victims' varies between very hot and lukewarm, with Julia Child representing the writers who don't mind.

FRANCESCO GHEDINI

FRANCESCO GHEDINI
40 recipes from *North Italian Cooking*
He won't object in person because his book was published posthumously.

RICHARD OLNEY
39 recipes from *Simple French Food* allegedly recognised in *Richard Nelson's American Cooking*
'What irritated me is not that this idiot lifted ideas; one publishes ideas to be shared. What irritated me most of all is that he lifted my own language and writing style.' Through his lawyer Joseph Santora: 'Copyright infringement and unfair competition': $50,000 in damages, $1 m in punitive damages.

JULIA CHILD
21 recipes
'Frankly I don't care. Once they're published it's like the good old three-star chefs – once they do things, everyone copies it.'

JULIA CHILD

JAMES BEARD
16 recipes
'There can be a similar approach to a recipe, but I don't think any two people write in exactly the same way. I think it's very hard sometimes to tell – if you've been in this business as long as I have – who wrote a recipe.'

CRAIG CLAIBORNE
9 recipes
'I think it's appalling, unmitigated gall to steal something of mine and use it.'

RICHARD OLNEY

PAULA WOLFERT
7 recipes
'You don't steal. Period. That's what I think it's about. . . . I think recipes generally have a source, and we food writers must be scrupulous about assigning credit.'

CLAUDIA RODEN
Many recipes from *Middle Eastern Food*
'It is tragic when food writers add or take away an ingredient to make a lifted recipe "their own", and pass it off as authentic. They are falsifying tradition. This is how a culture ends up garbled and destroyed in the lap of another.'

CLAUDIA RODEN

say all these writers were robbed

PAULA WOLFERT

CRAIG CLAIBORNE

JAMES BEARD

The Olney/Nelson suit has prompted many American food writers to rake over the ashes of an earlier quarrel.

The case of Pamela Harlech of British *Vogue* was journalist v journalists, and as Katha Pollitt said in *The Nation*, 'Journalistic ethics are to real ethics what Velveeta is to cheese.' In Lady Harlech's *Feast Without Fuss*, published by Atheneum in 1977, there were said to be 165 unacknowledged recipes from *Gourmet*. The authors of the recipes, as analysed by Paula Wolfert and William Bayer in *New York* magazine, included James Beard, Jane Grigson and Evan Jones. James Beard raged, but *Gourmet* did not sue. And when Lady Harlech's next book came out in 1981, *Pamela Harlech's Practical Guide to Cooking, Entertaining & Household Management*, James Beard praised it. The upper crust is intact and impressive.

Jane Grigson thinks too much fuss is made about plagiarism. Julia Child is similarly generous, and was the first to telephone Richard Nelson to give him her support.

It is undeniably true that using a cook's recipes is flattering to the creator. Only the court case will tell if publishing them is the most expensive form of flattery.

This report on plagiarism was largely plagiarised from the work of various excellent American Foodie journalists: principally Liz Logan of the *Orlando Sentinel*, but also Robert Shoffner of *The Washingtonian*, Peggy Katalinich of *Newsday*, Alf Collins of the *Seattle Times*, Jane Salzfass Freiman of the *New York Post*, Candy Sagon of the *Dallas Times Herald*, Barbara Durbin and Paul Manley of the *Oregonian*, and Karen Brooks – and you must admit that too many cooks have made a spicy broth.

Old Jewish food joke
When Marilyn Monroe was married to Arthur Miller, his mother always made matzo ball soup. After the tenth time, Marilyn said, 'Gee Arthur, these matzo balls are pretty nice, but isn't there any other part of the matzo you can eat?'

Foodie cookery schools

Places one can learn to cook have increased by 1000 per cent in the last five years, if you count all the château and palazzo courses where the amateur can perfect her knowledge of charcuterie, pâtisserie, eau de vie or merely joie de vivre. Famous chefs are the pin-ups of female Foodies, like ski instructors or tennis pros to less sexy women. Michel Guérard, Roger Vergé, Pierre Troisgros (plus, it must be admitted, other big names without bulging white hats – Paula Wolfert, Claudia Roden, Ken Hom, Marcella Hazan, Simca) are constantly wooed to teach a week's course at this place or that to American women, many of whom make a career of tasting the cookery classes of Europe. Meanwhile, other Americans are making a career setting up cookery classes in Europe. The brochure may show the Mediterranean, the booking is in Manhattan.

Foodies who want a professional training are wary of getting immured in the wrong cookery school, the sort where stone walls do a Parisian make. There are two main types of these old fortresses, at opposite ends of the social scale. One is the catering college or vocational college, which trains future chefs to do old-fashioned French (or, in America, German) style cooking. The other is the school for ladies, which teaches the same dishes to debs and divorcees. *Culinary Arts News*, an American quarterly edited by Camille Cook [yes!] which reports on cookery schools, calls them Toque Blanche schools and Cordon Bleu schools. To the Foodie, they are alike and equally the enemy – 'Fossils!', 'Flour and butter mountains!'

Your sort of college is La Varenne and its equivalents. You accept that less flour costs more money. *Culinary Arts News* pointed out in the winter of 1983 that to get a grand diplôme at La Varenne costs more than twice as much as a training at

the Culinary Institute of America and 260 per cent as much as at Tante Marie in England. But that just illustrates the point. The CIA is a catering college, the Tante Marie teaches ladies. The proof of the pudding is in the eating – you will find, when applying for a job, that Foodie restaurateurs *do* prefer graduates of Foodie schools. Such as the following.

Foodie-approved cookery schools

To keep abreast of courses, read *Culinary Arts News* ($25 a year – add postage if outside USA – Box 153, Western Spring, Illinois 60558, USA. 312 246 5845).

Britain

Main courses

● La Petite Cuisine, 50 Hill Rise, Richmond, Surrey. (01) 940 7583. Run by Lyn Hall, who has worked with top chefs in France. An intensive 3-month diploma course for 20 students starts Jan, April, Sept. Good training, and best professional demonstration kitchen in Britain (half-day classes for the public), but school does not aim to train chefs. No accommodation (can arrange it). £2,000 a term.

● Leith's School of Food and Wine, 36a Notting Hill Gate, London W11. (01) 229 0177. Prue Leith founded this but Caroline Waldegrave and Sally Proctor run it for her as joint principals. The one-year diploma course for 48 pupils starts in October (there are shorter, more amateur courses). No accommodation (they will help find it). The teachers trained at Leith's, Cordon Bleu, and other schools. The diploma includes a wine certificate: £3,640 plus VAT.

Small courses

● Ken Lo's Memories of China Cookery School, 14 Eccleston Street, London SW1. (01) 730 7734. Day or evening demonstrations of Chinese cooking. £14 each lesson day (£65 for five), £15 evening (£70 for five).

● Jane Mann's School of Cookery, 10 Trawley Road, London SW10. (01) 736 5108. 3-month advanced course (non-boarding) starts April, 12 students. They get a certificate as being of restaurant, though not chef, standard (also beginners' courses). Mrs Mann is Leith-trained. £1,320 plus VAT.

● Claudia Roden, 8 Wild Hatch, London NW11. (01) 455 7898. Occasional 2-day courses on Middle Eastern food: about £50.

● Miller Howe Hotel, Windermere, Cumbria. (09662) 2536. 5-day courses by the extrovert John Tovey, whose hotel is in the Foodie address book, demonstrating his own recipes. Price includes meals and room: Sun–Thurs, £250.

I'm a big fish in a big pond. Paul Bocuse often demonstrates in Japan, but here, he shows loup de mer en croûte to Professor Tsuji's students at Lièrgues

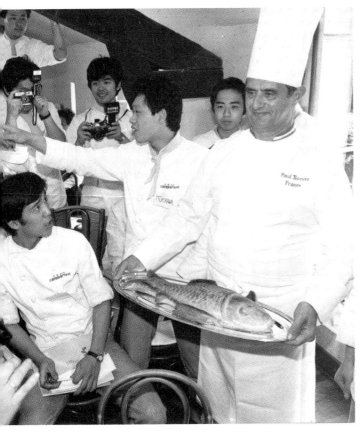

At leith I'm trying. Students at Leith's in London learn to make meringues

• Sonia Stevenson's Sauce Cookery, The Horn of Plenty, Tavistock, Devon. (0822) 832528. Another Foodie chef who teaches. Five people at a time, staying locally, eating at the restaurant. Price is inclusive: Fri–Sun, £185; Fri–Tues, £265.

France

Main course

• Ecole de Cuisine La Varenne, 34 rue Saint-Dominique, Paris 7e. (1) 705 1016. Founded by Anne Willan from Yorkshire, principal is Susy Davidson, an American, but classes in French (with translation). 36-week grand diplôme for 20 pupils starts Oct. There are about 20 other pupils doing shorter courses. Nouvelle and classic techniques taught, with 6 weeks' career training – restaurant management and so on. No accommodation (will help find it). Demonstration kitchen: public can come if there are places. Diploma course: 116,500F/$15,535. 10 places for student trainees – no fee, masses of work, grand diplôme.

Small courses

• Marie-Blanche de Broglie Cooking School, 18 avenue de la Motte-Picquet, Paris 7e. (1) 551 3634. Day- and week-courses in English, French and Spanish run by Princess M-B de B in her Paris appartement most of the year: intensive Mon–Fri diploma course, 3,250F. Boarding courses at her Normandy château in Aug and first week Sept: Sun night to Sat morning, $1,000/8,000F.
• École Lenôtre, 40 rue Pierre Curie, Hameau des Gatines, 78370 Plaisir. (3) 055 8112. Various 5-day courses in French from a chef: eg pâtisserie, 5,300F, including breakfast.
• Paris en Cuisine, 78 rue de la Croix-Nivert, Paris 15e. (1) 250 0423. Courses (in English) and tours arranged by American Foodie Robert Noah, whose programmes include a 4-day course with Pierre Troisgros in Roanne: 16,750F. Day tours, from 150F.
• Madeleine Kamman, an American, ran courses in Annecy for professionals but now does 2-week summer seminars there only, for 6 students, intensive, in English, with excursions to 3-star chefs. Kamman Classes, Spencer Associates Inc, 130 S Bemiston, St Louis, MO 63105, USA.
• La Grande Carte d'Aquitaine, Chamber of Commerce and Industry, 12 place de la Bourse, 33076 Bordeaux. (5) 690 91 28. As well as the International Institute of Wine and Spirits, the Chamber of Commerce runs two cookery courses of a week each year, spring and autumn, for pros, taking them to visit Michel Guérard, André Daguin and other near-by chefs.

What makes Foodie salads always praised?
★ The Emperor's New Dressing.

KNOCK KNOCK.
Squawk squawk.
WAITER, MY QUAIL'S EGG
HAS AN EAGLE IN IT!

Lièrgues again, 30 kilometres from Lyon. Eighty Japanese students attend the equivalent of a post-graduate college for chefs

Other cookery courses can be arranged for groups. Prices include accommodation and most meals.
● Yetabo, Pailly 89140 Pont-sur-Yonne, (86) 663228. Cooking (la grande cuisine bourgeoise) and language school in an 18th-C farmhouse in Burgundy. Teaching in French by Jean La Roux. From 5,687F a week, including meals and lodging.
● Roger Vergé's L'Ecole du Moulin, Mougins, 06250 Alpes-Maritimes. (93) 757824. Or The World of Oz, 3 East 54th Street, New York, NY 10022. (212) 751 3250. 5-day course in French (with translation), also trips. With accommodation, and meals at Vergé's Le Moulin de Mougins: 4,200F.

Italy
Small courses
● Marcella Hazan School of Classic Italian Cooking. Booking: PO Box 285, Circleville, NY 10919. (914) 361 3503. Week-courses in English run in Bologna by Marcella Hazan and her husband Victor, author of *Italian Wine*, April–Sept. Price includes most meals but not accommodation.
● Giuliano Bugialli's Cooking in Florence. Booking: Mrs Bernard Berman, 2830 Gordon Street, Allentown, PA 18104, USA. (215) 435 2451. Courses in English of varying length by Giuliano Bugialli: in Florence, Montecatini Terme (week) and tours. June–Oct but minus Aug. Price includes meals and lodging: 6 days in Florence, $1250; 1 week in Florence, $1500; tour, $2450.
● Hotel Cipriani, Isola della Giudecca 10, Venice. (041) 707744. Marcella Hazan and other famous cooks teach courses here. Prices include accommodation and meals, eg a Marcella Hazan week in Oct 1984 was $1,850/£1,291.90. (Booking for Marcella Hazan: see above.)

Japan
Main course
● Ecole Technique Hôtelière Tsuji, Abeno, Osaka. (6) 623 7741. Professional course, April to March, for 2,500 students run by Professor Tsuji with a staff of 220. Pupils from all over Japan, also some Chinese and Koreans. The course is in four parts: Japanese, Chinese, Western and pâtisserie. The school also has an establishment where 80 Tsuji graduates can complete their expertise in France, the Centre de Perfectionnement at Lièrgues near Villefranche sur Saône.

USA
Main courses
● The New School, 27 West 34th Street, New York, NY 10001. (212) 947 7097. 18-week certificate course to turn out fast-cooked pros. Classes of up to 90 start every 6 weeks. Several La Varenne graduates teaching, none from Culinary Institute of America. Last 6 weeks is training in the school's restaurant. No accommodation. $4,200.
● California Culinary Academy, 215 Fremont, San Francisco, Ca 94105, USA. (415) 543 2765. Principal

is Danielle Carlisle, who founded it in 1977. 16-month diploma course for pros; terms start Sept, Jan, May. 250 students in the school. Last 6 weeks is training in the school's 200-seater restaurant. No accommodation. $2,300 a term.

The central body
● The International Association of Cooking Schools, 1001 Connecticut Avenue NW, Suite 800, Washington DC 20036 (202) 293 7716, has over 700 members, whose names and adresses they will supply. The difficulty is to know which are the good (the Foodie) ones. After this year, they should all be morally good – the Association intends to 'impose appropriate sanctions' on members caught stealing recipes from other cooks. In 1984 they announced: 'The International Association of Cooking Schools does not condone the practice of the unauthorized and unattributed use of the recipes and other intellectual property of another. Recent media attention to several instances of alleged misappropriation or misattribution of such materials have highlighted the need for strict adherence to the highest ethical standards in this regard.' Good for you, IACS! But you won't find it easy to keep *this* surface clean. (See *Plagiarism*, p 108.)

EXORCISING A FOODIE

If the creature's stayed too long with you
Then make an EXORCISM ROUX.
Of butter take a quarter pound,
Of flour take a lot.
Stir in curry powder
Over low heat in a pot.
Pour in stock from stock cubes,
Saying to your guest:
'This makes a most delicious sauce
For a cold chicken breast.
My mother taught it to me.
And since *you're* staying here
I'm going to make my own ice cream –
I flavour it with beer.'
At once the frightened Foodie
Will make excuse and go.
So *don't forget this recipe*.
It's a ruse you need to know.

PART FOUR

A FOODIE WHO'S WHO

LE RÈGLEMENT DU CHEF

Article I - Le Chef a raison.

Article II - Le Chef a toujours raison.

Article III - Même si un subalterne a raison, c'est l'article I qui s'applique.

Article IV - Le Chef ne mange pas, il se nourrit.

Article V - Le Chef ne boit pas, il goûte.

Article VI - Le Chef ne dort pas, il se repose.

Article VII - Le Chef n'est jamais en retard, il est retenu.

Article VIII - Le Chef ne quitte jamais son service, il est appelé.

Article IX - Le Chef n'entretient pas de relations avec sa secrétaire, il l'éduque.

Article X - Le Chef ne lit jamais son journal pendant le service il l'étudie.

Article XI - On entre dans le bureau du Chef avec des idées personnelles, on en ressort avec les idées du Chef.

Article XII - Le Chef reste le Chef, même en caleçon de bain.

Article XIII - Plus on critique le Chef, moins on a de primes.

Article XIV - Le Chef est obligé de penser pour les autres.

A

ELIZA ACTON (1799–1859) is the first and most plagiarised of the Victorian cookery writers. Her *Modern Cookery for Private Families* was published in 1845: Elizabeth David has called it 'the greatest cookery book in our language'. Her recipes represent the taste of pre-industrial England, which was changing as she wrote (eg Bird's custard powder appeared in 1840).
& p 10, 108, 120

ALI-BAB is the pseudonym of Henry Babinski, who wrote the important *Gastronomie Pratique*, subtitle *Etudes culinaires*, published in 1928. He says in this very well-written book of over 1100 recipes that he discovered food at 25, when working as a mining engineer in 'les pays perdus' – or rather, he began to invent recipes and study the basic principles of cooking, because the food he was offered was so bad. Some of the conclusions he came to are similar to what the nouvelle cuisine chefs believe today. Ali-Bab says 'C'est l'étude des associations végétales et végéto-animales qui constitue la base des créations gastronomiques.' He calls it 'la science du bon'. An American edition, in the 1970s, was cut by almost half.
& p 10, 42–43

FERNANDE ALLARD, born in Burgundy, has been in the restaurant business for more than 30 years, having started at 20, when she and her husband opened Allard in Paris. She is the daughter-in-law and inheritor of the recipes of Mère Allard. Allard is 'the last and most honest of the great Parisian bistros', according to Gault-Millau, who commend her chocolate charlotte: 'so good you would sell your soul to the devil for a slice.' *Address*: 41 rue St André des Arts, 75006 Paris.
T: (1) 326 4823.

PIERRE ANDROUËT (b 1915) 's *Guide du Fromage* (1971) is the last word on cheese. He also runs Androuët's restaurant in Paris, where you can eat cheese for every course. A Foodie ought to do this once; but once is enough. *Address*: 41 rue d'Amsterdam, 75008 Paris.
T: (1) 874 2690.
& p 42–43, 64

GERALD ASHER (b 1932) is a Foodie's Grapie. He writes a regular column on wine for *Gourmet*, the American Foodie mag, in which he describes the food that accompanied the wine in a way that, to Foodies, raises him above a mere wine writer. He started as a London wine merchant but now lives in San Francisco, where he directs the Mosswood Wine Co for Foremost-McKesson. He presides each spring over New York's Four Seasons

Foodies don't often talk about the Last Supper – last meals are not a nice thought. But if you did pick your Leader and twelve disciples, it might be these, as drawn for the article in Harpers & Queen (1982) which christened Foodies. (That Judas Paul Levy should be painted out)

restaurant's Barrel Tasting – the American Grapie's most important annual do.
& p 70, 107

B

CHARLES BARRIER (b 1916) is the chef-patron of the restaurant at Tours that bears his name. He is one of the great names of nouvelle cuisine, but at 67, in December 1983, he was convicted of fraud and sentenced to six months in prison. His crime, in the words of the *International Herald Tribune*, was to 'pick up restaurant bills that his guests had paid and then discarded, usually on the table, when they left. He then destroyed the bills

Claudia Roden ★   Arabella Boxer ★   Richard Olney ★   Julia Child ★   Anne Willan ★   ★ Caroline Conran

and failed to record the amounts in his records.' Foodies were stunned that a charge for this very common practice should be brought against such a hero.

Barrier's earlier misfortunes included the loss of his third Michelin star. Famous dishes made by him include his own smoked salmon, warm oysters with endives, and baby pigeon cooked with an infusion of thyme flowers, garlic and preserved cabbage. *Address*: 101 Avenue Tranchée, 37100 Tours. T: (47) 542039.
& p 60–61, 62, 63

JAMES BEARD (b 1903, Portland, Oregon) is the Grand Old Man of American Foodism. He published his first cookery book, *Hors d'Oeuvres and Canapés*, in 1940; by the Fifties he had started giving cookery classes – in what has since become the kitchen of Lutèce in New York. A bachelor, James Beard has encouraged and helped many younger cookery writers and chefs. One of these writers, Jackie Mallorca, helps him with his syndicated column, which appears in papers throughout the USA.

Other books include *The James Beard Cookbook* (1959), *James Beard's American Cookery* (1972), *Beard on Bread* (1973) and *The New James Beard* (1981).

The sharp-tongued food historians John and Karen Hess write: 'Of the three dominant figures in the gourmet biz – Child, Claiborne, and Beard – only Beard seems from his work actually to enjoy cooking and to write well about it.' But Beard, a former actor, who is good at appearing in commercials, is also heavily into Foodiebiz. Endorsements by him for Iowa steaks have recently appeared in American magazines.
& p 42–43, 78, 99, 104, 107, 110, 112, 113, 133, 138

SIMONE BECK, 'Simca' (b 1904, Normandy) is best known to Foodies as Julia Child's collaborator on *Mastering the Art of French Cooking* (vol I, 1961; vol II, 1970). This book grew out of the Paris cookery school, the Ecole de Trois Gourmandes, which Simone Beck, Julia Child and Louisette Bertholle started in 1951. (LB helped write the first volume of *Mastering*, then dropped out.) Before going into Foodieteach, Simca had been a heroine of the Resistance, then a Paris hostess. Henri-Paul Pellaprat taught her to cook at the Cordon Bleu, then *she* hired *him* to cook for dinner parties.

Elizabeth David ★   Alan Davidson ★   ★ Elisabeth Lambert Ortiz   ★ Fay Maschler   ★ Jane Grigson   ★ Prue Leith   ★ Paul Levy

She has written two books on her own, *Simca's Cuisine* (1972) and *New Menus from Simca's Cuisine* (1980).
& p 114, 123, 137

MARION ROMBAUER BECKER

(1903–1975) was the daughter and co-author of Irma S. Rombauer (d 1962) of St Louis, who wrote *The Joy of Cooking* and had it privately printed in 1931. In 1936 mother and daughter enlarged the book to its present encyclopaedic format. They were well-off, well-educated Americans of Austro-Hungarian descent, used to having servants, but their book became the bible of the middle-class housewife who could not expect to employ domestic help. It is to Americans of the second half of the twentieth century what Fannie Farmer was to the first.

Foodies consider that the 1975 *Joy of Cooking* is almost up to date. It introduced couscous and rijsttafel to middle America, but it is still thickening sauces with flour.
& p 27, 42–43, 128

ISABELLA BEETON

(1836–1865), the best-known English cookery writer, was educated in Heidelberg. She was already a journalist and pianist when she married Samuel Orchard Beeton, publisher of the *Queen* among other magazines, in 1856. Her huge work on the whole subject of *Household Management* was published by him in 24 monthly instalments between 1859 and 1861. It made her name a household word. She said in the preface to the first collected edition of 1861: 'I must frankly own, that if I had known, beforehand, that this book would have cost me the labour which it has, I should never have been courageous enough to attempt it.' In the cookery chapters, she 'attempted to give ... an intelligible arrangement to every recipe, a list of the *ingredients*, a plain statement of the *mode* of preparing each dish, and a careful estimate of its *cost*, the *number* of people for whom it is *sufficient*, and

Mrs Beeton at 24

the time when it is *seasonable*.' Only Eliza Acton before her had tried to be systematic in setting out recipes.

Mrs Beeton imposed order on existing material. She had no time to invent recipes of her own, or even to cook more than a small proportion of the ones in her book. She acknowledged that her recipes came largely from readers of *The Englishwomen's Domestic Magazine*.

She died at 28, of puerperal fever after the birth of her fourth son. Biographies: Nancy Spain (1948), Montgomery Hyde (1951), Sarah Freeman (1977): *Isabella and Sam*.
& p 10, 13, 42–43, 44, 108

LÉA BIDAUT,

'Léa de Lyon', is the last of Lyon's mères, as women chefs are called there. Her predecessors Mère Guy, Mère Filloux and Mère Brazier presided over their stoves in the small, unpretentious restaurants that the Lyonnais call bouchons, which serve dishes such as Léa Bidaut's own tripe dish, tablier de sapeur. When it is on the menu Chez Léa (formal name: La Voûte), it consists of beef tripe, simmered in a court bouillon, then coated in breadcrumbs and fried in oil, and eaten with a mayonnaise flavoured with white wine, shallots and tarragon. *Address*: 11 Place A.-Gourju, 69002 Lyon. T: (7) 842 0133.

MARIUS BISE,

'Père Bise' (d 1968) founded the restaurant that bears his name at Talloires, on Lake Annecy in the Haute Savoie, in 1928. By 1931 his wife's cooking had won three Michelin stars. He was a friend of Fernand Point and had similar habits – they drank six bottles of champagne between them when they spent a day together. His son, François, is the present chef of the restaurant; its specialities still include the fish of the lake: trout, perch and the rare omble chevalier, Arctic char. *Address*: Auberge du Père Bise, 74290 Talloires. T: (50) 607201.
& p 54, 60–61

GEORGES BLANC

(b 1943) is chef-patron of his family's establishment, La Mère Blanc at Vonnas near Mâcon; as the name implies, the cooking is in the Lyonnais tradition. His enormous wine list impresses even those wine-anti-snobs the Foodies. *Address*: p 59.
& p 52, 60–61, 98

RAYMOND BLANC

(b 1949, Besançon) is the chef-owner of Le Manoir aux Quat' Saisons in Oxfordshire, the only British restaurant-with-rooms comparable to the great French establishments. Blanc is the youngest of England's important chefs, but he received a star from Michelin almost as soon as he set up on his own with the Quat' Saisons restaurant in Oxford in 1977. This he now runs as a bistro, having moved his main ambition, and his two Michelin stars, to the manoir in 1984. He is self-taught. *Address*: p 81.
& p 52, 77, 90, 135

SONIA BLECH

(b 1940), née Romano, a Frenchwoman with an Italian father, is the chef at Mijanou in London, owned and run by her with her British husband Neville, an accountant. Sonia Blech is the only woman chef of the first rank in London. She studied for a career in linguistics, but gave it up to cook after the Bleches bought the Crown Inn,

Whitebrook, near Monmouth in Wales. Her efforts won a star in Michelin, the only one in Wales. Since the Bleches set up in London in 1980, however, and applied the higher standards of experience, Michelin have quirkily withheld their favours.

Sonia Blech's cooking is original and features fruit and nuts in unexpected places. Her menus emphasise vegetables, and her gâteau salé has been copied by other restaurants. Mijanou is close enough to Parliament to attract half the Cabinet to lunch there some days. *Address*: 143 Ebury Street, London SW1. T: (01) 730 4099.
& p 32, 81

PAUL BOCUSE (b 1926 at

Collonges au Mont d'Or, near Lyon) is the most famous chef in the world, and synonymous with nouvelle cuisine. Bocuse was the name that stuck in

Paul Bocuse deserves a big bouquet

people's minds, with Guérard, when the style being practised by a group of Fernand Point's former pupils was christened by Gault and Millau in 1973. As fervently as any Catholic longs to visit Lourdes, Foodies long to visit Bocuse's restaurant in his birthplace.

Bocuse is largely responsible for the improved financial and social position of the chef. It is he who has made them like movie stars. And if he does quite well out of Foodiebiz himself, why should anyone complain?

Bocuse's *Cuisine du Marché*, published in France in 1976, then in

translation in America (1977) and Britain (1978), acknowledges using the recipes of Point, and says of the recipes of Alfred Guérot that they are 'the most perfect in existence, and in this book I draw on them extensively. In cooking one does not invent.' But Bocuse is an honest man. He is often away from his kitchen, so his menu frankly credits his chef, Roger Jaloux. *Address*: p 59.
& p 19, 30, 38, 42–43, 52, 56, 60–61, 62, 98, 100, 105, 124, 130

X. MARCEL BOULESTIN

(1878–1943), born in Poitiers, first worked as a writer (he was 'secretary' to Colette's Willy), then as an interior decorator. His Anglophilia led him to London. It was purely by chance that he wrote his first cookery book, *Simple French Cooking* (1923) at the invitation of a publisher. Following its success, and the popularity of his articles for *Vogue* and the *Evening Standard*, he opened a Restaurant Français in Panton Street, then launched Boulestin, in the present premises in Southampton Street, Covent Garden, in 1927.

He also gave the first television cookery programme on the BBC, in 1937.

JEAN-ANTHELME BRILLAT-SAVARIN (1755–1826), Foodie

philosopher, became the mayor of his home town of Belly, north of Chambéry, in 1793. He was a lawyer and gastronome. At the outbreak of the

Illustration from 'La Physiologie du Goût'

revolution he left France, first for Switzerland and then for America, where he gave French lessons and played the violin in a theatre orchestra. In 1796 he returned to France, and in 1825 published the book by which he is known, *La Physiologie du Goût*. It includes the famous aphorisms (in M. F. K. Fisher's great translation): 'Animals feed themselves; men eat; but only wise men know the art of eating', 'The destiny of nations depends on how they nourish themselves', and 'Tell me what you eat, and I shall tell you what you are'.
& p 129

WILLIAM BUCKLAND (1784–

1856), English geologist, mineralogist and Dean of Westminster, was a Foodie pervert. He said that until he ate a bluebottle, he had always thought 'that the taste of mole was the most repulsive he knew' (according to Catherine Caulfield in *The Emperor of the United States of America*, 1981). On being shown a liquefying relic of the blood of a holy martyr in a cathedral, Buckland dipped a finger in it, sucked it, and pronounced the liquid to be bat's piss. Probably the strangest thing he ever ate was a bit of the embalmed heart of Louis XIV of France, which the Archbishop of York had bought from a grave-robber during the French Revolution. There is a British dining society named after Buckland, based in the Midlands. But they do not try to outBuckland Buckland.

C

ANTONIN CARÊME (1784–

1833). Some reference books give his name as Marie-Antoine, but his books are all signed Antonin (food for thought: Marie Antoinette was beheaded in 1793). Carême has a good claim to be the most important chef in history. His ideas dominated the whole of the nineteenth century. He was born in Paris, the son of a stonemason, and

★ What do Foodies eat at the cinema?

Carême caramels.

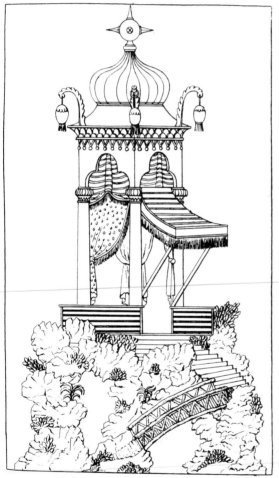

Le Pavillon Indien. No wonder Carême thought himself superior to architects

L'Ermitage sur un Rocher

Carême's own drawings for his pièces montées

taught himself to read (so he could consult cookery books) and to draw. One of his cookery teachers was Germain Chevet, entrepreneur, who had supplied flowers to the Queen.

In Carême's twenties, he was apprenticed to Bailly's pâtisserie. Pastry chefs were called in when a great house needed one, and Carême went both to Talleyrand and Napoleon. Talleyrand reinforced his taste for culinary display; Carême disapproved of Napoleon.

Carême went briefly to cook for the Prince Regent at the Royal Pavilion in Brighton. One day, the royal glutton complained of the temptation, and Carême answered, as he wrote in *Cuisinier Parisien*: 'Your Highness, my duty is to tempt your appetite; yours, to control it.'

He went to Russia, where he learned, but came to dislike, service à la russe, the method we use today – the carving done in the kitchen or at table and the food served hot in separate courses. Carême's fondness for display required the older French service – everything placed on the table before the start of the meal. His famous food sculptures, the pièces montées, for which we have his own drawings, were often of pastry. He had folie de grandeur about his marzipan Chinese pagodas and meringue pyramids. Anatole France quotes him as saying: 'The fine arts are five in number, to wit: painting, sculpture, poetry, music, architecture – whose main branch is confectionery.' He loved cooking for huge parties, such as the military dinner in the Champs Elysées for 10,000 guests. The tables stretched from the Place Louis XV to the Barrière de l'Etoile.

But his real influence was in the kitchen itself, where he tried to improve working conditions for the near slaves who still cooked over vast charcoal fires. Carême came close to codifying the methods of cooking. His classification of the grand sauces into four – béchamel, espagnole, allemande and velouté – influenced chefs into our own times. Carême wrote eight books,

including *La Pâtisserie Royale* (1815), *Le Maître d'Hôtel Français* (1822) and *L'Art de la Cuisine Française au Dix-Neuvième Siécle* (1833).
& p 128, 139, 142

ROBERT CARRIER (b 1923, Tarrytown, New York), American writer, journalist, television cook and restaurateur, stayed in Britain after the war. This dark, handsome, affable bachelor had a great vogue in the Sixties, when his recipes, lusciously illustrated with colour photographs, inspired many British housewives to pay attention to the look of food. He was thus the prophet of the dinner-party boom. Consequently Foodies say he's last year's flavour. His books include *Great Dishes of the World* (1963), and he started cookery cards.

Robert Carrier is the only British (-based) Foodie who endorses food products – the showbiz-y side of Foodiebiz so noticeable in France and America. *Address*: Carrier's, 2 Camden Passage, London N1.
T: (01) 226 5353.
& p 99, 102

ALAIN CHAPEL (b 1937) is a top nouvelle cuisine chef who trained at La Pyramide and Chez Juliette before taking over his family's one-star restaurant at Mionnay, near Lyon, when his father died in 1969. It is now an elegantly austere three-star (1973) restaurant. Chapel takes delight in dishing up oddities, such as his calves' ears 'farcie comme en Bugey', stuffed with sweetbreads flavoured with truffles, or his 'ragoût fin de crêtes and rognons de coqs', cock's kidneys and combs (the traditional garnish for sauce financière) served with morels and crayfish. His desserts are spectacular. *Address*: p 59.
& pp 42–43, 56, 60–61, 100

JULIA CHILD (b 1912 in America) learned to cook after the war at the Paris Cordon Bleu. In 1951, she, Simon Beck and Louisette Bertholle founded the Ecole des Trois Gourmandes in Paris, where they taught a lot of American ladies to cook. With the same two collaborators, Mrs Child wrote the very influential *Mastering the Art of French Cooking* in 1961. Volume II, by Julia Child and Simone Beck, followed in 1970.

Julia Child became the world's greatest television cook in the Sixties, when she began appearing on the

Six foot and six-shooters. Julia Child at Santa Barbara in 1983 on the set of her TV series 'Dinner at Julia's'

educational channel in Boston. Her gawkiness (she is over six foot) and proneness to disaster encouraged viewers. She once dropped a cooked salmon on the studio floor, but said quickly 'I'm so glad that happened; I *did* want to show you how to reconstruct a fish.'

Her breathy New England drawl and relaxed manner were misunderstood by a BBC executive, who thought she must be using the brandy for more than cooking and failed to buy her series for British television. Thus the British got Delia Smith instead.

Julia Child started late. *People* magazine claim that when she went to the Paris Cordon Bleu at the age of 37, 'Julia cooked as if the way to a man's heart was through his stomach pump.' Even later on, Foodie critics John and Karen Hess say of some of her recipes: 'Black beans and olive oil in Alsace, sesame paste in Soissons, "Flied Lice" in risotto, and many more anomalies reflect a disregard for the inner nature of a dish and for the region and the people who created it.'

But Mrs Child has won every award imaginable, and has written many books, eg *Julia Child's Kitchen* (1978), though none has had the impact of the first volume of *Mastering*.

Julia Child is the moving spirit behind – and has contributed much of the money to – the American Institute of Wine & Food founded in 1981. & p 20, 29, 42–43, 106, 107, 108, 112, 113, 118–119, 119, 133

GLYNN CHRISTIAN (b 1942) is a
New Zealander who has lived in London since 1965. He is the great-great-great-great-grandson of Fletcher Christian who led the 1789 mutiny on the *Bounty*, and author of a biography of that Mr Christian (1982). London Foodies know Glynn as the Mr Christian who started Mr Christian's delicatessen just off Portobello market, and he is a popular BBC television cook (*Pebble Mill at One* and *Breakfast Time*). He is also a magazine journalist

and author of several books – eg *The Delicatessen Cookbook* (1984) and *Glynn Christian's World Guide to Cheese* (1984).

CRAIG CLAIBORNE (b 1920,
Mississippi) is the power-broker of the American food world. He has been food editor of the *New York Times* for 27 years. He is far from boring, however, and stunned American Foodies in 1982 when he published *A Feast Made for Laughter*, an autobiography larded with recipes. It was not his ghastly Curried Sweetbreads with Fettucine that shocked, but his admitting that, as a child, he had been sexually molested by

his father. 'Nothing in recent cookbook history matches the personal nature of Claiborne's revelations,' gasped the *Chicago Sun-Times* food editor.

The book contains Claiborne's interesting 'recommended cookbook library' of 114 titles. Of his own fifteen, he includes the two he thinks indispensable: *The New York Times Cook Book* (1961) and *The Chinese Cookbook* (1976), written with Virginia Lee. The *NYTC* has sold over a million copies.

After wartime service in the US Navy, Claiborne went to hotel school in Switzerland. He joined the *NY Times* in 1957; he now reigns there with his friend and occasional collaborator on books, Pierre Franey.

Claiborne is very kind to younger food writers, and has helped the careers

of Marcella Hazan, Virginia Lee, Madhur Jaffrey and Ken Hom, to name four. But he does have at least two enemies. The Hesses make him the chief villain of 'the Pepsi generation of gourmet writers' who brought the 'gourmet plague' and 'taught Americans to be ashamed of their own great food heritage.' & p 11, 27, 30, 36, 62, 99, 104, 110, 112, 119, 126, 129, 131, 132, 141

CAROLINE CONRAN (b 1939),
née Herbert, started her Foodie career by editing Ambrose Heath on the *Queen* in the early Sixties, then was *Nova*'s food editor for three years, then a food editor and writer on the *Sunday Times* magazine for thirteen years.

She wrote *Poor Cook* (1971) and *Family Cook* (1972) with Susan Campbell, *British Cooking* (1978) by herself and *The Cook Book* (1980) with her husband. CC is also the NC book translator, first Michel Guérard's *Cuisine Minceur* (1977), then Guérard's *Cuisine Gourmande* (1978), Roger Vergé's *Cuisine of the Sun* (1979) and the Troisgros brothers' *The Nouvelle Cuisine of Jean and Pierre Troisgros*. & p 42–43, 118–119

Lady Conran is married to:

SIR TERENCE CONRAN
(b 1931), knighted 1983. He is a designer, restaurateur (the Neal Street Restaurant in London), writer (*The Kitchen Book*, 1977; *The Cook Book*, with his wife, 1980), tycoon (Conran shops, Hepworth's, Mothercare, Heal's, etc) and bringer of taste to the masses (Habitat shops and the Boilerhouse

modern-design museum inside the Victoria & Albert). Terence Conran is responsible for what the Foodie kitchen looks like, and also for what a lot of Foodie restaurants look like. Before he founded stripped-pine culture (though he denies ever having sold stripped-pine furniture), Conran had a restaurant in Wilton Place called the Soup Kitchen, his first business. He is still a good cook, in the vast kitchen of his country house in Berkshire. He is a Foodie hero on both sides of the Atlantic and in Japan.
& p 90, 126

MARGARET COSTA (b 1917 in

Umtali, Southern Rhodesia) was educated at home by her mother. She won a scholarship to Oxford to read mediaeval French, and became a journalist on the *Sunday Pictorial*. She had been cooking since the age of four, and got the job of food and wine editor on the *Sunday Times*, then moved to the colour supplement as food and wine editor when it started in 1962. She also wrote for *Queen* and *Gourmet*.

In 1968 she advised Marks & Spencer on opening food departments. In 1967 she had married Bill Lacy, at the time chef at the Écu de France. They opened their own London restaurant, Lacy's in 1970 (closed 1982). Margaret Costa gave up the *Sunday Times* when the restaurant ate up too many hours.

Her books include *The Country Cook* (1968), *England at Table* (1968, published by *Gourmet*) and *the Four Seasons Cookery Book* (1970). And she anglicised the *Time-Life* foreign food series.

ROBERT J. COURTINE (b 1910

in Paris) is the no-nonsense premier Foodie journalist of France. He writes the restaurant column for *Le Monde*, and edited the 1967 and 1984 French editions of the *Nouveau Larousse Gastronomique*.

Courtine is anti nouvelle cuisine, preferring vieux country cuisine. His book *Grand Livre de la France à Table*,

1982, is an excellent province-by-province guide.
& p 105, 131

QUENTIN CREWE (b 1926),

patrician journalist, writer and restaurateur, changed British restaurant criticism by his column in *Queen* in the Sixties. He described ambiance and his fellow diners. This was useful, as new money and new professions were giving quite different people restaurant power. Quentin Crewe is in a wheel-chair, but this was unknown to most head waiters.

Crewe has now joined the gamekeepers, as a partner in the Brasserie St Quentin in London (opened 1981). He is the author of two Foodie scriptures, the *International Pocket Food Book*, 1980 (its Foodie vocabularies are essential for travellers) and the earlier *Great Chefs of France*, 1978 (full of new material, from interviewing chefs in their restaurants).
& p 2, 42-43, 54, 60-61, 103, 136

CURNONSKY, the pen name of the

food critic Maurice Edmond Sailland (1872–1956), was called 'the prince of gastronomes', and most good Paris restaurants kept a table permanently reserved for him. Curnonsky was brilliant but vast, and when he ate – usually surrounded by friends and onlookers – his huge dewlaps wagged. He was an early champion of French regional cooking, which he distinguished from haute cuisine and from middle-class home cooking. His most important book was *Le Trésor Gastronomique de France* (1933).

He founded the Académie des Gastronomes in 1930 and presided over its dinners until 1948. The Foodie world loved him. In 1979, the 'Association des Amis de Curnonsky', who included Roger Vergé, Richard Olney and Michel Guérard, published a tribute to *Curnonsky et Ses Amis*, which gives his favourite recipes (eg tarte Tatin and Fernand Point's crayfish salad).
& p 54, 105

D

ELIZABETH DAVID (b 1913).

English Foodie goddess. The only person everyone in the Foodie world agrees about. Her seven beautifully written books have influenced two generations of cooks and eaters, but to the just-post-war British she opened up a new life. American Foodies such as Richard Olney and Alice Waters were influenced by Mrs David as well, and the French Government has made her a Chevalier of the Ordre du Mérite Agricole (1977). The British have meanly limited her honours to an OBE (1976), but she is also an honorary doctor of the University of Essex and a Fellow of the Royal Society of Literature.

Brought up in Sussex, the second of four daughters of Rupert Sackville Gwynne, a Conservative MP, Mrs David left school at sixteen and went to France for eighteen months, to study at the Sorbonne and live with a French family. She returned to England determined to teach herself to cook.

She was one of the beauties of her time, and she worked for a short while as an actress; then as a vendeuse at Worth in London. During the war she worked for the Admiralty and the Ministry of Information in Egypt and Greece – she was the Librarian at Alexandria. From 1944 to '60 she was married to an army officer, Lt-Colonel David of the Bengal Lancers. As a result of her own travels and his postings, she has lived in France, Italy, Egypt, Greece and India.

When she returned to England after the war she published her first articles, in British *Harper's Bazaar*. Her first book, *Mediterranean Food*, was rejected by several publishers before John Lehmann published it in 1950, with John Minton illustrations. *French Country Cooking* followed in 1951, and in 1954, after a year of on-the-spot research, *Italian Food*. The next year, *Summer Cooking* came out; then *French*

Provincial Cooking, her fattest book, in 1960. But it was the publication of the books in paperback by Penguin, starting with *Mediterranean Food* in 1955, that put them on every bookshelf.

Spices, Salt and Aromatics in the English Kitchen (1973) was the first of the scholarly, specialised books she now prefers to write, followed by *English Bread and Yeast Cookery* (1977), for which she won the Glenfiddich Writer of the Year award. In 1984 she published a collection of her journalism called *An Omelette and a Glass of Wine*. She opened a kitchen shop in London, called Elizabeth David, in 1965 but parted company with it in 1973.

Mrs David pursues her studies, most recently in ice cream. As Auberon Waugh once wrote of another woman, in a just world she'd be made a duchess.

& p 11, 25, 26, 27, 32, 37, 42–43, 44, 104, 106, 109, 110, 111, 118, 118–119, 126, 128, 130, 131, 132, 133, 136, 139, 143

ALAN DAVIDSON (b 1924) is the leader of the British Scholar Foodies. He gave up a distinguished career in the diplomatic service (he retired as Ambassador to Vientiane, capital of Laos, with the CMG, or Call Me God as diplomats say) to pursue a new career as Foodie author and publisher (Call Me Greedy?). When Head of Chancery in Tunis, he had written, at the request of his American wife Jane, a guide to *Seafish of Tunisia and the Central Mediterranean* (1963), so she could identify the fish in the market. But he was not quite set on his Foodie course: next year he wrote about the largely inedible *Snakes and Scorpions Found in the Land of Tunisia*. In 1972, he published his definitive *Mediterranean Seafood*, which caught the Foodie imagination with its combination of recipes and pedantry. (Davidson has taught Foodies to use the scientific Latin names of plants and animals, ending the confusions caused by conflicting common names.)

He went on to write *Fish and Fish*

Dishes of Laos (1975) and the more comprehensive *Seafood of South East Asia* (1976); then an edition, with Jane Davidson, of *Dumas on Food* (1978); and, the next year, the encyclopaedic *North Atlantic Sea Food*.

Alan Davidson was the founder in 1979, with Elizabeth David, Jill Norman, Richard Olney and others, of a publishing imprint for food history: Prospect Books, and its journal *Petits Propos Culinaires*, recent issues of which contained articles on 'Diets, Plasters and Wound Drinks: Some Alimentary Aspects of Mediaeval Medicine' and on ancient forks dug up from the mud of the Thames. (Subscription £8, three issues a year.)

Davidson is currently writing *The Oxford Companion to Food*. He is active in the Foodie world, and serves on the board of directors of the American Institute of Wine & Food. Since 1979, the chief event in the Foodie calendar has been the Davidson-inspired (and formerly Davidson-organised) Oxford Symposium on Food at St Antony's College. *Address*: Prospect Books, 45 Lamont Road, London SW10.

& p 11, 13, 32, 39, 40, 42–43, 44, 66, 105, 106, 107, 118–119, 136, 138, 143

JUSTIN DE BLANK (b 1927 in London) is the Foodies' grocer. He had a Dutch grandfather and lived in Holland and France as a child. After war service in the Navy, he joined the company that became Unilever, selling fats to bakers and chocolate-makers, then became production manager for Stork margarine. Sacked from Unilever (he's *always* been able to tell Stork from butter), he went into advertising at J. Walter Thompson, then to Conran as marketing diirector.

He opened his first London shop, in Elizabeth Street, in 1968, to supply good-quality brands of food not easily obtainable in Britain. When he found that many brands had been driven out of business by the new supermarkets with their cheaper goods, he began making his own, specialising in very

expensive, very good, very *fresh* things. He now has fingers in every corner of the Foodie pie. Turnover has risen from £25,000 in 1968 to £1½m in 1984. J. de B. believes this reflects the growth of Foodism in Britain, helped along by himself. In 1979, he opened Shipdham Place in Norfolk, a 'restaurant with rooms' on the French pattern.

& p 90, 91, 92

LOUIS DIAT (1885–?1958) added chives and cream to his mother's recipe for leek and potato soup and christened it Crème Vichyssoise; at the time he

It would be nicer with chives and cream in it...

was chef of the Ritz-Carlton in New York. He was born near Moulins and at fourteen became apprentice to the best pastry shop there. Once trained, he went to Paris. In 1903 he became Soup Chef at the Ritz under César Ritz, and when a Ritz was opened in London in 1906, he moved there, until 1910. He then went to New York as chef for the opening of the Ritz-Carlton.

Diat's books, such as *Cooking à la Ritz*, turned several generations of Americans into serious cooks. *Gourmet Basic French Cookbook* (1961) was published posthumously by *Gourmet* magazine, for whom he ostensibly wrote a column, 'Menu Classique'. In fact, this was by Helen Ridley and edited by the young Craig Claiborne.

& p 27

JOSCELINE DIMBLEBY (b 1947), née Gaskell, is one of Britain's most original writers of recipes. She has lived abroad in several countries – her stepfather was a diplomat – and acquired a taste for high seasoning and combinations of spices. In 1967 she married David Dimbleby, the broadcaster and newspaper proprietor. Her reputation was made by her first book, *A Taste of Dreams* (1976), and consolidated by a series for Sainsbury's supermarkets. Her 1979 *Book of Puddings, Desserts and Savouries* won the André Simon memorial award, and in 1983 *Favourite Food* came out, with a dust-jacket of a Tessa Traeger cover photograph showing the author's cleavage. Josceline Dimbleby says she did not mind the 'gastroporn' comments – she admits to equating food with sensuality. She has been cookery correspondent of the *Sunday Telegraph* since 1982.

CHANDRA DISSANAYAKE is

the leading cookery writer of Sri Lanka. Her *Ceylon Cookery* (1968, 2nd ed 1976) is the definitive work on this small subject.

CHRISTOPHER DRIVER

(b 1932), editor of the *Good Food Guide* of Britain from 1970 to '82, was born in India. Some people say nostalgie d'Inde was one of the two guiding principles of the *Guide* under his editorship, the other being Christianity (he wrote *A Future for the Free Churches?* published in 1962). But the *Guide*'s penchant for informal, downmarket and ethnic restaurants springs from its method, not from editorial prejudice. Foodies distrust judgements based on reports from hundreds of unqualified readers whose own palates are not subject to inspection.

Driver himself is clever, discriminating and learned. Educated at Rugby and Christ Church, Oxford, he has worked as a journalist since 1958. He was features editor of the *Guardian* in the heady Sixties and published *The Disarmers: a study in protest* in 1964 and *The Exploding Universe*, about student protest, in 1971. But his longest-lasting work will be *The British at Table 1940–*

1980 (1983), which describes the British Foodie's roots. His latest book is *Pepys at Table*, 1984, with Michelle Berriedale-Johnson. He also owns a bookshop in Shaftesbury, Dorset.
& p 2, 29, 42–43, 138, 140, 143

SIR JACK DRUMMOND (1891–

1952), British nutritionist and apostle of wholemeal bread, became professor of biochemistry at University College, London at only 31 after his research into butter and margarine. With his second wife, Anne Wilbraham, he wrote the pioneering book *The Englishman's Food: a history of five centuries of English diet* in 1939.

Very early in the war he became an adviser to the Ministry of Food. He and Lord Woolton, appointed Food Minister in 1940, collaborated closely, and faced with shortages and rationing, gave the nation a diet that was actually healthier, and whose influence lasted.

Drummond died in a famous murder, killed with his wife and daughter while camping in Provence; Gaston Dominici, a farmer, confessed but later retracted his confession.
& p 143

FÉLIX URBAIN DUBOIS (1818–

1901), born in Trets, was once chef at the Prussian court. He was responsible for the universal adoption of service à la russe – each course brought in hot from the kitchen – which drove out service à la française – all the food placed on the table beforehand. His *Cuisine Classique* (2nd edn, 1864) was addressed to the professional chef, and widened the gulf between the pro's haute cuisine and the housewife's cuisine bourgeoise. His other influential books included *Cuisine de tous les pays* (1868) and *Cuisine Artistique* (1872–74). He died in Nice.

ALEXANDRE DUMAS père

(1802–1870), the grandson of a French count and a black Haitian, was the author of *The Three Musketeers, The Count of Monte Cristo, The Black Tulip* and *Twenty Years After* as well as of his

really important book, the *Grand Dictionnaire de Cuisine*, published posthumously in 1873.
& p 126

E

GEORGES AUGUSTE ESCOFFIER (1846–1935) was born

the son of a blacksmith at Villeneuve-Loubet, near Nice, where, at 13, he went to work in his uncle's Restaurant Français. At 19 he became the chef at the Petit Moulin Rouge in Paris. (He was so short that he had to wear built-up shoes to reach the stoves.) During the next eighteen years he was chef to a Russian grand duke, chef de cuisine to the general staff of the French Army of Rhine at Metz (and later at Mainz) during the Franco-Prussian war, and worked at three great Paris hotels, and at the Grand Hotel, Monte Carlo, and the Hotel National in Lucerne, whose manager in 1884 was César Ritz.

Ritz persuaded Escoffier to go to London with him, and first at the Savoy, then at the Carlton and the Ritz in Paris and London, the Ritz-Escoffier team invented the splendour of the Edwardian dream hotel. The smooth running was not only for the guests: one of the first things Escoffier did was to improve working conditions for the cooks. He banned smoking and drinking in the kitchen, decreed that orders were no longer to be shouted, and did what he could about the heat. He ruled that cooks were not to be seen in dirty 'whites' by the public, and must change before going out on the street.

Escoffier rationalised the work-pattern of the kitchen, so that several specialised chefs de partie could work at once on a single dish, in assembly-line fashion, and the diner stood a better chance of getting his food hot.

In spite of the flaming bombe Nero and flamboyant pêche Melba associated with Escoffier, his motto was 'faites simple', and he practised what he

Escoffier (facing camera) at a café

preached. André Simon suggested that chefs of Carême's time probably developed their rich sauces to camouflage meat, game and fish in pre-refrigeration days: 'Escoffier is to Carême what the New Testament is to the Old.' Simon writes that Escoffier 'wanted his sauces to help and not to hide the flavour of whatever dish they adorned. He introduced, and he had the greatest faith in, fumets and essences, that is, evaporated stock obtained by allowing the water, milk or wine in which meat, game, fish or vegetables happen to be cooked, to steam away slowly so as to leave behind a fragrant concentrate as a basis for whatever sauce will be served with them.' There we have the first description of the current nouvelle cuisine doctrine of making sauces by reduction.

Above all, Escoffier was a great codifier, and his rules of conduct as well as his recipes still reign in most professional kitchens. His *Guide Culinaire* (1903, new English edition, 1979) contains 5,000 recipes, and his late work, *Ma Cuisine* (1934), still in print, is many an old-fashioned domestic cook's bible.

Escoffier is also the father of Foodiebiz. Michel Guérard has a letter

of his in which he endorses Maggi's products – indeed, many of his recipes called for ham, anchovy or mushroom essence – and his association with Maggi was certainly on a commercial basis.

Unfortunately for Escoffier, in 1898 the directors of the Savoy caught him out at the chef's oldest trick: arranging with his suppliers to be invoiced for more than was actually received, and pocketing a 5 per cent commission. The Savoy forced a very broke Escoffier to sign a confession and pay back £500 of the £8,000 he owed. Another £8,087 was recovered from the tradespeople. Escoffier and Ritz, who had been in on the larceny, left the Savoy for Claridge's, the Carlton and the Paris and London Ritz. It remains a mystery why, when Escoffier died in Monte Carlo in 1935, he left very little.
& *p 10, 42–43, 60–61, 100, 139*

F

FANNIE MERRITT FARMER
(1857–1915) was the most important American cookery writer of the

nineteenth and early twentieth century. *The Boston Cooking-School Cook Book* (1896), called *The Fannie Farmer Cookbook* in its dozens of posthumous revised editions, was the basic text of the American kitchen before the *Joy of Cooking* took over from it.

Fannie Farmer was born in Boston. Partially paralysed by a stroke in her youth, she could not go on into higher education, but she learned to cook, at the Boston Cooking School. She graduated from there, aged 32, in 1889, and promptly took it over and ran it from 1891 to 1902. She then opened Miss Farmer's School of Cookery in Boston, which trained housewives rather than cookery instructors.

Fanny Farmer was the founder of the American cook's obsession with accurate measurements – particularly difficult in a system that uses volume measurements rather than the more accurate weight measurements of British and European cooks. Foodie historians John and Karen Hess hold her responsible for the degeneration of American cooking: 'Before her, women wrote of cooking with love; she made it a laboratory exercise. She embodied, if that is not too earthy a word, all the major ills of twentieth-century culinary teaching. She was the maiden aunt of home economics.'
& *p 42–43, 108, 120*

M. F. K. FISHER (b 1908, Albion, Michigan) is the Elizabeth David of American Foodie writers. Brought up among the orange groves and vineyards of southern California, Mary Frances Kennedy Fisher's childhood, about which she has written often, is a reminder of a more genteel America, a civilization and a culinary tradition different from its European original but not inferior. It disappeared after the war, and American Foodies began to yearn to read about their roots. Mrs Fisher, who had gone to live in France in 1929 with Al Fisher, her first husband, had the feeling and the prose to satisfy them.

She started writing about food in

1935, when she discovered that the man sitting next to her in the Los Angeles public library was reading 'very old, fine-smelling' Elizabethan cookery books, which *she* began writing about, to amuse her husband. These essays turned into her first book, *Serve It Forth* (1937). By the time it was published she had left her husband to marry Dillwyn Parrish, who was a painter, as was his cousin Maxwell.

Parrish was the great love of her life. They went to live in Europe, and stayed in Switzerland until war broke out. Then, in 1941, the idyll was terminated by his death. The same year she published *Consider the Oyster*, then her wartime book *How to Cook a Wolf* in 1942, and the next year, *The Gastronomical Me*. (These titles are collected in the omnibus *The Art of Eating*, 1976.) In 1949 she published her translation of Brillat-Savarin's *The Physiology of Taste*.

Mrs Fisher now lives in Sonoma County, California, in a house designed for her by her friend and neighbour, British architect David Pleydell-Bouverie. The kitchen is the central room of the house. M. F. K. Fisher has written fifteen books in all, and W. H. Auden was probably right when he said 'I do not know anyone in the United States today who writes better prose.'
& *p 39, 42–43, 107, 121, 142*

JEAN-LOUIS FLANDRIN

(b 1931 in Grenoble) is the chief academic Foodie of France. Professor Flandrin is director of studies in social sciences at the University of Paris VIII-Vincennes at St Denis, and has done research into the history of books, the history of sexuality and the history of taste. His articles on the history of gastronomy enliven the French journal *L'Histoire*.

CHARLES ELMÉ FRANCATELLI (1805–1876),

French maître d'hôtel and chef to Queen Victoria, wrote several books, including *The Modern Cook* and *The Cook's Guide*, but his most entertaining

was *A Plain Cookery Book for the Working Classes* (1852), which he wrote out of reforming zeal. It includes recipes such as 'No 239. How to prepare a Large Quantity of Good Soup for the Poor.'

PIERRE FRANEY (b 1920 at St

Vinnemer, Burgundy) is Craig Claiborne's collaborator on his *New York Times* column and several books. Claiborne met Franey when PF was chef for Henri Soulé at Le Pavillon, then the best restaurant in America. After a disagreement about overtime and staff wages, Franey left in February, 1960, and Soulé had to close the restaurant temporarily. Franey then became an anti-Foodie, and accepted a post as vice-president of the Howard Johnson fast-food empire.

He was also keeping constant company with Claiborne, who says that Franey contributed most of the recipes to the column, although unpaid and seldom credited. He has since got a by-line. He has written two books on his own, *Pierre Franey's 60-Minute Gourmet* (1979) and *Pierre Franey's More 60-Minute Gourmet* (1981) – more haste, less grammar.

The dirty-minded will want to know that the heterosexual Franey lives near Claiborne at East Hampton with his wife Betty and their children.
& *p 99, 124, 132, 141*

FU PEI-MEI is Taiwan's television

cook, and the author of the Chinese recipe book most coveted by Foodies, *Pei-Mei's Chinese Cook Book* (1969). Pei-Mei herself (it is called *Pei-Mei's Chinese Cook Book*, not Miss Fu's) was born in Fushan in China and has been cooking on the telly since it was first introduced to Taiwan in 1962.

G

HENRI GAULT (b 1929) was a

journalist on *Paris-Presse* with Christian Millau when his grumbles about being bored got him assigned to do a

restaurant column on Paris, which was edited by Millau. In 1962 they joined together to write the *Guide Juillard* to Paris, which was an instant success.

In 1969 G. and M. started their own monthly magazine, the *Nouveau Guide Gault-Millau*, and began to publish the *Gault-Millau* guides – to France, Paris, New York, London, Italy, and, in November 1984, a *Guide du Vin*.

In 1973 they published a manifesto in the October issue of the *Gault-Millau* magazine with the cover-line 'Vive La Nouvelle Cuisine Française'. This did not invent the new movement; it merely baptised it, but the baptism brought it to the notice of the world. Gault is now more and more occupied with editing a quarterly, *Ma Maison et La Table*.
& *p 7, 8, 11, 15, 54, 55, 56, 60–61, 62, 95, 105, 118, 121, 130, 135, 136, 140*

FRÉDY GIRARDET (b 1937),

Swiss chef-proprietor at Crissier. *Address*: p 59.
& *p 60–61*

HANNAH GLASSE (d 1770) is the

author of *The Art of Cookery Made Plain and Simple* (1747), the most famous English cookery book of the eighteenth century. Hannah Glasse has been much misrepresented. Her contemporary, Dr

Johnson, claimed that *Cookery Made Plain and Simple* was written by a man. Several dictionaries of quotations ascribe to her the line: 'First catch your hare.' She nowhere wrote that; though she did write a sentence beginning 'Take your hare when it is cased …'. She also received scarcely any benefit from the great success of her book, as she was declared bankrupt in 1754 and lost the copyright.

Mrs Glasse's permanent claim to Foodie attention is that she was the first writer to give recipes in easy-to-understand language, so that they could be used by cooks and servants and not merely by the educated mistress of the household. And she seems to have been the first English writer to give a recipe for curry.
& p 36, 44

RICHARD GRAFF (b 1937), is chairman of the AIWF.
& p 106, 107

JANE GRIGSON (b 1928), née McIntyre, is a distinguished British Foodie. Since 1968 she has been the cookery writer for the *Observer* colour magazine, and is responsible for its pre-eminence in British Foodie circles. Jane Grigson was born in Yorkshire and educated at Newnham College, Cambridge. She then worked for publishers and translated from the Italian (she won the John Florio prize in 1964).

Mrs Grigson's food books are also notable for their writing. Her first was the specialised *Charcuterie and French Pork Cookery* (1967); then *Good Things* (1971); *Fish Cookery* (1973); *English Food* (1974); *The Mushroom Feast* (1975); *Jane Grigson's Vegetable Book* (1978); *Food with the Famous* (1979); *Jane Grigson's Fruit Book* (1982); *The Observer Guide to European Cookery* (1983), and *The Observer Guide to English Cookery* (1984).

Jane Grigson is married to the poet, critic and naturalist Geoffrey Grigson.
& p 26, 37, 42–43, 44, 97, 106, 108, 113, 118–119, 133, 136, 139

MICHEL GUÉRARD (b 1933, Vétheuil), worked for a caterer, Kleber Alix at Mantes-la-Jolie, then at several restaurants and hotels. He gained the

Michel Guérard in the dining-room at Eugénie-les-Bains

chef's supreme award, Meilleur Ouvrier de France, in 1958. With little backing, he went to the Paris suburb of Asnières and opened the tiny Pot-au-Feu in 1963.

Guérard got his first star in 1967 and second in 1971. Then coincidence struck. Pierre Troisgros introduced him to Christine Barthélémy, whose father owned several spas. Guérard himself was getting fat from too much kitchen work and too little sleep. They discussed slimming and marriage in 1972, and in 1972 took over M Barthélémy's Les Prés et Les Sources d'Eugénie, where Guérard got his figure back on his own regimen, which he called Cuisine Minceur.

This menu is served only to spa guests. Everyone else eats gourmande food. Michelin gave him his first star the year he opened and his second the year after. When they got around to awarding the third in 1977 it was an anticlimax, as these things go in Foodie politics, for Gault and Millau had already proclaimed Guérard the most original chef of the lot. Eugénie-les-Bains is peculiar in one respect: it remains closed all winter, so Guérard has to engage a new staff each spring. This means he has to do an unusual number of jobs in the restaurant himself. Tant mieux. *Address*: p 59.
& p 11, 30, 42–43, 56, 60–61, 62, 93, 95, 98, 99, 114, 115, 121, 124, 125, 128

ALFRED GUÉROT (d 1965). French chef and cookery writer, author of *La Cuisine et la Pâtisserie Française*.

Paul Bocuse acknowledges drawing on recipes from this for his *Cuisine du Marché*, because they are 'perfect'.
& p 105, 121

H

PAUL HAEBERLIN (b 1923) comes from a family who kept an auberge at Illhaeusern in Alsace. He fought for the Free French during the war, then trained in Paris and under Edouard Weber. In 1950 he reopened his family's restaurant as L'Auberge de l'Ill, gaining his first Michelin star in 1952, his second in 1959 and the third in 1967. His younger brother Jean-Pierre is maître d'hôtel. Paul Haeberlin makes a feature of frogs' legs, and is the inventor of potage aux grenouilles, with froggy quenelles in frog consommé, and of gâteau of frog, with little morsels of frog inside a moulded mousseline – both often imitated. Haeberlin was also the first to serve a warm salad of rabbit with its sliced liver, sprinkled with truffles and sauced with vinaigrette. This dish is attributed to Paul's son Marc, and gives diners hope for continuity. *Address*: p 59.
& p 60–61

PHILIP HARBEN (d 1970) was the first British television cook, when BBC Television reopened after the war in June 1946. Harben, who never had a formal cookery lesson, learned to cook because his parents were on the stage and toured a lot: he spent his time in the kitchen. In 1938 he took up catering, and when the war ended he was appointed director of a large industrial catering company – nowadays, this would disqualify him, but it was just what the country seemed to want of a telly cook when food was still rationed. And Harben looked the part, with his beard and striped apron. His Penguin paperback, *Cooking*, was also what the public wanted in 1960, despite the availability of Elizabeth David's books. Harben's book

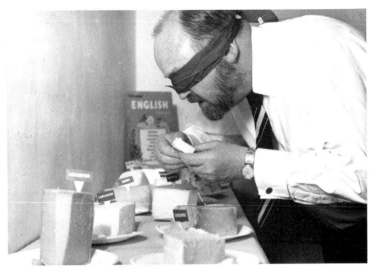

English cheeses in a blind tasting by Philip Harben, 1960

explained a good deal of the science of cooking, a different angle on the subject.
& p 29, 138

PAMELA HARLECH (b in New York), née Colin, is a food columnist for British *Vogue.* Lady Harlech is the second wife of Lord Harlech, who, as David Ormsby Gore, was British Ambassador to Washington during the Kennedy era. Her books are *Feast without Fuss* (1977) and *Pamela Harlech's Practical Guide to Cooking, Entertaining and Household Management* (1981), which Foodies are forever consulting to learn how to remove red wine stains (but she does not give the favoured Grapie method, which is to pour *white* wine over the stain as quickly as possible).
& p 113

DOROTHY HARTLEY (b 1893, in Yorkshire) should be called Hartley of England. A scholarly, inquiring spinster, she was among the first to be interested in the everyday life and skills of country people from mediaeval times to her childhood. She illustrates her own books: *Life and Work of the People of England* (6 vols), *Water in England* (1961), *The Land of England* (1979) and others. Most important to Foodies is *Food in England* (1954), which documents a lost rural cuisine. She lives in Clwyd, Wales.

MARCELLA HAZAN (b in Cesenatico, Emilia-Romagna, Italy) rescued Italian food for Foodies in 1973 with *The Classic Italian Cookbook* (USA; Britain, 1976). She stressed that real Italian food is home-made, and showed up the trattorie of Little Italy and Soho alike as travesties and haunts of cliché. Out of the window went Luigi with his two-foot pepper mill. Mrs Hazan began her book: 'The first useful thing to know about Italian cooking is that, as such, it actually does not exist.'

She is a small blond Italian married to Victor Hazan, an Italian-born American, author of *Italian Wine.* Mrs Hazan got a PhD in biology from the University of Ferrara and went to New York in 1967. There she began giving cooking lessons in her apartment, got discovered by Craig Claiborne, and became the most famous Italian Foodie since Catherine de Medici.

Her book was followed in 1978 by *More Classic Italian Cooking* (published in Britain 1982 as *The Second Classic Italian Cookbook*). Mrs Hazan divides her time now between New York, her Marcella Hazan cookery school in Bologna and cookery courses she gives in Venice. *Address:* PO Box 285, Circleville, NY 10919, USA. T: (914) 361 3503.
& p 29, 42–43, 74, 97, 114, 116, 124

AMBROSE HEATH (1891–1969) was an old-fashioned British cookery journalist of good prose and prodigious output. He produced more than 100 books, mostly compiled from his various newspaper columns, which began in the Thirties with *The Morning Post.* He worked also on the *Manchester Guardian*, the *News Chronicle*, the *Evening Standard*, and until as late as 1964 on *Queen* magazine. His style was friendly and elegant, and he had the best illustrator in contemporary cookery publishing until Elizabeth David's books came along: Edward Bawden (see *Good Food*, Faber, 1932).
& p 124

JOHN L. and KAREN HESS are distinguished New York journalists, but they are the married couple least loved by the American Foodie Establishment. Their book *The Taste of America* (1977) is a devastating attack on the eating habits of Americans and on the writers who brought the 'gourmet plague'.

John Hess was a prize-winning investigative reporter for the *New York Times.* He was based in Paris for nine years (he won the Ordre de Mérite), then was Raymond Sokolov's successor as the *NY Times's* food critic for nine months in 1973 and 1974. He was admired for the work he did in this post, except perhaps by other food critics, for few of whom he has a kind word; Robert Courtine and Mimi Sheraton are the exceptions.

Newsweek magazine once called Karen Hess 'the best American cook in Paris'. Brought up in a small town in

Nebraska, Mrs Hess has done research into culinary history, and written for the *NY Times, Atlantic, Harper's* and other magazines. In 1980 she Americanised Elizabeth David's *English Bread and Yeast Cookery*, which was attacked in a review in the *New York Times* by Claiborne and Franey, who said they had followed the recipe for crumpets religiously and ended up with something that had a texture like boiled rope. A correspondence ensued, in which it was pointed out that boiled rope was quite a good description of the texture of a properly made crumpet.

John Hess, asked by the *NY Times* not to write about *living* subjects, has now begun a career on television as a professional curmudgeon.
& p 11, 36, 99, 108, 119, 124, 128, 140

KEN HOM (b 1949, Tucson, Arizona) is a first-generation Chinese American. Brought up by his widowed mother in Chinatown in Chicago, he learned to cook at eleven in an uncle's Chinese restaurant. He has now reached the top of the Foodie tree, as presenter of the 1984 BBC TV Chinese cookery series. The BBC hope this will succeed like Madhur Jaffrey's *Indian Cookery*. If it does, the book of the series will also sell like hot egg rolls.

The BBC chose Hom for his clear American English: other candidates flunked the oral.

Hom lives in California, where he gives cookery lessons. Every year he takes a party of Foodies for expensive on-the-spot training in Hong Kong. His American book, modelled on Jacques Pépin's *La Technique* (French cookery methods in photographs) shows Chinese methods: *Chinese Technique* (1981). It was written with Harvey Steinam.
& p 114, 124

ROSEMARY HUME (1908-1984) was a very professional cook in the French haute cuisine style, though she founded that famous cookery school for

amateur young ladies, the British Cordon Bleu. She had studied at the Paris Cordon Bleu, and in 1931 opened her own Cordon Bleu school in Sloane Street in London. Here she taught debs how to increase men's waistlines.

The school was closed in 1939 because of the war, but in 1945 Rosemary Hume reopened it with Constance Spry the flower-arranger (1886–1960), in Marylebone. They also opened a boarding-school, Winkfield Place in Berkshire.

Rosemary Hume's best-known book was a joint effort with Mrs Spry called *The Constance Spry Cookery Book* (1956). With her business partner Muriel Downes, she wrote the *Penguin Cordon Bleu Cookery Book* and in 1967 a Cordon Bleu part-work. This ran for 72 weeks and was selling 100,000 copies by 1968. Foodies consider Miss Hume's influence disastrous – cuisine dodo. Today's debs adore nouvelle – cuisine kiwi.
& p 29

MADHUR JAFFREY (b 1933, Delhi) is a Hindu who introduced Indian methods and spices to Britain in 1982, when she demonstrated them in the BBC 2 series *Indian Cookery*. Her beauty and presentation helped – she is well-known as an actress from Merchant-Ivory films like *Shakespeare Wallah*. The book of the series, *Madhur Jaffrey's Indian Cookery* (1982) was on the British best-seller list for weeks.

As a drama student at RADA in London, Madhur Jaffrey was shocked to find that the hundreds of Indian restaurants were almost all inauthentic. She got her mother in Delhi to send her recipes, and taught herself to cook. Her first book, *An Invitation to Indian Cookery* (USA, 1973; Britain, 1976) was mainly about Delhi province. In 1981 she brought out *World-of-the-East Vegetarian Cooking*, giving dishes from India, Bali, Japan and China.

Madhur Jaffrey currying favour

She lives in New York with her husband, a black American violinist.
& p 11, 28, 42–43, 124, 132, 133

HUGH JOHNSON (b 1939 in London) is the man who brushed the snobwebs from wine. Before he published *The World Atlas of Wine* in 1971, France and Germany were the chief and almost the only countries credited with decent wine. But Johnson pointed out that all the other countries with vineyards were in ferment. Germany was passing new wine laws, Italy delimiting wine areas every month, California and Australia starting to export, North Africa pouring wine into Russia, oenocetera.

Johnson has been Secretary of the Wine and Food Society (appointed by André Simon), editor of *Wine & Food* (1963–65) and *Queen* (1968–70) and is now wine editor of *Cuisine* and president of the Wine Club started by the *Sunday Times*, as well as writing on gardening and trees. Other Grapie books: *Wine* (1966), *The California Wine Book* (1976, with Bob Thompson), *Hugh Johnson's Pocket Wine Book* (annually from 1977), *Understanding*

Wine (1980), *Hugh Johnson's Wine Handbook* (1982), *Hugh Johnson's Wine Companion* (1983) and a video, *How to Handle a Wine* (1984). In his spare time he plants trees in Essex.
& p 70, 140

EVAN (b 1915) and JUDITH JONES (b 1924).

Judith Jones works for Knopf in New York and is the best-known cookery editor in America. Her authors include Elizabeth David, James Beard, Julia Child, Jane Grigson, Madhur Jaffrey, Elisabeth Lambert Ortiz and Claudia Roden.

Evan Jones has written a profile of Mark Twain as gastronome, 'Sourdough and Hardtack', in *The American Heritage Cookbook* (1969). His books are *American Food: the gastronomic story* (1975) and *The World of Cheese* (1976), published in Britain as *The Book of Cheese* (1980).
& p 113

K

DANNY KAYE (b 1913) was born

Daniel Kominski in New York. He wanted to be a doctor but became a Hollywood actor. His greatest success was *The Secret Life of Walter Mitty*, in which the hero excels in many professions. Since then, Kaye has in real life performed open-heart surgery, piloted a 747 and conducted a symphony orchestra. He is in this book because he has also cooked with several of the world's greatest chefs. His great love is Chinese food, and he has built a kitchen in his Hollywood house that has a professional two-wok stove and tacky restaurant tables. (Though you wok through a storm ... in a kitchen like this, you'll never wok alone.)
& p 107

PIERRE KOFFMANN (b 1947),

chef-proprietor of La Tante Claire in London. *Address*: p 81.
& p 135, 140

L

VINCENT LA CHAPELLE.

Eighteenth-century cookery writer and plagiarist. See *François Massaliot*.

NICO LADENIS (b 1934 in

Tanzania, then Tanganyika) is the son of a French father and Greek mother. He is chef-proprietor of Chez Nico restaurant in an insalubrious part of Battersea in London; where he has won two stars from the British Michelin inspectors and an equally praising two toques with 15/20 points from Gault-Millau. Nico is as famous for his fiery personality as for his duck liver mousse; his warm mousseline of white fish and salmon with a chive-flavoured beurre blanc; his veal kidneys and a shallot and mustard sauce; and his grilled rare, thinly sliced breast of duck with herbes de Provence. *Address*: p 81.

FRANÇOIS PIERRE DE LA VARENNE published the first great

French cookery book, *Le Cuisinier françois*, in 1651. Its recipes make a clean break with those of the Middle Ages. There is no longer almond milk with everything, and flavours other than sweet-and-sour are encouraged. La Varenne had several advantages: the adoption of the pottery plate instead of the stale-bread trencher meant that knives and forks could be used, and that not everything had to be hashed or

LARKS IN A SWEET SAUCE

minced; also more interesting liquid dishes could be served. (The pre-plate use of the trencher is the reason that the British still eat baked beans and spaghetti on toast.)

L.S.R., the anonymous author of *L'Art de bien traiter* (1674) attacked La Varenne viciously, in one of the first of the controversies that recur repeatedly in gastronomic history. According to Jean-François Revel (from whose *Culture and Cuisine* the following account is quoted), 'La Varenne was relatively conservative and addressed himself to a cautious bourgeoisie.' L.S.R.'s was an 'avant-garde polemic':

'I believe that in these pages the reader will not see the absurdities and the disgusting lessons that the Sieur de La Varenne dares to put forth and argue in favour of, with which he has for so long deceived and hoodwinked the stupid and ignorant populace by passing off his productions as so many infallible truths ... Do you not shudder at the description of a teal soup with hippocras, of larks in a sweet sauce? Can you look without horror on his soup of leg of beef with lemon slices, cooked in a vulgar stewpot?'

La Varenne's first post was with the Duchesse de Bar, who was the sister of Henri IV, which meant that La Varenne came into contact with Catherine de Medici's Florentine chefs. La Varenne later worked for the Marquis d'Uxelles, to whom he dedicated his book. It went through 30 editions and remained an important work for several generations. A second book, *Le Parfaict confiturier*, was published in 1667 with La Varenne's name on the title page, and another book, *Le Pâtissier françois* (published in the Hague, 1721) is traditionally attributed to him.
& p 134

PRUE LEITH (b 1940 in South

Africa) presides over a Foodie empire in London. She is food editor of the *Guardian* and writes a column for a trade publication, *Hotel and Caterer*. She sits on the board of British Rail – to which she was appointed during the regime of her country neighbour, Sir Peter Parker, to see if she couldn't do something about British Rail food. (She did what she could – which wasn't much.)

In addition to Leith's Restaurant, Prue Leith owns Leith's School of Food & Wine, which trains boardroom-lunch Sloane Rangers as well as professional cooks, and she has her own catering firm.

She is married to Rayne Kruger, a South African writer. Her many books include *The Prue Leith Cookery Course* (1980) and *The Cook's Handbook* (1981). *Address*: Leith's, 92 Kensington Park Road, London W11. T: (01) 229 4481. *& p 13, 114, 118–119*

A. J. LIEBLING (1904–1963) was the by-line of Abbott Joseph Liebling, a great American journalist and gastronome. The son of an Austrian Jewish immigrant with a wholesale fur business, he had an agreeable upbringing that included Dartmouth College and travel in Europe. As a war correspondent he crossed the Channel with the troops on D-Day; but he was best known as *The New Yorker*'s press critic, for his column 'Wayward Press'.

His writing on food was collected in *Between Meals: An Appetite for Paris* (1962, but most of the pieces had appeared in *The New Yorker* in 1959). *& p 141*

LIN YUTANG (1895-1976) Chinese artist, novelist and gastronome, was born in China and educated at Harvard and Leipzig. After 1923 he lived mainly in the USA, though he returned three times to China and travelled widely in Europe. With Dr Lin's help, his wife Tsuifeng and daughter Hsiang Ju wrote *Chinese Gastronomy* (1969, most recent edition 1982), the most important, reflective book ever written on Chinese food and food customs. *& p 42–43, 57*

KENNETH LO (b 1913, Fuzhou, China) studied physics in Peking and English literature at Cambridge. He

came to England in 1936, and stayed on as a diplomat during the war. He loves tennis, and in 1946 played for China in the Davis Cup. He has often played at Wimbledon – he was Veteran Doubles Champion of Britain in 1976.

In 1966 he became a writer and consultant on Chinese food, and he has published more than 20 books. In 1980, he opened a first-rate, and expensive, London restaurant, Memories of China. He also runs Chinese cookery classes. *Address*: Memories of China, 67 Ebury Street, London SW1. T: (01) 730 7734. *& p 114*

M

FRANÇOIS MARIN was, with Menon, one of the 'nouvelle cuisine' chefs of the eighteenth century. His 1739 book, *Les Dons de Comus, ou les délices de la table*, went into edition after edition in the 1740s and '50s. Stodge-thickened sauces were coming in – Marin may well have invented sauce béchamel (named after Louis XIV's maître d'hôtel, the Marquis de Bechameil) – but Marin's preferred sauces were the old jus, coulis and restaurants (in its original sense – a very rich, restoring stock).

Marin, like Menon, seems to have been addressing himself to both the aristocracy and the bourgeoisie. He warned the eighteenth century Foodie Noovs: 'many bourgeois, wishing to imitate the great, exceed the limits of their position, covering their tables with dishes that cost a great deal of money, but without doing themselves any honour, for, to be successful, these dishes must be dressed by a clever hand.'

FAY MASCHLER (b 1945, in India), née Coventry, won a competition to become the restaurant critic of *The Standard*, London's evening paper. As the only full-time serious restaurant critic in London,

Mrs Maschler wields enormous power. But she is a very fair-minded Foodie, able to appreciate humble Indian flocked-wallpaper eateries as well as the temples of nouvelle cuisine. She was the Newspaper Association's Critic of the Year in 1978, an astonishing accolade from the anti-Foodie philistines who usually make the British press awards so boring.

Mrs Maschler has a mere fraction of the budget the *New York Times* gave Mimi Sheraton; she also has a fraction of Mimi Sheraton's waistline. *& p 106, 118–119*

FRANÇOIS MASSIALOT (1660–1773), born in Limoges, died in Paris, was the real successor to La Varenne. His *Le Cuisinier roïal et bourgeois*, which appeared in 1691 in Paris, was the first book to acknowledge that any non-aristo might require a recipe. It is also the first to give recipes in alphabetical order. Despite its title, though, the book is concerned almost entirely with dishes suitable for the court. Quantities are rarely given. Like his predecessors, Massialot was writing for professional cooks who calculated the quantities by the numbers and ranks of the guests.

The English book, *The Modern Cook* (1733) by Vincent La Chapelle, plagiarised Massialot. Scholar Foodie translators Philip and Mary Hyman have shown that one third of La Chapelle's recipes in the first edition were stolen from Massialot's 1712 *Nouveau cuisinier royale et bourgeois*. Scholar Foodie Barbara Wheaton wonders whether Massialot did not get his revenge by pinching the 54 of La Chapelle's recipes that appeared in his next edition, in 1734. Foodies have ever been so. (Up to now, books have said nothing was known about Massialot as a person; the Hymans supplied the new dates and facts about him which are given here.)

JACQUES MAXIMIN (b 1948), chef at the Hotel Negresco in Nice. *Address*: p 59. *& p 42–43, 52, 54, 55, 60–61*

JACQUES MÉDECIN (b 1928) is the Foodie Mayor of Nice, a position that is nearly hereditary in his family. He was Secretary of State for Tourism in Chirac's government from 1976 to 1977, and is wildly right-wing – he professes unbounded enthusiasm for Ronald Reagan, and speaks perfect English with a cowboy accent (he is married to an American heiress). He recently exchanged discouraging words with novelist Graham Greene about gangsterism in Nice, and successfully sued him for libel.

This colourful man has also written the best book on Niçoise cooking, published in France in 1972 as *La Cuisine du Comté de Nice* and in English translation by Peter Graham in 1983 as *Cuisine Niçoise*.
& p 36, 42–43

MARC MENEAU (b 1944), chef at L'Esperance, St-Père-sous-Vézelay.
Address: p 59.
& p 60–61

MENON was a French chef of the mid eighteenth century. Nothing personal is known about him, not even his first name: evidence that the status of the chef before the Revolution was not high. Menon was an important transitional figure between the cooking of the aristocracy – cut short by the Revolution in 1789 – and that of the bourgeoisie. He also apparently invented the phrase 'la nouvelle cuisine'. His first book was *Nouveau Traité de la Cuisine* (1739); its sequel in 1742 was *La Nouvelle Cuisine* 'avec de nouveaux menus pour chaque saison de l'année, qui explique la façon de travailler toutes sortes de mets, qui se servent aujourd'hui, en gras et en maigre; très utile aux personnes qui veulent diversifer une table par des ragoûts nouveaux'. This mouthful had several points of contact with today's nouvelle cuisine – including an appreciation of pasta.

Menon wrote many books in many volumes and they went through many editions. *La Cuisinière Bourgeoise*, 1746,

was the first cookery book for women. It was chiefly addressed to the aristocracy. The title was probably inspired by the vogue among French aristocrats of the 1740s and '50s for things bourgeois.
& p 134

CHRISTIAN MILLAU (b 1929) eats 350 meals a year for professional purposes, as the chief author of the Gault-Millau series of restaurant guides. He eats only half-portions. 'Scion of an old established family of parfumeurs, Dubois-Millot (he has changed his name to avoid trading on the association)', is how *Time* magazine described him in its cover story for 18 February 1980.

Millau studied international relations at the Institut de Sciences Politiques, then read law for five years at the Sorbonne. 'Like everybody else with my degrees,' he told *Time*, 'I didn't know what to do next.' So he became a journalist – deputy editor-in-chief of *Paris-Presse*, where he edited Henri Gault's Paris restaurant column. In 1962 they joined forces to write the *Guide Julliard* to Paris, which became the *Guides Gault-Millau* to other cities and countries after they launched the very successful monthly magazine *Le*

Christian Millau reads an improving book
Nouveau Guide Gault-Millau in 1969. An unsigned article in this in 1973 gave the name 'nouvelle cuisine' to the kind of food cooked by chefs who had trained with Fernand Point at Vienne.

Millau now runs the *Guide* side of their operations. His face is well-known

to restaurateurs in several continents, which is not surprising, as his criticism is very personal. In answer to the suggestion that a known diner like himself gets better food and service than the invisible Michelin man, he says: 'People who say that just cannot have any idea of how a restaurant is run. The menu is determined and the shopping done in advance. There is very little a chef can do from that point on, except to cook well or badly. It is possible to have a bad meal in a good restaurant. Indeed, it happens all the time, and one must learn to make allowances for it. But it is impossible to have a good meal in a bad restaurant.'
Address: Gault-Millau, 210 rue du Fabourg St Antoine, 75012 Paris.
T: (1) 367 8500.
& p 7, 8, 11, 15, 54, 55, 56, 60–61, 62, 95, 105, 118, 121, 129, 130, 136, 140

MONTMIREIL, nineteenth-century chef to the French writer and diplomat Chateaubriand (1768–1848), invented steak Chateaubriand, twentieth-century Businessman's treat. André Simon thinks it was originally done by grilling a thick slice cut from the middle of the fillet between two inferior steaks, which having given their juice to the better meat were thrown away.

ANTON MOSIMANN (b 1947, Solothurn, Switzerland) is the greatest chef now cooking in England. Since 1976 he has been Maître Chef des Cuisines of the Dorchester Hotel. There are now other chefs in England, such as Pierre Koffmann of Tante Claire and Raymond Blanc of Les Quat'Saisons, who have a claim to the top class, but they do not yet move in the culinary jet set. Mosimann lectures in Hong Kong, Singapore and California, for example.

Mosimann began his career as a child in Switzerland by cooking in his parents' restaurant. He used to give lunch parties for grown-up friends in the kitchen – a practice he continues in his tiny kitchen-within-a-kitchen at the Dorchester.

His books are *Cuisine à la Carte* (1981), basically intended for professionals, and *A New Style of Cooking* (1983), aimed at domestic cooks, and published by the Sainsbury supermarket chain at under £1. A new book is scheduled for 1985. He has a

Anton Mosimann in his whites

personal collection of 4,000 old cookery books. *Address:* p 59.
& *p 20, 44, 52, 55, 59, 60–61, 81*

N

DOMINIQUE NAHMIAS

(b 1952) cooks at the tiny Olympe restaurant in Paris (formerly on the rue Montparnasse, hence the name) which she and her husband own and run. He was an academic sociologist, she is the daughter of a Corsican lawyer and studied acting at the Toulon conservatory before going to take Paris by the stomach. Gault-Millau, who give her three toques and a score of 17/20, say she is the best practitioner of 'cuisine de femme' in the world. The restaurant has panels from the old Orient Express. *Address:* 8 rue Nicolas-Charlet, Paris 15e. T: (1) 734 8608.

EDOUARD NIGNON (1865–

1935) was one of the most influential French chefs of this century. 'Nignon

was a free spirit, a poet of a chef,' says Quentin Crewe. He emphasised creativity in the way that became characteristic of nouvelle cuisine chefs. The recipes in his *Les Plaisirs de la Table* (1926) and *Eloges de la Cuisine Française* (1933) are purposely vague about quantities and even cooking times – they are to finished dishes what a sketch is to a painting, and they often inspire cooks to do great things.
& *p 60–61*

JILL NORMAN (b 1940) is the single most important Foodie publisher in Britain. She built up the cookery list at Penguin in the Sixties and Seventies, in the great days when Elizabeth David, Jane Grigson, Claudia Roden and Alan Davidson (the nucleus of the Scholar Cooks group of Foodies) were all Penguin authors. She set up her own imprint in 1979, and all her authors went with her. Since then, she has discovered Nathalie Hambro, a real original (*Particular Delights*, 1981), and introduced Richard Olney to Britain (*Simple French Food*, 1981). She is married to antiquarian bookseller Paul Breman.
& *p 126*

O

RICHARD OLNEY (b 1927, Marathon, Iowa) is a cult figure whose first two books, *The French Menu Cookbook* (1970) and *Simple French Food* (1974), over-excited a generation of Foodies. The recipes, though complicated enough to make Foodies feel proud of their craftsmanship, produce clear and distinct flavours. Olney's highest praise of a sauce or a flavour is that it is 'clean'. He also likes dishes that are 'agrestic' (rural, rustic). Olney went to France in 1951 to paint, and his food and wine writing began as a hobby. He was known as an innovative cook, and in 1963 *Cuisine et Vins de France* asked him to be a contributor. This forced him to learn to

write in French (no mean feat at 36).

He is now the owner of the most photographed hands in history, as they appear on nearly every page of his 27-volume Time-Life *Good Cook* series, published between 1978 and 1983, a volume every two months. Time-Life insisted that every recipe in the anthology in each volume should come from some published work, not from Richard Olney's head. Olney, however, wanted to write his own

Richard Olney at home in France

'teaching' recipes. This clash may have had something to do with the launching by Alan Davidson, Olney and others of the world's most recherché Foodie journal, *Petits Propos Culinaires*, in 1979. The recipes signed 'Tante Ursule' and 'Nathan d'Aulnay', which first appeared in *PPC* and then in *Good Cook*, are suspiciously clean and agrestic.

Olney pleased other food writers by suing fellow American Richard Nelson in 1984 for breach of copyright – he said he recognised recipes from *Simple French Food* in *Richard Nelson's American Cooking*. There has not been a recipe-robbery case for 40 years and whatever the result, Olney is a Foodie hero.

He is also deeply Grapie. His next book will be on Château d'Yquem.
& *p 42–43, 104, 108, 109, 110, 112, 113, 118–119, 125, 126, 136, 142*

ELISABETH LAMBERT ORTIZ (b 1928) is the foremost

Foodie expert on Latin American food.

Born in London, educated partly in Jamaica, married to a Mexican United Nations official, Mrs Ortiz has knocked around the world a bit.

The Book of Latin American Cooking was published in America in 1979 and won a Tastemaker award. There are rumours of a French translation; but the British edition, although printed in 1982, did not appear until 1984. The American binder went bankrupt and the sheets were seized ... it was one hell of an enchilada. Elisabeth Ortiz writes regularly for *Gourmet*, and has written *Caribbean Cooking* (1973), *The Complete Book of Japanese Cooking* (1976) and a book on high-fibre dishes. She lives in London, and is working on a book on British chefs.
& p 42–43, 118–119, 133

LOUIS OUTHIER (b 1930, Belfort) comes from a family of millers in the Franche-Comté – his people were not in the restaurant business but they were in the *food* business. At nine he knew he wanted to be a cook, and at sixteen his family sent him to the local Grand Hôtel du Tonneau d'Or. His master there was Denis Michalland, who had worked for George V, and when Michalland died, Outhier went to Fernand Point's kitchen, where he stayed from 1951 to '53.

The remarkable part of Outhier's story is that he began his restaurant

Louis Outhier in dinner-jacket

L'Oasis at La Napoule, near Cannes, as a pension. He finally bought it in 1956, and began to cater for outsiders as well as residents. By 1963 it had become a one-star restaurant. He kept the boarders until 1968, and his third star followed in 1970. Outhier is old-fashioned for a nouvelle cuisine chef in that he still holds that hard work is of more value than publicity.

His food makes few concessions to his Mediterranean location – you are as likely to find North Sea turbot as loup de mer on his menu, but all the ingredients will be as good and fresh as any in France that day. Outhier's really magical dishes are the ones he is inspired to do on the day, and sometimes adds to the menu by hand. His menus often offer some of Point's best dishes (which you are unlikely to get any longer at Vienne). Look out for the foie gras en brioche, the fillet of John Dory (Saint-Pierre) au noilly and the loup en croûte Fernand Point.
Address: p 59.
& p 60–61

SRI OWEN (b 1935, Central Sumatra) has lived or travelled in most parts of Sumatra, Java and Bali, and now lives in England. She is the author of *The Home Book of Indonesian Cookery* (1976) and its revised version, *Indonesian Food and Cookery* (1980), both published by Prospect Books. Foodies consider her books models for how to deal with a foreign cuisine, both because she explains Indonesian table manner and eating habits, and because she gives the proper Latin names of things like the vegetable talas – which is sometimes given as tales, or keladi, or birah keladi, or taro, or herklots, or dasheen, but is, correctly and unequivocally, Colocasia antiquorum var. esculentia. Mrs Owen is also learned and careful enough to tell you to boil or bake it 'long enough to destroy the calcium oxalate crystals that form in some (not all) varieties. These can taste unpleasantly acrid, or even cause mild inflammation in the mouth and throat.'

Now that's telling it like Foodies like to hear it. Incidentally, C. antiquorum is used as a substitute for sweet potato or yam.
& p 42–43

P

HENRI-PAUL PELLAPRAT (1869–1949) was 'Professeur' at the Cordon Bleu school of Paris from 1902 until 1932, interrupted by military service in the First World War. Born in Paris, he was apprenticed to a pastry-cook at thirteen for three years. He then worked in confectionery with Forest at Bourges, and returned to Paris a year later to work at the Café de la Paix with Père Lapy, followed by La Maison Dorée with Casimir Moisson and stages with Bignon, Maire and Prillard.

After he retired from the Cordon Bleu, he wrote several important books: *La Pâte Feuilletée* – puff pastry (1932); *La Cuisine au Vin* (1934) with Raymond Brunet, *Les Sandwiches et les Pains Fourrés* (1934); then, in 1935, his massive *L'Art Culinaire Moderne*.

The Cordon Bleu's aim always was to teach some of the skills of the male chef – trained, full-time, and physically strong – to the housewife – amateur, part-time and who could never stand the heat of the professional kitchen. Oddly enough, the target of the Cordon Bleu was always the rich young woman who could afford to employ a cook, like 'Simca' (Simone Beck), who became a noted Foodie.
& p 42–43, 119

JACQUES PÉPIN (b 1935, Bourg-en-Bresse) has been personal chef to three Presidents of France, including Charles de Gaulle. He has worked at the Plaza Athenée in Paris and at Le Pavillon in New York. He has lived in the USA since 1959. Pépin must be the best-educated chef in history, as he has two degrees from Columbia University

– a BA in French literature and philosophy and an MA in eighteenth-century French literature.

A power in American Foodie politics, Pépin was 'culinary adviser' to the World Trade Center. He has become a peripatetic cookery teacher, giving classes all over America based on the material in his photographic cookery books, *La Technique* (1976) and *La Méthode* (1979). His other books are *The Other Half of the Egg* (with Helen McCully), *The Great Cooks Cookbook* (with James Beard and others) and *A French Chef Cooks at Home* (1975).
& p 132

CHALEUNSILP PHIA SING

(c 1898–1967) has been called 'an extraordinarily versatile man, a sort of Laotian Leonardo da Vinci' by Alan Davidson, who edited Phia Sing's manuscript recipe book under the title *Traditional Recipes of Laos* (Prospect Books, 1981). Phia Sing was born at Luang Prabang, the ancient capital of Laos, and became royal chef at the Palace there. He was, moreover, the Royal Master of Ceremonies, says Davidson, 'at a court of many and beautiful ceremonies; a physician, architect, choreographer, sculptor, painter and poet.'
& p 42–43

ROGER PHILLIPS (b 1931) has

created a new form of Foodie illustration, by developing a technique that allows him to make photographs that are as clear as drawings. He has produced the first successful book of photographs of *Mushrooms* (1981) that has ever been done. Roger Phillips worked for several years in advertising in London before becoming a photographer; his first three books, in which his technique was developed, were not Foodie: eg *Wild Flowers of Britain* (1977).

Phillips's most recent book is *Wild Food* (1983), and he is currently photographing the mushrooms of North America.
& p 42–43, 55

JACQUES PIC (b 1932), chef-patron at Valence, son of André.
Address: p 82.
& p 43, 60–61

FERNAND POINT (1897–1955). Father of nouvelle cuisine.
& p 11, 54, 55, 56, 60–61, 62, 120, 121, 125, 135, 137

RAYMOND POSTGATE (1896–1971) was a British novelist, historian and political journalist who founded the Good Food Club in 1950, and the following year, collected and edited its members' restaurant recommendations as the first *Good Food Guide*.

Postgate was a bubbling pot of contradictions. Son of a famous classical scholar, he kept up his own Latin and Greek throughout his life. But he was on the far left of the Labour party, and married George Lansbury's daughter, Daisy. G. D. H. Cole, with whom he collaborated on *The Common People 1746–1946*, was a brother-in-law.

With Philip Harben, the television cook, he founded the Half Hundred dining club, whose members took it in turn to comment on the food and drink at the club's dinners. In 1949, Stephen Potter (of *Gamesmanship*) asked Postgate to write some articles for the *Leader Magazine*, which he edited, on British catering: and Postgate started by proposing a Society for the Prevention of Cruelty to Food. The Good Food Club, and then the *Guide*, grew out of the *Leader* articles.

Christopher Driver, his successor on the *Good Food Guide*, says that 'Postgate – the "Public Stomach Number One", who had to insist that the OBE granted him by the Wilson government was in recognition of his work as a labour historian, not as a restaurant critic – owed his status as a food commentator largely to his circle of friends.'

He was actually more a Grapie than a Foodie, and in 1951, the year of the first *Good Food Guide*, caught the rising post-war wine tide with *The Plain Man's Guide to Wine*. The first *Good Food*

Guide sold 5,000 copies. It now sells ten times that.
& p 11

MARCEL PROUST (1871–1922) was the great Foodie novelist of the twentieth century. Not only does *A La Recherche du Temps Perdu* begin with food, the petite madeleine the narrator dips into his tea, but Proust saw Françoise's boeuf à la mode as a metaphor for the process of writing his novel. 'My work,' the narrator says in the last volume, 'would resemble that of Françoise … in a book individual characters, whether human or of some other kind, are made up of numerous impressions … so that I should be making my book in the same way that Françoise made that boeuf à la mode which M de Norpois had found so delicious, just because she had enriched its jelly with so many carefully chosen pieces of meat.'
& p 26

R

MAJOR PATRICK RANCE

(b 1918) is a one-man campaign to save British cheese. As the author of *The Great British Cheese Book* (1982), Major Rance is the world's foremost authority on his subject. He is also an expert on foreign cheeses, many of which he sells at his Wells Stores, at Streatley, Berkshire, the world's ripest smelling shop. T: (0491) 872367.
& p 64

JEAN-FRANÇOIS REVEL

(b 1924) is a French political philosopher and journalist, former director of *L'Express* and columnist for *Le Point*. Of course Foodies admire his *Without Marx or Jesus* (1971) and *The Totalitarian Temptation* (1976), but they reserve their highest praise for *Culture and Cuisine* (1982) – originally published in 1979 as *Un Festin en Paroles* – subtitled 'a journey through the history of food.'

Reviewers said it stands 'in the

tradition of the "new" and influential *Annales* school of French historiography,' but Foodies don't let that kind of talk put them off *their* dinner. The hero of Revel's book is Carême. Revel refuses to accept that French cookery was revolutionised by the Italian cooks of Catherine de Medici in 1533, and insists that Italy's contributions to cuisine were only two – the refinement of table manners and the invention of pastry.
& p 133

CÉSAR RITZ (1850–1918) was born in Niederwald, Switzerland, the son of a shepherd. His first hotel job was in 1870 as a waiter at Voisin, then the smartest restaurant in Paris. He heard almost immediately about Escoffier (who was on the point of becoming chef to the Army of the Rhine). When both were older they loved to reminisce about the Franco-Prussian war, when Voisin bought two elephants from the zoo during the famine, and the menu listed 'tronc d'éléphant sauce chausseur.'

Ritz's next posting was Vienna, at the Imperial Pavilion. Then, aged 23, he went to the Grand Hotel, Nice, as restaurant manager. It was at the National Hotel at Lucerne that Ritz first began to attract attention. He spent the winters in the south of France, and before long, he actually met Escoffier, either at Lucerne or at the Grand Hotel, Monte Carlo. Ritz was discovered in 1888 at the Minerva in Baden-Baden by Richard D'Oyly Carte, who lured him to London as the restaurant manager of his new Savoy Hotel, which opened in August, 1889. By 21 December, Ritz had become General Manager.

He had brought with him his own staff, including Escoffier as chef, and a man called L. Echenard as maître d'hôtel. This is the part of the record that is public. What is hitherto unknown is that, by 1898, the Savoy had sacked Ritz, Echenard and Escoffier.

Following a wrangle and a counter-claim against the directors of the Savoy, in 1900 Escoffier confessed to being 'on commission'. And Ritz confessed that he had allowed it to happen; that he had abused his position to help himself and his friends to freebies to the extent of £6,377; that he had violated his contract and taken part in business not connected with the Savoy; and that he had committed at least fifteen other pieces of serious impropriety. He denied, however, that he and his assistant, Echenard, had ever been guilty of 'appropriating or applying to their own use the monies of the Savoy Hotel Company, or taking monies by way of presents or commissions from the tradesmen of the Hotel.'

Like Escoffier, Ritz was made to grovel, and Sir Arthur Sullivan and Richard D'Oyly Carte reserved the right to make whatever use they liked of the confessions. But the Savoy party nobly held their tongues, even when Ritz and Escoffier went on to make a success of the very business deals they had cooked up in the Savoy's time. (The Ritz Hotel Syndicate Ltd had been registered in London as early as 1896.) The Savoy allowed it to be put about that Ritz had quarrelled with the head housekeeper, and did not even squeal when the Prince of Wales

cancelled a party at the Savoy because Ritz had left.

Claridge's had already been rebuilt by Ritz – with Savoy money. Ritz had moved on to the Carlton while the unpleasantness at the Savoy was still going on, then to the Paris Ritz – his greatest achievement – and to the London Ritz, opened in 1906.

He was taken seriously ill in 1901 while preparing the Carlton to become the social headquarters for the coronation of Edward VII. He was physically broken – possibly by the conclusion of the Savoy scandal the year before – but carried on, and did not die for seventeen years, at 68, in a clinic at Kusnacht near Lucerne. This is the first time the true story has ever been told.
& p 60–61, 100, 126, 127, 128

CLAUDIA RODEN (b 1936) the world's foremost expert on the food of the Middle East, was born in Cairo, into a prosperous family of Sephardic Jews. Her great-grandfather, Haham Abraham Ha-Cohen Douek, was Chief Rabbi of the Ottoman Empire. Inspired by the examples of Elizabeth David and Jane Grigson, and nostalgic for the tastes of her childhood, Mrs Roden (who had come to England as an art student in the Fifties) collected recipes

Claudia Roden serves tradition to students

from, among others, her own family for *A Book of Middle Eastern Food* (1968). This book practically discovered the food of this vast region for the English-speaking reader.

Mrs Roden is also the author of books called *Coffee* (1977) and *Picnic* (1981, and expanded with a new title, *Everything Tastes Better Outdoors*, in the US, 1984). She is doing research for the definitive book on Jewish food.
& p 7, 11, 29, 32, 42–43, 106, 110, 111, 112, 114, 118–119, 133, 136

IRMA S. ROMBAUER. See *Marion Rombauer Becker.*

EGON RONAY was born in Budapest, into a restaurant-owning

A tea-tasting, 1980. Egon Ronay and his inspectors, 'masked to elude future recognition'

family. He trained as a lawyer in Hungary, but came to England in 1946, and opened the Marquee restaurant in Kensington in 1952. Since 1956 he has published a restaurant and hotel guide, and other guides to pubs and inexpensive meals out. His attacks on the standard of motorway catering made some impact in Britain.
& p 56, 105

WAVERLEY ROOT (1903–1982) was an American journalist who lived most of his life in Paris. He wrote *The Food of France* (which has never been out of print) in 1958 and *The Food of Italy* in 1971, both of which are indispensable to the Foodie traveller. At his death he left several filing

cabinets full of material for an encyclopaedia of food.
& p 42–43

ALBERT (b 1935) **and MICHEL ROUX** (b 1941) are the chef-proprietors of the most expensive restaurants in Britain, Le Gavroche (London) and The Waterside Inn (Bray).

Born in France, both Roux brothers had conventional catering careers, except that each of them spent some time in private service – Michel for a Rothschild and Albert for Lady Astor, Sir Charles Clore and Peter Cazalet. Some of their former employers have given the Roux brothers the financial backing that has allowed them in turn to become the benefactors of Pierre Koffman at La Tante Claire (London), Jean-Louis Taillebaud at Interlude de Tabaillau (London), Christian Germain at the Château de Montreuil (France) and Peter Chandler at Paris House (in the grounds of Woburn Abbey, Bedfordshire). They are thus the centre of a charmed circle, but are not well-known internationally, despite the Gavroche's three stars in the British Michelin. (Bitchy Foodies say this only proves how bad Michelin's judgement is. Gault-Millau give the Gavroche one toque and only 14 points.) The Roux published their *New Classic Cuisine* in 1983, and are soon going to be associated with a new restaurant in Santa Barbara, California.
& p 90, 91, 101

S

ALAIN SENDERENS (b 1941), chef at L'Archestrate, Paris. *Address:* p 59.
& p 60–61

MIMI SHERATON retired as the *New York Times* restaurant critic in 1983, saying she was 'going on a diet'. Foodie scourges John and Karen Hess

approve of Mimi Sheraton; they call her 'one of the few food writers who do honor to the trade.' She wrote a shopping column for *New York* magazine before moving to the *Times*. Her restaurant column was all-powerful in New York.

Mimi Sheraton's vast budget made it possible for her to be scrupulously fair – it was the policy of the paper to visit every establishment reviewed at least three times. But she became obsessed with anonymity, and guests reported that she took almost as much time choosing her wig as she did choosing the restaurant. Once, appearing on French television with several three-star chefs whom she had slated, she insisted on wearing a paper bag over her head so that she could not be recognised by future chef victims.
& p 131, 134

SIMCA. See *Simone Beck.*

ANDRÉ LOUIS SIMON (1877–1970) was born in Paris, but moved to London when he married in 1900. He worked as export director for a French wine firm, and wrote books about wine as a hobby, until he resigned in 1933 and founded The Wine and Food Society, 'to bring together and serve all who take an intelligent interest in the pleasures and the problems of the table.' André Simon ran it himself until 1963, and was a much-loved figure in the stomach world.

His major works are *A History of the Wine Trade in England* (4 vols, 1908–1910) and *A Concise Encyclopaedia of Gastronomy*, whose publication in parts began in 1939, but was interrupted by the war, and was first published in full in 1952 and in paperback in 1983. He also founded the Condé Nast magazine *Wine & Food* and edited it until he was 86, in 1963, when he took on Hugh Johnson as editor and Secretary of the Wine and Food Soc.

In *The British at Table*, Christopher Driver is critical of Simon: 'His output of books and articles was prolific to the point of blatant pot-boiling. A peasant at heart, as he was the first to acknowledge, Simon was treated by his monied but in those days small circle of British – and American – wine-lovers with deferential respect, as the lovable representative of a gastronomic culture whose superiority was universally conceded.'

André Simon had a famous collection of old food and wine books, and is commemorated by annual awards made for books on food and wine, and by a semi-annual award of a food fellowship, made by the André Simon Memorial Trust in London. *& p 64, 66, 106, 127, 128, 132, 135*

RAYMOND SOKOLOV (b 1941),
Arts and Leisure editor of *The Wall Street Journal* and gastronomic columnist for *Natural History,* has a large Foodie following in the US. Born in Detroit, educated at Harvard and Oxford, Sokolov began his career on *Newsweek.* It was as a foreign correspondent for the *New York Times* in France that he was the first to report, in 1972, to the English-speaking world that there was a new food movement not yet called nouvelle cuisine. He became food editor and restaurant critic of the *New York Times,* and published *Great Recipes from the New York Times* in 1973, *The Saucier's Apprentice* in 1977, a life of Foodie journalist A. J. Liebling in 1980, and *Fading Feast,* on American regional foods, in 1981. *& p 42–43, 62, 131*

HENRI SOULÉ (1903–1966) was
the greatest – some would say the only great – restaurateur in America. Born in south-western France, Soulé began his career at Biarritz. From the start, he was 'front of house.' He moved to the Mirabeau Hotel in Paris and then the Claridge. Still only 23, he was said to be the youngest maître d'hôtel in Paris. In 1939 he was chosen to go to New York as general manager of Le Restaurant du Pavillon de France at the World's Fair.

When the Fair ended in 1941, Soulé opened the restaurant that became the best in America, Le Pavillon, on East 55th Street. In 1957, he moved it to East 57th Street and opened La Côte Basque in the 55th Street premises. Pierre Franey, Craig Claiborne's colleague, was Soulé's chef at Pavillon for 25 years, until Franey left for Howard Johnson's. After Soulé's death, Le Pavillon went to pieces. *& p 53, 129*

ALEXIS SOYER (1809–1858), born
at Meaux en Brie, became chef of the Reform Club in London. He was caricatured by Thackeray, and a popular figure in the pages of *Punch.* But he was a creative cook as well as a culinary social reformer, who designed soup-kitchens for the Irish during the famines of the Forties and went to the Crimea in 1855 to improve catering and hygiene for the British Army. His adventures with Florence Nightingale make funny reading: see Helen Morris, *Portrait of a Chef* (1938). Probably his greatest contribution to cooks' welfare, though, was to introduce gas-fired ovens in place of the older coal-fired ranges, whose fumes poisoned chefs.

T

Guillaume Tirel, **'TAILLEVANT'** (d c 1395) is the only mediaeval cook about whose life anything is known. In 1326 he was a kitchen boy in one of the French royal households. Twenty-five years later, records show him to have been, successively, in the service of Philip VI and the Dauphin, who, in 1364, became Charles V. Still serving the same master, Taillevant was described in 1373 as 'premier queu du roi' – chief cook. He was still alive in 1392, when his name figures on a list of royal chefs who had received new knives. He was also granted arms: on his tombstone, he is portrayed wearing armour and carrying a shield decorated with three marmites.

Le Viandier, the cookery book that bears Taillevent's name, survives in one manuscript that dates from before 1392, says Barbara Ketcham Wheaton in *Savouring the Past;* so it is possible that he actually did have something to do with it. Mrs Wheaton points out that two texts from very early in the century (certainly predating Taillevent's birth), contain 'the core' of the recipes in *Le Viandier,* but adds, 'it would be inappropriate to reproach the historical Taillevent with plagiarism.... Most cooks were illiterate, holding their knowledge in their heads, hands and palates. When the rare literate cook wrote down – or the illiterate cook dictated – what he knew, he drew on traditional knowledge.'

BENJAMIN THOMPSON, Count
Rumford (1753–1814) is venerated by scientifically-minded Foodies. Born in Woburn, Massachusetts, he went to England in 1776, and held various administrative positions, while experimenting with gunpowder in his spare time. In the 1780s he went to work for the Elector of Bavaria, and put down a beggars' rebellion. He lured them into alms-houses, locked the doors and fed them on a cheap and nourishing soup of his own invention. For this and other services he was knighted in 1784, and in 1791 made a Count of the Holy Roman Empire. He took his title from his wife's American

home town of Rumford (later Concord), New Hampshire. After returning to England in 1795, he invented an improved kitchen range (1800) with ovens and hobs that could be regulated separately – the ancestor of all modern ovens. He also discovered that boiling coffee destroyed the flavour that comes from its volatile oils, and designed a very practical coffee-maker. *& p 10, 32*

RAYMOND THUILIER (b 1897), owner and formerly chef of Baumanière

M Thuilier. Foodies live for ever

and Mayor of Les Baux-de-Provence. *Address*: Oustaù de Baumanière, 13520 Le Baux-de-Provence. T: (90) 973307. *& p 54, 60–61*

JEREMIAH TOWER (b 1942) was born in America, but brought up in England and France. He trained as a marine architect at Harvard, but became a chef instead. He is the leader of the San Francisco Bay Area 'California cuisine' movement, with its distinctive mesquite-charcoal grilling. Jeremiah Tower, who was a major collaborator with Richard Olney on several of the Time-Life *Good Cook* volumes, cooks at The Santa Fe Bar and Grill. His famous dishes include fried black bean cake with chillies and sour cream, mesquite-grilled thresher shark with ginger scallion butter and fresh Dungeness crab cioppino with tomatoes and coriander. *Address*: p 83. *& p 106*

JEAN (1926–1983) **and PIERRE TROISGROS** (b 1928). Brothers, chef-patrons of the famous three-star restaurant that bears their name at Roanne, near Lyon. *Address*: p 59. *& p 42–43, 51, 56, 60–61, 62, 63, 100, 114, 115, 124, 130*

SHIZUO TSUJI (b 1933) is head of the Ecole Technique Hôtelier Tsuji in Osaka, the largest establishment for training chefs in Japan. Professor Tsuji's father was a baker, but he graduated with a degree in French literature from Waseda University in Tokyo and became a journalist on the *Yomiuri Shimbun*. He decided to become a chef and cookery teacher himself after writing a feature on Japanese cooking schools. After some years of studying Japanese cooking, he went to France and trained with several chefs.

In 1960, Professor Tsuji returned to Osaka and expanded his father-in-law's small domestic cookery school into the present 2500-student academy, which teaches one-year courses in Japanese, French and Chinese cooking.

Professor Tsuji is the chief Foodie of Japan. He has written 29 books on food, travel and music – including his private (500) edition of Carême's drawings of pièces montées, one of the heaviest books ever published. He owns a huge collection of Bach recordings, and is an honorary Meilleur Ouvrier de France. His most important book in English is *Japanese Cooking: A Simple Art* (1980), with an introduction by M. F. K. Fisher. *Address*: p 116. *& p 42–43, 74*

U

LOUIS EUSTACHE UDE was a contemporary of Carême at the turn of the eighteenth century, and, like Carême, came to Britain to work. His employer, the Earl of Sefton, paid him 300 guineas a year (a lot then) and left

I wouldn't order the chef's special today

him 100 a year in his will. At Crockford's Gaming Club, where he later worked, he was renowned for his arrogance and bad temper.

Ude's book *The French Cook* was published in London in 1813.

V

LA VARENNE. See under L.

HENRI VATEL (1635–1671). Maître d'hôtel to Nicholas Fouquet, Mazarin's finance minister. *& p 66*

ROGER VERGÉ (b 1931), chef-

Roger Vergé, chef, Foodiebiznessman

proprietor of the Moulin de Mougins, near Cannes. *Address*: p 59. *& p 42–43, 60–61, 62, 63, 98, 114, 116, 124, 125*

JEAN-CLAUDE VRINAT

(b 1936), proprietor of Taillevent in Paris. *Address*: p 59.
& p 60–61, 105

W

ALICE WATERS

(b 1944) is the chef-proprietor of Chez Panisse in Berkeley, California, the best restaurant on the West Coast. Born in Chatham, New Jersey, she was educated at Berkeley, where she took a degree in French cultural history. Alice Waters also trained as a Montessori teacher in London. While travelling in France as a student of 19, she developed a passion for French regional food and fell under the spell of Elizabeth David's books. When she returned to Berkeley to teach during the Sixties, she made the dishes she had learned for her 'extended family' – which included most of the prominent members of the New Left.

In 1971 she founded Chez Panisse (named after the character in the Marcel Pagnol trilogy), which serves one never-repeated, fixed-price, five-course dinner every night. In 1980 she opened the Café Chez Panisse, above the main restaurant, which serves the best pizza in the world. She published *The Chez Panisse Menu Cookbook* in 1983. *Address*: p 83.
& p 27, 125

ANNE WILLAN

(b 1938) comes from Yorkshire. She read economics at Cambridge – and cooking in Paris and London. After marrying Mark Cherniavsky, an international economist, she moved to America, where she worked first on *Gourmet*, then as food editor of the *Washington Star*. She edited the 20-volume *Grand Diplôme Cookery Course*.

In 1975, when Mark Cherniavsky's job took them to Paris, she founded l'Ecole de Cuisine La Varenne, of which she remains a director, though she and her family have moved back to Washington. She is the author of *Entertaining* (1980), *Great Cooks and Their Recipes*, the very successful *Observer French Cookery School* (1980) and *French Regional Cooking* (1981).
& p 42–43, 62, 63, 115, 118–119

ECKHART WITZIGMANN

(b 1942), chef of the Aubergine in Munich. *Address*: p 59.
& p 60–61

PAULA WOLFERT

(b 1944) is an American food writer and cookery teacher, one of the Scholar Cooks. She is known both for journalism (for *Vogue* and other magazines) and for her books, which include *Couscous and Other Good Food from Morocco* (1973) and *Mediterranean Cooking* (1977). She won a 1983 Tastemaker award for *The Cooking of South-West France*. Oddly enough, this makes some of her recipes double-prize-winning – a few had appeared unacknowledged in a book by her pupils which won a Tastemaker award the year before. See *Plagiarism*.
& p 112, 113, 114

LORD WOOLTON,

Frederick James Marquis, 1st Baron (1883–1964), was a Conservative politician and businessman, born in Liverpool, who had had a scientific education. He was made a peer in 1939 to give him a seat in Parliament, and in April 1940 became Minister of Food. He and Sir Jack Drummond, the nutritionist, formed a working alliance – Woolton's scientific background was the key to the success of their collaboration.

Together, says Christopher Driver (in *The British at Table 1940–1980*) they 'ensured that whatever it was prudent to explain was explained; and that whatever humour could be found in the situation was duly extracted.' Drummond said that Woolton always took account of the psychological effects of his policies, whatever 'the recommendation of the scientists'. Thus rationing was kept simple, and confined, says Driver, 'to goods whose

supply could be guaranteed, with a safety margin in ample quantities of unrationed bread and potatoes.'

It is now a cliché to say that the British were better nourished during the war than afterwards. This was achieved by healthy things such as the National Loaf, grey in colour and of 85 per cent extraction – including some of the bran and wheatgerm normally discarded in the 72 per cent extraction white loaf – and the 'Woolton Pie'. This resembled the beloved steak and kidney pie, but was filled only with vegetables bound in a béchamel. Ugh. The recipe can be found in *Food Facts for the Kitchen Front*, by Anon, no date, foreword by Lord Woolton. Also Lord Woolton's *Memoirs* (1959).
& p 127

Z

THEODORE ZELDIN,

Fellow of St Antony's College, Oxford, and organiser with Alan Davidson of the Oxford Symposium on Food, is an important historian of France, whose *Intellect, Taste and Anxiety* (vol 2 of *France 1848–1945*), 1977 (paperback, 1980, under the title *Taste and Corruption*) was the first ever history of France to give food its rightful high place. There is also a chapter on food in Zeldin's *The French* (1983).
& p 11, 13, 32

ACKNOWLEDGEMENTS

The Publishers would like to thank the following for their kind permission in allowing us to use their recipes: Michael Joseph p 27; Penguin p 36; A P Watt Ltd p 59; Macmillan pp 62, 97; Jill Norman p 109.

The publishers would like to thank the following for their kind permission to reproduce illustrative material in the book:

J Allen Cash pp 69, 89; Anthony Blake pp 24, 37, 49, 50, 98, 112, 115, 117, 121, 130, 132, 136, 137, 138, 142, 143; Doubleday/ William Bayer p 113 (top); Mary Evans pp 46, 66; Robert Golden p 102; Tara Heinemann p 70; Denis Hughes-Gilbey pp 34, 96; Hulton Picture Library pp 120, 121, 128; Keystone Press Agency p 28; John Lee pp 63, 64; Mansell Collection p 10; Tim Mercer p 9; Richard Olney pp 112, 136; Press Association pp 8, 74; Rex Features pp 115, 116, 135; Frank Spooner Pictures pp 57, 71, 75, 85, 91; Topham 6, 19, 45, 84, 112, 123, 131, 140, Dan Wynn p 113; and John Springs for the cartoon on pp 118–9.

ANSWERS

1 C
2 C
3 C The Prince of Wales likes old-fashioned plain food, eg smoked salmon.
4 C President Reagan eats jelly beans. According to *The Times*, 30 December, 1983, Mrs Thatcher 'often boils a plump fowl when she prepares dinner at No 10 Downing Street. She then beats up two egg yolks with cream and sherry, thickens the mixture over a low heat and pours it on the cold chicken.' She misnames this dish Véronique.
5 C They represent toques (chefs' hats).
6 C
7 C
8 C
9 C
10 C
11 C

Score 20 points for each C, 10 points for each B, 0 for A.
140–220 points: You're a true Foodie.
100–130: You're a 'gourmet', whatever that means.
60–90: You're just greedy.
Under 60: You're not having dinner with *me*.